Youth Homelessness

YOUTH HOMELESSNESS

The Construction of a Social Issue

Susan Hutson and Mark Liddiard

Consultant Editor: Jo Campling

MACMILLAN

First published 1994 by
THE MACMILLAN PRESS LTD
Houndmills, Basingstoke, Hampshire RG21 2XS
and London
Companies and representatives
throughout the world

ISBN 0–333–55055–2 hardcover
ISBN 0–333–55056–0 paperback

A catalogue record for this book is available
from the British Library

Printed in China

To Larry and May; Beechey and Cynthia; and John

Contents

List of Figures and Tables   x
List of Boxed Material   xi
Acknowledgements   xii

1   Youth Homelessness in Context   1
    1.1   Introduction   1
    1.2   A historical context   1
    1.3   A homelessness context   3
    1.4   An international context   15
    1.5   A basic approach to social problems   23

2   Defining and Measuring Youth Homelessness   26
    2.1   Introduction   26
    2.2   Defining homelessness   27
    2.3   Homelessness statistics   30
    2.4   Gender and ethnicity   41

3   Explaining Youth Homelessness   46
    3.1   Introduction   46
    3.2   Issues in explaining youth homelessness   46
    3.3   Approaches in explaining youth homelessness   67

4   The Public Presentation of Youth Homelessness   73
    4.1   Introduction   73
    4.2   Patterns in the presentation of homelessness   74
    4.3   The media, public opinion and policy making   92

5   **Agency Viewpoints**   **99**
   5.1   Introduction   99
   5.2   The range of agencies   100
   5.3   Agency presentations to an outside audience   110
   5.4   Classifications within agencies   117

6   **Young People's Viewpoints**   **123**
   6.1   Introduction   123
   6.2   The experience of homelessness   124
   6.3   Explaining homelessness   134
   6.4   Defining homelessness   137

7   **Solutions to Youth Homelessness**   **143**
   7.1   Introduction   143
   7.2   Agency solutions   143
   7.3   Politicians' solutions   156
   7.4   Young people's solutions   160

8   **The Construction of Other Social Issues**   **165**
   8.1   Introduction   165
   8.2   The issues   166
   8.3   Definition and measurement   168
   8.4   Explanations   171
   8.5   Public presentation   173
   8.6   Agency viewpoints   175
   8.7   The viewpoints of 'victims'   177
   8.8   Solutions   178

9   **Conclusions**   **181**
   9.1   Introduction   181
   9.2   Youth homelessness in context   182
   9.3   Defining and measuring youth homelessness   183
   9.4   Explaining youth homelessness   185

Contents

9.5   The public presentation of youth homelessness   187
9.6   Agency viewpoints   188
9.7   Young people's viewpoints   189
9.8   Solutions to youth homelessness   190
9.9   The construction of other social issues   192
9.10 The construction of a social issue   193

Bibliography   196

Author Index   208

Subject Index   212

List of Figures and Tables

Figures

1.1 Vagrants, paupers and the unemployed   13
2.1 Households accepted as homeless by local authorities
 in England, 1978–1992   35
2.2 Homeless applications and acceptances in England,
 1992   36
2.3 Previous night's accommodation of young housing
 clients   44
3.1 Stock of dwellings by tenure in Great Britain,
 1971–1991   48
3.2 Unemployment rates by age in the United Kingdom,
 January 1993   51
4.1 Little beggars   76
4.2 Street homelessness in London   80
4.3 Two views on young beggars   84
6.1 Feelings about the total experience in London whilst
 homeless   132
6.2 Responses to the question 'Do you see yourself as
 homeless?'   138
8.1 Offences involving violence dealt with
 by selected police departments in Edinburgh and
 Glasgow in 1974   170

Tables

2.1 Estimate of 'unofficial homelessness': actual and
 potential, England, 1990s   38
2.2 Gross weekly earnings of full-time employees in
 Great Britain: by sex and type of employment, 1990   42
3.1 Average gross weekly pay for full-time males and
 females, Great Britain, 1992   52

List of Boxed Material

2.1 Situations of homelessness   28

2.2 Local authorities' legal duties towards homeless people,
Housing Act 1985   34

4.1 Two drama documentaries   88

4.2 An agency account   90

4.3 Press coverage of a government homelessness package   94

7.1 Agency solutions to youth homelessness   146

Acknowledgements

We have worked together as researchers in the field of young people and homelessness since 1988. This book has been very much a joint endeavour. Responsibility for the research and the writing has shifted between us on a number of occasions.

We would like to thank the funding bodies who made this possible – the Joseph Rowntree Foundation and the Children's Society. We are also grateful for the support of our two departments – the Department of Sociology and Anthropology, University College Swansea, and the Department of Social Policy and Administration, London School of Economics.

We would like to thank the following for their comments on and contributions to the text: Chris Harris and John Hutson, University College Swansea; Kay Parry, West Glamorgan Probation Service; Maurice Cove, South Glamorgan Social Services; Mandy Jones and Bridget Price, Swansea City Housing Department; Irene Glasser, Eastern Connecticut State University; Karen Ingram, Network, Cardiff; and Graham White, Liverpool Institute of Higher Education. We would also like to thank the publisher's reviewer for the constructive comments that were made on the first draft.

In particular, we would like to thank the agency workers and young people who gave up their time to talk to us. Our special thanks go to John, Anita, Holly and James for their interest, support and encouragement.

Susan Hutson
Mark Liddiard

The authors and publishers wish to thank the following who have kindly given permission for the use of copyright material:

Association of Metropolitan Authorities for 'Local authorities' legal duties towards homeless people, Housing Act 1985', in *Homelessness: Programme for Action*, 1990, p. 27, London.

B. T. Batsford Ltd for a graph from M. A. Crowther, *Workhouse System 1834–1929*, 1981, p. 253.

Cambridge University Press for adapted material from M. Liddiard and S. Hutson, 'Homeless young people and runaways: agency definitions and processes', *Journal of Social Policy*, 1991, 20, 3.

Express Newspapers plc for 'Lambs to the slaughter', *Sunday Express*, 24.6.90.

The Free Press, a division of Macmillan, Inc., for table from R. Emerson Dobash and Russell Dobash, *Violence Against Wives: A Case Against the Patriarchy*, p. 247. Copyright © 1979, The Free Press.

Guardian News Service Ltd for 'Destitute teenager faces jail penalty' and 'Young beggars governed by law of the bullring', *Guardian*, 3.1.90.

The Controller of Her Majesty's Stationery Office for Crown copyright material.

Newspaper Publishing plc for 'Little beggars', *Independent Magazine*, 3.12.88, and 'Benefit cuts force more teenagers to sleep rough', *Independent*, 8.1.90.

Routledge for tables from D. Brandon, K. Wells, C. Francis and F. Ramsky, *The Survivors*, Routledge & Kegan Paul, pp. 52 and 57.

Joseph Rowntree Foundation for figures from *Homelessness in Britain* and *House Research Findings*, No. 48.

School for Advanced Urban Studies, University of Bristol, for material from G. Bromley, 'The definition and measurement of homelessness', in G. Bramley, K. Doogan, P. Leather, A. Murie and E. Watson (eds.), *Homelessness and the London Housing Market*, Occasional Paper No. 32, School for Advanced Urban Studies, 1988.

Shelter for table, 'Estimates of unofficial homelessness: actual and potential', from *Homes Cost Less Than Homelessness*.

Solo Syndication for 'The wild West End', *Mail on Sunday*, 26.5.91.

Every effort has been made to trace all the copyright-holders, but if any have been inadvertently overlooked the publishers will be pleased to make the necessary arrangement at the first opportunity.

1
Youth Homelessness in Context

1.1 Introduction

Homelessness has long shocked the public and concerned the authorities in many countries. That citizens should beg and live on the streets of states with welfare systems is a puzzle. That families and others should live for years in hostels or temporary accommodation contradicts the expectations and promises of western industrial economies. The homelessness of young people is, however, particularly shocking. Sleeping on the streets is the very opposite of what one expects to see provided for children and young people.

This book examines the issue of youth homelessness and has two main objectives. First, in consolidating what is currently known about the problem, both on a national and an international level, it will address many of the questions that are often raised about youth homelessness: How is it defined? What is its scale and extent? What has caused the dramatic growth in youth homelessness? How can the problem be resolved? However, it is soon clear that there are no straightforward answers to these questions. Little is uncontentious, from the causes of youth homelessness to the way in which young homeless people are presented in the press. The book's second objective, therefore, is to set out and examine the different, and even contradictory, viewpoints that surround youth homelessness. This involves looking at all those people who present the issue – in this case, the media, agencies, academics, politicians and young homeless people themselves.

1.2 A historical context

The concern about children and young people on the streets is nothing new. Many elements in the following UK account are common to other western industrial countries. In 1803 it was reported that three-fifths of all beggars in London were children. Many orphaned and unwanted children took to the streets of Great Britain following the industrial changes of the eighteenth and nineteenth centuries. Others were sent out to beg by their parents or travelled with them from workhouse to workhouse (for an account of child begging and vagrancy 1815–1939, see Rose 1988, pp. 37–44; 130–8). In 1876 Dr Barnardo estimated that among the 27 000 or so 'dossers' in London's registered houses, 6,000–7,000 were under 16. Over all, it was estimated that there were 30 000 homeless youngsters in London if all venues were taken into consideration, including sleeping rough, casual wards and unregistered houses (ibid., p. 136).

There was evidence that begging led boys into thieving and crime, and led girls into prostitution, so various philanthropic societies such as the Ragged School Movement (1844) and Barnardos (1866) responded by providing schools, orphanages, boarding out and emigration schemes for homeless youngsters or 'street Arabs' as they were sometimes called. Various factors led to a marked reduction in the number of homeless youngsters from the 1890s. The introduction of compulsory education in 1876 and the dwindling opportunities for child labour took children off the streets. In the 'Children's Charter' of 1908, parents could be punished for causing their children to beg and these children could be put in orphanages. At the same time, the National Society for the Prevention of Cruelty to Children (NSPCC) and workhouse authorities removed the children who were travelling with itinerant adults.

In terms of homelessness, children and young people then largely disappear from view in many countries, although a number of factors were moulding their reappearance in the 1960s and 1970s – such as the emergence of 'adolescence' or 'youth' as a distinct life stage in the 1950s. The increase in homelessness among young people was noted from the late 1960s. In the USA, comment focused on runaways and, in the UK, concern was particularly for young people going to London with nowhere to stay. This led to the opening of accommodation and advice agencies for young people throughout the 1970s and 1980s. The 1975 television documentary *Johnny Go Home* exposed the risks of homelessness for young people going to London and placed the problem of youth homelessness firmly on to the public agenda (see Chapter 4). Nevertheless, the recommendations of the Government Working Group that was subsequently set up in 1976 were not implemented, and young people were not included as a priority group in the 1977 Housing (Homeless Persons) Act (Beacock 1979, p. 131).

However, it was a variety of socio-economic factors that largely lay behind the increasing numbers of young homeless people in the 1980s in many western industrial countries. By the time the children of the 'baby boom' generation hit the labour market, traditional industries such as shipbuilding and mining had collapsed and newer industries were not taking on the same volume of unskilled labour. In the UK, youth training schemes were introduced partly to remove young people from the unemployment registers. Many young people moved between government schemes, low-paid casual work and unemployment (Coffield et al. 1986). Large-scale youth unemployment led to fears in government circles that the demands of young people would increase the national cost of welfare and led to media headlines that young people were living off the state on the 'Costa del Dole' (Brynin 1987). The subsequent clampdown on benefits for those under 25 was itself to increase homelessness (see Chapter 3). While the income of young people in many countries was falling and less secure, the accommodation suitable for them had become more expensive and difficult to access. The private rented sector, commonly providing low-quality accommodation for young people, was contracting with urban renewal, gentrification and other opportunities for capital investment. Few single young people could take advantage of the increase in owner occupation and, where public housing did exist, families generally took precedence. This account of youth unemployment, a reduction in benefits for young single people, and a reduction in suitable accommodation could be similarly detailed for the USA and other western industrial countries.

One must be aware that tracing youth homelessness historically can imply a continuity that does not in fact exist. Young people who are homeless in the 1990s are homeless in very different housing and labour market conditions to those that prevailed in the 1890s and before.

1.3 A homelessness context

In the UK the term 'youth homelessness' generally refers to homelessness among young single people between the ages of 16 and 25, and it is on this age category that this book will focus. However, it is important to recognise that youth homelessness is part of a wider homelessness problem and has close links with a number of other similar issues. Therefore, before focusing on young homeless people, as the rest of the book will do, we will first compare and contrast their situation with that of runaways, homeless families and the older single homeless. There are a number of distinctions between these categories of people, which rest in part on their age and on their position in relation to legislation. It is important to appreciate these differences, as well as their common homeless situation. When a discussion about homelessness fails to make these distinctions, then the picture presented can be confusing. Moreover, the reaction to the increase in youth homelessness from the 1970s rests on earlier homelessness legislation and images of and attitudes to other categories of homeless people.

Runaways

Traditionally, little distinction is made between runaways and young homeless people. Surveys and media reports often merge the two groups together (O'Connor 1988; Robertson 1990) and several of the reports that first alerted policy makers and the public to the problem of youth homelessness and young people living on the streets of western industrial cities focused upon runaways (Sereny 1984). This blurred distinction between young homeless people and runaways is understandable; nevertheless, there are some important distinctions.

Differences

The basic difference between youth homelessness and running away rests on the age at which a young person can legally leave home or care. Runaways, by reason of their age, have left home or care illegally. In contrast, homeless young people have left home or care legally or have been legally evicted, and thus they are not breaking the law in the same way.

The laws concerning the age of majority are complicated in all countries. This is illustrated by the situation in the UK, where a young person must be in the care of a parent, a guardian or the state up to the age of 16. Between 16 and 18, a young person can leave with the permission of their carers. However, if carers report a young person missing who is under the age of 17, the police usually have to return them if they are found. Additionally, the police have the legal power to detain anyone aged under 17 if they believe them to be in physical or moral danger. For this reason, the age of 17 is an important watershed and the definition of a runaway in the UK is:

A young person, aged under 17 years or in local authority care (which in some circumstances can be extended to 19), who has either left home (or residential care) of their own accord but without agreement or is forced to leave, and is missing for one or more nights (De'Ath and Newman 1987, p. 14).

In contrast, youth homelessness campaigns and reports in the UK primarily refer to people aged between 16 and 25, who have left home or care legally. Youth homelessness agencies provide services for those aged 16 and over and are usually not allowed by law to accommodate those aged under 16. However, this is not necessarily the case in other countries. For example, although Australian youth shelters have to inform social services (FACS), they can accommodate those aged under 16. The homelessness issue is presented as one of homeless children and the campaign is phrased in terms of 'child rights' both within the state and within the family (Burdekin 1989; O'Connor 1988). Similarly, in the USA, little distinction is made between runaways and homeless young people. For example, surveys and agencies working in the field can cover young people living away from a secure base in a wide age range from 13 to 25 (Price 1990; Robertson 1990).

Similarities

The most obvious similarity between young homeless people and runaways is their shared experience. Both groups usually experience very significant difficulties with accommodation and are often susceptible to the same risks. The vulnerability of young men and women to sexual exploitation is often stressed in the media, but there are other equally invidious risks, such as offending on the run – whether this be taking and driving cars or stealing food or goods to survive (Hutson and Liddiard 1989a, p. 22; Robertson 1990, p. 7).

In the same way that many young homeless people experience repeated episodes of homelessness, so many runaways run repeatedly. In a study of runaways in London, for example, 7 out of 10 had run before (Newman 1989, pp. 146–7). Just as repeated episodes of homelessness can increase the likelihood of problems (see Hutson and Liddiard 1991), so can persistent running. For example, persistent running can have a highly detrimental effect on education or care programmes. It can cut young people off further from their families and can itself lead to a young person being taken into care. Once in care, repeated running can lead to a young person being held in increasingly secure placements.

The reasons for young homeless people and runaways finding themselves in their respective situations are also similar. For instance, family conflict and abuse are commonly reported by young homeless people as the main factors forcing them to leave home, and this is similarly the case with young runaways (see De'Ath 1987; Hutson and Liddiard 1989a; Newman 1989). Certainly, the image of the runaway as simply an adventurer or fun seeker, heading for the bright lights of the city, has long been refuted. For example, in a study of 532 young people who used a London safe house for runaways in 1985–7, 18 per cent (29 per cent of females and 6 per cent of males) had been sexually abused at some time (Newman 1989, p. 133). In a comparable study in the USA, 37 per cent had left home at least once because of physical abuse and 11 per cent because of sexual abuse (Robertson 1990, p. 7). One in five of these 13–17-year-olds had been removed from their homes, prior to living on the streets, because of family abuse. Accounts from Australia also stress the connection between family conflict, physical and sexual abuse and running (O'Connor 1988, pp. 25–41). Abuse is also closely linked to youth homelessness, and one UK study suggests that four out of ten homeless young women have experienced earlier sexual abuse (Hendessi 1992).

Young people with a background in local authority care make up a high proportion of both young people who run and those who are homeless. While 1 per cent of young people in the UK are in care, 34 per cent of London runaways had run there from care (Newman 1989, p. 23). Similarly, young people with a care background make up between 20 and 40 per cent of those in youth homelessness surveys (Hutson and Liddiard 1991, p. 25; O'Mahony 1988, p. 10; Randall 1988, p. 22). In a study of young people from street sites in Hollywood, Los Angeles, 41 per cent had previously been in foster placements (Robertson 1990, p. 7). In Australia, many of the young people surveyed were also wards of the state (O'Connor 1988, pp. 65–8).

There is also evidence that running away can later lead on to homelessness. More than one in five of the young homeless people we interviewed in Wales had run away from home or care before they were 16 years old (Hutson and Liddiard 1991, p. 46), while just over half of the homeless young people in one Australian survey had first been on the streets at 14 years or under (O'Connor 1988, p. 14). This is not surprising, for a background in care and family abuse or conflict can be precipitating factors in both situations.

Homeless families

A common distinction is often made between the single homeless and homeless families, or homeless people with dependent children. A large proportion of homeless people in most countries are in fact homeless families. Although in many respects their experiences of homelessness are similar to those of single people, homeless families are often in a different legal and social position.

Differences

In 1966 the film *Cathy Come Home* showed the British public that ordinary families could become homeless. It was not surprising that the increasing numbers of young couples seeking housing of their own were faced with a national shortage. War damage, slum clearance, and property speculation all led to a decline in the private rented sector. A series of surveys in the UK outlined this increase in homelessness (Greve 1964; Glastonbury 1971; Greve et al. 1971). It was against this background that the 1977 Housing (Homeless Person's) Act was passed in the UK, since replaced by Part III of the 1985 Housing Act. These Acts make an important legal distinction between homeless families on the one hand and single homeless people on the other. In simple terms, the state has a statutory duty to re-house homeless families, or homeless people with dependants. The state, with only a few exceptions, does not have such a duty towards single people who are homeless.

In other countries, the distinction between family and single homelessness may not be laid out so clearly by statute. However, there is generally a recognition, in practice if not in theory, that the needs of homeless people with dependants are greater than the needs of single homeless people. For example, in the USA the state seldom has duties to re-house any homeless people. Yet welfare payments, which in theory cover rent, are more easily obtainable by women with children than by single able-bodied men (Handler and Hasenfeld 1991, p. 112).

However, even when the state has a duty to re-house homeless families, as it does in the UK, this does not imply automatic access to housing. For example, the homelessness of many families is not accepted in the first place. In England, every working day 1,500 households apply to local councils for help on the grounds of homelessness. Just over a third are eventually accepted (1992 figures). Families must prove that they are 'homeless' by the Act's definition: that they have not made themselves intentionally home-less and that they have a local connection of some kind. If they can prove all this, being accepted as officially homeless may still mean a wait of a year or more in temporary accommodation. Even when they are re-housed, the choice of housing available to homeless families can be a very limited one, consisting of old or unpopular housing stock. Thus, having a legal right to accommodation does not ensure a smooth route into housing.

Similarities

The factors triggering homelessness may be very similar for both young single homeless people and homeless families. In the case of the young single homeless, a relationship breakdown, in particular a breakdown in parental relationships, can be a factor preceding homelessness. The breakdown in a relationship – be it with parents or a partner – is also a precipitating factor in the homelessness of many families.

The housing strategies that homeless families adopt are often very similar to those of the young single homeless. In the short term, for example, both may find accommodation with friends or family, although this is usually only a very temporary solution (see Bonnerjea and Lawton 1987). It is only really in the longer term that different strategies become apparent. Both homeless families and the young single homeless have to contend with shortages in the private rented housing sector and the prohibitive costs of home ownership. However, for homeless people with dependants in the UK, there is at least the possibility of gaining access to public-sector housing, although this may not be without problems.

Many homeless families are placed in temporary accommodation while their eligibility for housing is being investigated, or until permanent accommodation is available. There has been a massive increase in the number of households in temporary accommodation throughout the 1980s and 1990s. In June 1992, for example, a record of almost 63 000 homeless households were living in temporary accommodation in England (Burrows and Walentowicz 1992, p. 14). Of these, over 11 000 households were in 'bed and breakfast' accommodation, which is most commonly used in London.

The term 'bed and breakfast' has become synonymous with the problem of family homelessness in the UK, although it has also been widely used as a source of accommodation by the young single homeless. Much bed and breakfast accommodation is in hotels that are designed to cater for short-stay visitors such as tourists. However, in the UK it has increasingly been used to accommodate families for periods as long as 18 months to three years. The problems of families living in one room with distant and communal cooking facilities and shared washing facilities are evident. The dangers of overcrowding, the poor physical condition of the buildings, and the insanitary conditions have all been mentioned in surveys – along with reports of poor health, behaviour problems with children, and accidents (see Bonnerjea and Lawton 1987; Storie 1990; Thomas and Niner 1989). To this list of problems is added the fact that families are often accommodated far from their workplaces, family, friends and the children's schools. There is also evidence that children's health and schooling can suffer dramatically in temporary accommodation. It is estimated that the 1 million households accepted as homeless in the 1980s included some 1½ million dependent children (Grieve and Currie 1990, p. 8), with the overcrowding and often temporary accommodation that this involves.

In the same way that the young single homeless are often stereotyped and portrayed as idle and workshy – points that do not stand up well to empirical scrutiny (see Liddiard 1991b, p. 87) – so homeless families are also the subject of misrepresentation. It is often felt that families who gain council housing through the homelessness routes are working the system and jumping the queue. However, such deliberate strategies have not been confirmed by survey findings:

The overall impression was that respondents were confused and ignorant of the homelessness process in which they were enmeshed. The image of well-informed, demanding and undeserving people making unreasonable claims on the local authority is far from the picture revealed by the survey (Thomas and Niner 1989, p. 149).

It is commonly suggested that young girls become pregnant simply in order to become housed, although again the evidence that exists does not substantiate this view. For example, the majority of lone parents with young children who become homeless have experienced the breakdown of a marriage or other partnership, while almost half have previously had a permanent home of their own – as tenants or owners. Similarly, the average age of lone parents in accommodation for the homeless is in the mid to late twenties. Only a very small percentage are unmarried teenage girls (Greve and Currie 1990, p. 9). In fact, an understanding of the substantial hardships that most homeless families have to endure negates many of these misconceptions.

The older single homeless

While the homeless teenager is more likely to illustrate the issue of homelessness in the last decades of the twentieth century, the focus before that, in both the UK and the USA, was on the older single homeless: the 'tramp', the 'down and out', the 'vagrant', the 'hobo'. Interest in both countries has been considerable – whether the investigation was historical (Jones 1982), literary (Orwell 1933), journalistic (Wilkinson 1981) or sociological (Anderson 1923). In the UK the term 'homeless single person' was established by a report by the National Assistance Board (1966) and referred to itinerant persons, either single or effectively single, using accommodation provided for transients. As Leigh points out, the term is often used as a 'flag of convenience' to denote:

> **a disparate body of persons including the vagrant, the casual labourer, the itinerant navvy, the mentally ill, the physically disabled, and the old-age pensioner with no family ties** (1979, p. 95).

Differences

The most obvious difference between the older single homeless and their younger counterparts is that of age. Young homeless people are generally taken to be under 25 years old. In the UK, Income Support levels increase at this age. However, in much service provision and media reporting of youth homelessness, the focus is on younger age groups – namely 16- and 17-year-olds (Strathdee 1992) – while the responsibilities of local authorities under the 1989 Children Act cease at age 21 for care leavers (see Chapter 5). Whatever the exact age, the distinction between younger and older single homelessness is obviously an artificial one and, in simple terms, the older single homeless person can be seen as a young homeless person who has grown older. However, since the 1970s there have been moves in most countries to distinguish youth homelessness in terms of separate services and campaigning, so as to separate young homeless people from the stereotypical and negative images and lifestyles that have been associated with older homeless people.

Certainly, the older single homeless are usually identified as a more problematic group than their younger counterparts, although it is interesting that the problems that are emphasised have changed over time. In the UK, throughout the nineteenth century the threat the 'tramp' posed to society was moral, criminal and even political. For the Victorian, the 'vagrant' was an affront to the triple virtues of 'industrious habits, respectability and religion'. As Ribton Turner wrote:

No foreign heathen can compare with him in obscenity of language and his utter brutality and filthiness of life and action (cited in Jones 1982, p. 180).

There was fear of the 'habitual vagrant' who shunned work and lived off the ratepayers' charity. It was reported that such people turned down offers of poorly paid work, preferring the colour and change of 'a roving life' (ibid., p. 186). Throughout the nineteenth century, 'tramps', or 'unwelcome outsiders', were also blamed for much of the indictable crime, although it was later pointed out that many convictions were in fact for breaking the vagrancy laws (ibid., p. 182). They were also seen as a political risk, spreading 'moral pestilence' among the low-paid and the young (ibid., p. 207) as they moved from workhouse to workhouse, or 'spikes' as they were called, looking for casual work. There were attempts, both nationally and locally, to control the situation. In the Vagrancy Act of 1848 a fundamental distinction was made between the 'deserving' and the 'undeserving' poor. Relief was refused to able-bodied males. They were put to hard manual labour, such as breaking stones, in return for bed and board, before being moved on to another parish. In the USA, at the end of the nineteenth century, the term 'homeless' often referred to casual labourers, without families, who stayed in the 'flop houses' of the Skid row areas and then moved on.

However, since the 1950s, medical pathologies – particularly alcoholism and mental illness – have tended to dominate discussions concerning the older single homeless. As Bahr (1973) notes, speaking of the situation in the USA:

> **In the 1940s and 1950s, however, the stereotype of the skid row man's uncontrollable alcoholism gained currency and to some extent replaced uncontrollable wanderlust and congenital laziness as the primary characteristic of the homeless man** (p. 112).

Tidmarsh and Wood (1972), in their study of a London Reception Centre, found that 26 per cent of their sample of 8,000 males were alcoholics, 18 per cent suffered from mental illness, and 22 per cent from personality disorders. One South African study of 'vagrants' claimed that over 98 per cent of its sample were alcoholics (Department of Health and Welfare 1983, p. 15).

However, this image of the older homeless as mentally ill alcoholics has been questioned by a number of commentators. Leach (1979, p. 54), for example, questions the rates of mental illness found in studies of the older single homeless. Certainly, the high rate of problems identified with older single homeless people is not surprising given the aims of the surveys and the way in which the sample populations are drawn. Archard (1979) points out that if medical professionals construct questionnaires to tease out the medical and psychological problems of the older homeless, then a level of pathology will always be found (p. 21). Interestingly, alcoholism, mental illness, or even drug use do not feature to the same extent in surveys and reports of younger homeless people (Randall 1988, pp. 32–3). This partly reflects the different aims of the surveys, which are more often concerned with the effect of socio-economic policies on young people than with their medical and psychological problems.

Whether it is laziness, criminality or alcoholism, the older homeless person is almost inevitably seen to be personally respons-ible for their situation (Archard 1979, p. 21). What is surprising is that these individually based explanations of vagrancy have remained so prominent even in the face of other evidence indicating a strong link between such homelessness and economic conditions (see Crowther 1981; Jones 1982). It is possible to see in Figure 1.1, for example, that the rise in UK unemployment in the 1920s was

Figure 1.1 *Vagrants, paupers and the unemployed*

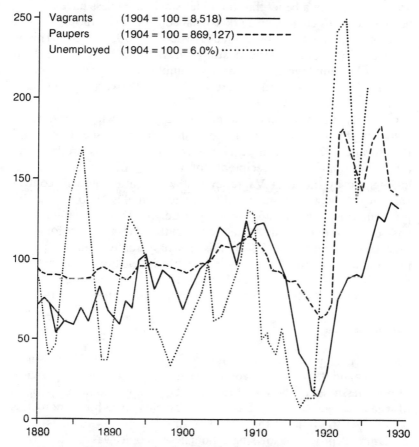

Number of vagrants relieved on the night of 1 January 1880–1930, compared with total number of paupers relieved on the same night, and with the average percentage of unemployed in certain trade unions 1880–1926

Source: Crowther 1981, p. 253.

followed, with a time lag, by a rise in charity to 'paupers', which in turn was followed by a rise in charity to 'vagrants'.

Although historical records convincingly show that there is a link between older homelessness and the economy, the way in which the problem has been dealt with and treated has consistently been in terms of individual blame. These individually based explanations arise in part from a belief that the older single homeless have already been given sufficient help and assistance. As such, those 'in that position must be there by choice' (Beacock 1979, p. 120). This is indicated by a South African study on vagrancy, where the high degree of unemployment among the sample is interpreted to imply that 'the vagrants concerned were predominantly workshy' (Department of Health and Welfare 1983, p. 35).

Certainly, the older single homeless are viewed with considerable suspicion by the public in almost all countries (see Cook and Braithwaite 1979), and there is a long history of this group being treated as undeserving recipients of welfare. In the UK, this is highlighted by the 1824 Vagrancy Act which attempted to control vagrancy by law and means that single homeless people can be prosecuted for just sleeping rough (see Leigh 1979). Although there has been considerable dissatisfaction with the Vagrancy Act for some time (see Home Office 1974), this has only really come to public prominence because of the way in which it is felt to be criminalising young homeless people (Carvel 1990), for whom it is accepted that homelessness may be the result of factors beyond their control.

Similarities

Clearly, the most obvious similarity between the older single homeless and their younger counterparts is their common experience of homelessness. In the UK, the majority of single homeless people, of whatever age, fall outside the statutory duty to re-house homeless people. At the time of the 1977 Housing (Homeless Persons) Act, government provision for single homeless people was limited to 21 Reception Centres or Resettlement Units, which were often descendants of the old workhouses, while the bulk of provision was provided by the voluntary sector in the form of hostels and day centres (see Beacock 1979). This emphasis on voluntary sector provision was continued in the face of increases in youth homelessness. Younger and older single homeless people often share the same night shelters and hostels, and it is generally the single homeless who sleep rough (see Steele 1989).

In addition, because surveys of both older and younger single homeless people tend to be of those using single homelessness hostels, men appear to predominate in both categories, but more so among the older homeless. For example, Tidmarsh and Wood (1972) show that 90 per cent of older single homeless people are male, and this proportion is replicated in most UK and US studies of older single homelessness.

1.4 An international context

In the same way that it is important to place the problem of youth homelessness in the broader context of homelessness in general, so it is also important that any consideration of youth homelessness is placed in a wider international context. In the next section, therefore, we briefly outline the problem of youth homelessness in four different national contexts – the USA, Australia, Europe and the Third World – and we consider the general issues involved in looking at youth homelessness cross-culturally.

USA

A recent study estimates that over 1 million people in the USA were homeless at some time during 1987. In the same year, 120 000 shelter beds were provided and 321 000 meals served for homeless people in American cities (Burt and Cohen 1989, pp. 5, 32). There was certainly a sharp rise in homelessness throughout the 1980s. Shelter users rose from 98 000 in 1983, to 275 000 in 1988 (Department of Housing and Urban Development 1989). Two pieces of legislation particularly mark this period of increase.

The 1981 Callahan Decree, following a case brought on behalf of four homeless men in New York City, set out that the state must provide shelter and that this shelter must be safe and decent. Similarly, in 1987, the Stewart B. McKinney Homeless Assistance Act released Congress funds for emergency shelters, but also authorised money for a range of programmes for homeless people in terms of health care and for the treatment of alcohol and drug abuse (Burt and Cohen 1989, p. 12).

Provision for homeless people has been largely in terms of shelters and soup kitchens. Many are provided by local charitable bodies, although government funding has increased (Burt and Cohen 1989, p. 6), and older single men make up the majority of shelter users, although the numbers of women and young people have increased. It is estimated that women and young people make up a quarter of the total (Hombs 1990, p. 5). Homeless individuals and families may also be accommodated on temporary vouchers in welfare hostels or single-room occupancy hostels (SROs).

Several reasons lie behind this increase in the numbers of shelter users (Burt and Cohen 1989; Marcuse 1990). Fundamentally, there has been a scarcity of low-income housing. State housing is rare in the USA and rent subsidies minimal. Gentrification and abandonment have eroded the private rented sector in many cities. Moreover, welfare benefit levels have not matched rent and cost of living expenses and, in 1981–5, nearly half a million recipients lost their disability benefits as regulations were tightened (Karn 1990, p. 73). In addition, the number of patients in pyschiatric hospitals has been reduced from 559 000 in 1955 to 123 000 in 1989, without adequate funds or plans for their accommodation in the community (Hombs 1990, p. 44).

In terms of youth homelessness, Robertson (1990) estimates that as many as 1.3 million young people go to emergency shelters or on to the streets in the course of a year in the USA. The common use of the terms 'runaways' and 'throwaways' indicate that many young people are leaving or being thrown out of their homes under the age of majority. These youngsters come under the responsibility of state child protection agencies, but many projects that offer accommodation, education and counselling to runaways and young homeless people, such as Covenant House in New York and The Bridge in Boston, are private charitable bodies. The Stewart McKinney Act guarantees access to education for homeless children with funds to develop programmes suitable for their needs (Hombs 1990, pp. 47–8). Some young homeless people qualify, as individuals, for state benefits (General Assistance), although money can also be made available to projects running education, health or drugs rehabilitation programmes. Free Greyhound bus fares are also available to runaways returning home (Gorder 1988, p. 108).

Australia

In Australia, as in the UK and the USA, homeless people live on the streets, and in squats and shelters. Others live in accommodation, such as rooming houses, that does not offer the permanency, security or facilities expected of a 'home'. In 1992 a government report estimated that there were well in excess of 10 000 people living in such conditions on any one night (Neil et al. 1992, p. vii). People with Aboriginal backgrounds are disproportionately represented in surveys of homeless people of all ages (*Sydney Morning Herald*, 11 July 1990). Government measures to relieve homelessness include mortgage and rent relief and funds to cover capital and revenue costs for crisis accommodation (Neil et al. 1992, pp. 76–7). Despite this, it was estimated that one out of every seven Australian households has a problem finding and paying for appropriate housing (Picton 1987, p. 48).

The increase in youth homelessness in Australia is shown by evidence that the proportion of those under 25 among the homeless rose from 7 per cent to 23 per cent in 1975–8 (Fopp 1989). The lack of jobs and suitable accommodation for young people lies behind this increase, as it does in the UK. In Australia, Youth Refuges, which are run by the state and by charities (mostly the church), cater for young people between 12 and 18 years. Attempts to target individual young people with the Young Homelessness Allowance have not been successful because of the difficulties of administering it (*Sydney Morning Herald*, 3 May 1988), but federal money is available for projects through the Youth Social Justice Strategy.

Concern over the numbers of homeless young people led to a two-year enquiry carried out by the Human Rights Commission and the publication of the Burdekin Report in 1989. The report accuses the government of neglecting state wards, failing to address problems in the juvenile justice area, and failing to provide homeless youth with appropriate health services (*Sydney Morning Herald*, 7 July 1990). It further points out the difficulties that children can face within their families in terms of violence and neglect (O'Connor 1988, p. 125). The response of Bob Hawke, the Prime Minister at the time, was a pledge that, 'by 1990, no Australian child would live in poverty' (Fine 1989, p. 11).

Europe

The increasing homelessness of young people has been the focus of several reports concerned with young people living in European Community countries (Burton et al. 1989a and b; Heddy 1990; House of Lords 1991). Under the Treaty of Rome, the Commission has no responsibility for housing and there are therefore no official European statistics or agreed definitions of homelessness. However,

the European Parliament accepted that 10 per cent of the population
of the EC could be classified as homeless (Burton et al. 1989a).

Homelessness in many European countries is linked with high rates
of youth unemployment. In 1989, unemployment of the 15–24 year
age group accounted, on average, for over a third of all unemployment in the EC member states (Heddy 1990, p. 39). Early leaving
from school and low rates of training for those over 16 were also
identified as leading to unemployment and a polarisation of young
people (House of Lords 1991, pp. 20–2). In many countries, young
people have born the brunt of benefit restrictions. Homelessness is
one of the interrelated problems faced by:

> **a small but significant group of especially disadvantaged young
> people who form an isolated or 'marginalised' element in society**
> (ibid., p. 8).

However, housing policies affect all young people, not only the
most disadvantaged. While housing is provided for students and
young people in military services, there are no policies to help other
young people gain independent accommodation. Having a child is
the threshold point for gaining state housing in many countries. The
employment mobility of young people is not encouraged by this
general lack of housing suitable for young people. In 10 out of 12 of
the countries of the EC, there is a minister who is, in some way,
responsible for youth policy or youth affairs. This is not so in the UK
or Italy (House of Lords 1991, p. 27). Despite this, there are few
general policies concerning young people and accommodation.
Youth homelessness is largely addressed by projects catering for
young people who are seen to be specifically at risk, such as young
drug addicts or people from care.

In France, Germany and Belgium there is also a tradition of hostels
for young workers and training is often provided alongside accommodation. However, often the most marginalised young people are
excluded from both worker and project hostels (Burton et al. 1989a,
p. 48).

The Third World

Children living on the streets is often accepted uncritically to be the
epitome of poverty, whether the scene is national or international. It
is the contrast between this poverty and the affluence of others that

makes the images so arresting. In western industrial countries, we are familiar with pictures of squatter settlements and young children on the streets in many Third World countries. Even when the economic conditions are barely comparable, there are some interesting parallels between homelessness in the two environments.

Many people in Third World cities are street homeless. They literally live and sleep in public places, such as parks, graveyards and railway stations, often because this is close to work which may, itself, be based on the pavement. For example, in Bombay 150 000 people live in makeshift huts on the pavements, which are often demolished by the authorities two or three times a year. Other people may live in such poor and overcrowded conditions that they would conventionally be defined as homeless. They may rent a room – in a city centre tenement, or house or on a squatter development – that whole families or groups of friends may share in order to keep down the cost.

One common response to being homeless in the Third World is to squat in buildings or on land that belongs to someone else. Squatting is basic to the survival of millions of poor people throughout the world. Squatter settlements usually mean illegal house construction on illegally occupied land, often around the city edge. It is common for between 30 per cent and 60 per cent of the population of Third World cities to live in illegal dwellings, while 70–95 per cent of all new housing in Third World cities is built illegally (Hardoy and Satterthwaite 1989, p. 12). While squatters or the homeless may be in a minority position in western industrial cities, in Third World cities they often make up the majority of the population. There is a strong element of organisation and self-help both in invading land for squatting and later building up public services through communal labour (ibid., pp. 83–5). For this reason, governments may turn a blind eye to squatter settlement, seeing it as a relatively cheap way of housing people necessary to the city's labour force. On the other hand, settlements can be an embarrassment or an inconvenience to the government (ibid., p. 39), and squatters may often be evicted or relocated. In more positive efforts to solve the problems of shanty towns, the most common strategy is to set up special projects rather than implementing general policies. While special projects may work where land and capital are provided, little is done outside the project boundary to resolve the problem for the vast majority of people. Comments about squatter settlements may stress the poverty – 'the teeming slums', the 'slums of despair' – but others stress the realistic strategies of the inhabitants for finding work and housing. Squatter settlements become:

> **Cities of pragmatists . . . where every square metre of material and every unit of currency is put to good use** (ibid., p. 17).

Many children live and work on the streets of Third World cities (Agnelli 1986; Aptekar 1988). In shanty towns where families may live in appalling conditions, many thousands of children share this situation. However, the term 'street children' generally implies that such children are living away from families. This may be because their families are living far away in rural areas, because the children have been permanently or temporarily evicted by their families or because their families cannot support them. Glauser (1990, p. 150) suggests that most children who lose ties with their families do so because of circumstances that drive them away. Most children do seek a stable alternative to the family such as kin, a shelter or an institution, but these are not always successful. Children may spend long periods on the street because that is their place of work – involving themselves in shoe shining, hawking or prostitution. Glauser, in a study of street children in Paraguay (1990), points out that children do not usually live on the streets continuously. They may spend weeks or months with relatives or back with their families. They may live with someone who takes charge of them out of compassion or offers them temporary work. He gives an example of an adult car thief who persuaded two children to leave a shelter and come on several trips to the Brazilian border. He needed children as partners and, in return for their thieving, he gave them food and shelter. Street children may spend time in institutions or shelters. However, between these episodes, they return to the streets. As time goes on the periods out on the street become longer and more frequent. Such children are clearly at physical risk when they sleep in the open, as well as being at risk from police harassment and violence.

Looking at youth homelessness cross-culturally

Similar factors lie behind the emergence of young people as a significant category among the homeless in many western industrial countries – youth unemployment, a reduction in state benefits, and a reduction in affordable housing that is accessible to young people. Similar factors put young people at risk of homelessness in many western industrial countries – conflict or abuse within the family or a background in state care. Government responses to youth homelessness are also remarkably similar – the setting up of schemes by voluntary agencies for special categories of young people. However, there is a danger, in stressing these similarities, that differing national structures and cultures will be discounted.

Any study of youth homelessness in a national context must take particular note of the responsibilities that the state has towards homeless people. These responsibilities may be laid out in legislation, such as the Housing Act in the UK or the McKinney Act in the USA. Often test cases such as the Callahan Decree are important in bringing change or clarification. It is in these Acts that homelessness is often defined. Where there is statutory responsibility, statistics will be collected. Surveys and accounts of homelessness will focus on those categories of people for whom the government has a responsibility (Karn 1990, p. 42). For example, in the USA numbers and accounts are predominantly of shelter users – older single men. Families are largely left out. In the UK, on the other hand, homelessness figures are predominantly of homeless families. In both countries, young single people are largely omitted.

Some women with children are found in the homelessness shelters in the USA (Sullivan and Damrosch 1987), but not in the UK. This reflects their disadvantaged position in the USA in relation to legislation and state housing, compared to the UK. However, Karn (1990, p. 95) suggests that, because the 1977 Housing Act did not itself create more housing, the advantageous position of homeless families in the UK is theoretical rather than real and the accommodation offered to them by the state can be far from adequate.

It is also important to understand the responsibilities that the state has towards children and young people in terms of child protection, child care and juvenile justice. For example, in Australia, Youth Refuges can accommodate children from the age of 12, although the statutory department concerned with children and families (FACS) will be informed if the young person is under 16. In the UK, all children under 16 must be returned home or be directly in the care of social services.

The way in which homelessness is funded will also vary from country to country. Provision may be funded directly from the government or the state may fund voluntary agencies in whole or part. Homeless young people may, or may not, be able to draw state benefits themselves. The working of the benefit system may influence who becomes homeless. In the USA the benefit (General Assistance) for able-bodied, non-contributing people with no dependants is minimal. In the UK, Income Support cannot usually be claimed by those under 18. Housing subsidies are more widely available to individuals in the UK than the USA. The availability of state benefits also affects the way homelessness provision is funded. In the USA, shelters and soup kitchens are often free, whereas in the UK, accommodation projects usually depend on Housing Benefit from residents.

National differences in both state structures and the expected role of the family can mean that the accommodation difficulties of young people are manifested in different ways. For example, Burton et al. (1989a) point out that the increase of street homelessness is more a feature of Northern Europe and relate this to the fact that there is more cheap, low-quality housing available in the Mediterranean countries because of lower land prices and less restrictive planning regulations. In Eastern European countries, many young people continue to live with their parents after marriage because of the shortage of housing units. However, the problem may only be 'hidden' in such situations. Street homelessness may be uncommon, but overcrowding and poor conditions may be widespread. Moreover, where the family plays such an important role in accommodation and support, the majority of young people who lack such ties may be in a particularly vulnerable position.

There are also interesting differences in the way that youth homelessness is presented to the public, which may arise from a number of factors. For example, in the UK and most European countries, the focus is particularly on the homelessness of young people aged 16 and 17. Campaigns and projects are concerned with better housing, jobs and benefits for young people. In the USA and Australia, however, the coverage tends to be wider. Government and media reports often include 12–18-year-olds. The problem is one of homeless *children* and the issue is often phrased in terms of children's rights. In the Burdekin Report, for example, homelessness is seen to result from a breach in children's human rights – by the state and by families. In reports of youth homelessness in Europe, however, the emphasis is more on the marginalisation of *young people* in terms of employment, income and housing. Homelessness is just one manifestation of this marginalisation, whether it be living on the streets, using hostels, or even being a single parent on isolated peripheral estates (Burton et al. 1989a).

In summary, it is suggested that the following can be used as a checklist of factors to be considered in order to construct the picture of youth homelessness particular to each country:

- State responsibilities and funding for homeless people.
- State responsibilities for young people – child care, runaways, juvenile justice.
- Housing markets particularly related to low income and young people.
- Education, training and youth labour markets.
- Benefits and rent subsidies.
- Factors affecting family structure such as divorce and marriage.
- Ages at which young people can leave school/home, take up a tenancy, etc.

However, it is also important, when looking at accounts of youth homelessness in any country, to be aware of who is presenting the issue and for what reason.

1.5 A basic approach to social problems

One of our main aims in this book is to set out the many diverse ways in which the problem of youth homelessness can be interpreted and presented by the media, agencies, politicians and by those directly affected – namely, young homeless people themselves. It is this bricolage of different meanings and interpretations that combine to construct a social issue.

In theoretical terms, this approach can be called an 'interpretivist' view of social issues, which takes for granted that the way in which one studies the subject matter of social science – that is, the social world – must be different to the way in which one studies the subject matter of natural science – that is, the natural world. This is because human beings, unlike atoms and molecules, interpret and make meanings of the world. Mankind, unlike natural matter, does not simply react to external stimuli, but contemplates and makes choices about how to act. In this way, people bring meaning to situations and react to external stimuli in light of the meanings that they attach to them. The use of an alarm bell is a good example. While it represents an external stimulus, it can mean a range of different things to the same person, who in turn can react in a range of different ways according to the meanings that they have attached to it. The external stimulus of an alarm bell can mean, for example, that it is time to get out of bed; that there is a fire; that there is a burglary; or that the temperamental car alarm has gone off again. How we react to this external stimulus essentially depends on the meaning that we attach to it and its context. As Hammersley and Atkinson note:

People interpret stimuli, and these interpretations, continually under revision as events unfold, shape their actions. The same physical stimulus can mean different things to different people and, indeed, to the same person at different times (1983, p. 7).

Adopting such an approach changes the aim and purpose of sociology. No longer should we simply aim to observe and measure aspects of society, such as crime or homelessness, as if they were objective facts. Instead, we should concentrate on understanding the meanings and interpretations that people apply to the social world and to social phenomena, such as youth homelessness.

Let us illustrate this by using the example of 'crime'. Traditionally, many sociologists have treated 'crime' as a feature of society that can be examined in the same way as a feature of the natural world. Namely, it is possible to measure the level of crime and make observations about the extent of crime and the characteristics of those involved in crime. Interpretivists, however, have stressed that such an approach is essentially flawed. They argue that simply looking at statistics and accounts of social problems is not particularly helpful, unless one also understands how and why these statistics and accounts are produced and used. For example, crime statistics tell us nothing about the basic issue of how meaning has been attached to certain behaviour to indicate that it is 'crime'. This is illustrated by the fact that, as we noted earlier, the 'meanings' attached to certain behaviour vary by their context. Killing a complete stranger, for instance, would usually be defined as a quite repugnant crime. Yet in wartime, it may be perceived as unproblematic or even admirable. Moreover, the way in which this action is defined, or the meaning that is attached to it, will obviously vary between different categories of people.

Interpretivists are therefore concerned with understanding more about the meanings that are applied to social phenomena. We are similarly concerned, throughout the book, with understanding more about the meanings and interpretations that people apply to youth homelessness, such as the media, agencies, politicians, academic commentators and young homeless people themselves. In the next chapter, we begin by examining the diverse ways in which youth homelessness can be defined and measured.

2

Defining and Measuring Youth Homelessness

2.1 Introduction

The study of any social problem logically begins with a definition. However, if a social issue can mean different things to different people at different times and in different contexts, how can it be defined? In the first part of this chapter we examine and discuss some of the difficulties involved in defining a social problem such as youth homelessness. Understanding the complexities inherent in defining social issues is fundamental, not least because the way in which a social problem is defined directly affects how it is measured.

Measurement is itself a crucial component in social problems. In deciding whether something is a 'problem' or not, its size is a critical factor. For a social issue such as youth homelessness to be addressed by policy makers, for instance, it is necessary to know how many people are affected and how this number is changing. These measurements are presented as statistics and great importance is often attached to them. However, it is ironic that youth homelessness statistics, in particular, actually tell us very little about the scale and nature of the problem. In the second part of this chapter, we examine and discuss some of the difficulties involved in measuring a social issue such as youth homelessness.

At the end of the chapter, we illustrate some of the issues surrounding the definition and measurement of youth homelessness by examining the scale of homelessness among young women and young black people. These groups are highly disadvantaged in both the labour and housing markets and there is a common consensus that they suffer disproportionately from homelessness. However, this is not always reflected in the statistics on homelessness and we examine why this is the case.

In summary, this chapter focuses upon three broad questions:

- Why is defining youth homelessness so important and yet so difficult?
- Why is measuring youth homelessness so important and yet so difficult?
- Why do young women and young black people often appear to be under-represented in statistics on the young single homeless?

2.2 Defining homelessness

When one considers the problem of youth homelessness, it is clear that there is little agreement about just what constitutes homelessness. There is, rather, a range of definitions. The most obvious definition, and one that dominates public viewpoints, is 'street homelessness' or 'rooflessness'. This includes as homeless only those people who are sleeping rough and living on the streets. In contrast, those who campaign against homelessness often take a much wider view, defining all those people who are in 'inadequate accommodation' as being homeless. In a sense, it is helpful to consider homelessness as a continuum of housing situations, ranging from those situations, such as sleeping rough, which almost everyone agrees represents homelessness, through more contentious circumstances that only some commentators would describe as homelessness. The nature of this continuum and the variety of circumstances that can be defined as homelessness are highlighted in Box 2.1.

These categories represent all those people who may be defined as homeless. Yet it is clear that some definitions of homelessness do not include all of these categories. Those people who define homelessness will draw their parameters at various points within this continuum. Some people will define only those individuals literally without a roof over their heads as homeless. Yet others will define homelessness in far broader terms, ranging from those without a roof to those living in another household who simply want to live independently. Most people attempting to define homelessness will draw a definition some way between these two extremes. However, all these definitions have boundaries that are often ill defined, and that can shift over time (see Chamberlain and MacKenzie 1992). For this reason, it is often difficult to judge whether someone is homeless or not. For example, can children who work and live on the streets of

Box 2.1 Situations of homelessness

1. People literally without a roof over their head, including those regularly sleeping rough, newly arrived migrants, victims of fire, flood, severe harassment or violence.
2. People in accommodation specifically provided on a temporary basis to the homeless (hostels, bed and breakfast, etc.).
3. People with insecure or impermanent tenures. This includes those in holiday lets, those in tied accommodation who change jobs, tenants under notice to quit, squatters and licensed occupiers of short-life housing, and owner occupiers experiencing mortgage foreclosure.
4. People shortly to be released from institutional accommodation, including prisons, detention centres, psychiatric hospitals, community or foster homes, and other hostels, who have no existing alternative accommodation or existing household to join.
5. Households who are sharing accommodation involuntarily. Sharing involuntarily with friends or relatives is the most common form of emergency accommodation. This can mean sleeping on the floor for a couple of nights or sharing accommodation for a longer period of time.
6. Individuals or groups living within existing households where either (i) relationships with the rest of the household, or (ii) living conditions, are highly unsatisfactory and intolerable for any extended period.
7. Individuals or groups living within existing households whose relationships and conditions are tolerable, but where the individuals/groups concerned have a clear preference to live separately. This includes cases where the 'potential' household is currently split, but would like to live together.

Source: Bramley 1988, p. 26.

a South American city be called 'homeless' when they may return to their families in the country during the winter or at other times of the year (Glauser 1990, p. 140)? Similarly, while people who sleep in cars are usually perceived as being homeless, is this the case with people who live in caravans?

The lack of any agreed definition of homelessness is exacerbated by the fact that different groups of professionals will be concerned with different categories of homeless people. For example, in many countries, workers in housing and social welfare departments may have statutory duties towards those people who are defined by legislation as 'homeless' (see later). Some of these people may have been placed in temporary accommodation by these agencies (point 2 in Box 2.1). Health, welfare or probation departments may have responsibilities for people leaving institutions (point 4). Voluntary agencies may work with homeless people across a wider spectrum, but particularly with the roofless (point 1), while housing and advice agencies may be approached by people threatened with homelessness (point 3). However, many people in unsatisfactory accommodation (points 5 and 6) or those seeking their own accommodation (point 7) do not approach agencies and so remain uncounted and invisible. For this reason, they are often referred to as the 'hidden homeless'. With such an array of housing situations and professional responsibilities, it is hardly surprising that there is no agreement over the definition of homelessness. Yet just why is defining homelessness so problematic?

In its broadest sense, the term 'homeless' means not having a 'home'. Of this there is no disagreement. The problem, however, lies in defining what one means by the term 'home'. A 'home', for example, clearly means far more than simply a 'house':

A 'house' is generally taken to be synonymous with a dwelling or a physical structure, whereas a 'home' is not. A 'home' implies a set of social relations, or a set of activities within a physical structure, whereas a 'house' does not' (Watson 1984, p. 60).

As such, defining the 'houseless' is fairly straightforward – it would simply include all those without any physical shelter. However, defining the 'homeless' is far more difficult, because a 'home' implies more than simply a physical structure. It is with regard to this grey area that the debate about how to define homelessness has raged. For example, should young people staying with friends or in hotels be defined as homeless or not? The complexity of this debate is highlighted by the self-definitions of young homeless people themselves. Watson and Austerberry (1986, p. 9) suggest that there is little doubt that young people sleeping rough are homeless. However, as we will discuss in Chapter 6, both ourselves and other authors – such as Brandon et al. (1980, pp. 52–5) – have noted that even young people sleeping rough may not necessarily view themselves as being homeless! The definition of homelessness is thus largely irresolvable.

If there cannot even be agreement about whether or not sleeping rough constitutes homelessness, so there can evidently be no overall agreement about how homelessness as a whole can be defined.

The definition of youth homelessness thus raises a range of issues. Yet the problem of definition is particularly crucial because of its impact upon how homelessness is measured. How a social problem is defined obviously determines its scale. If one defines homelessness as simply sleeping rough, or 'rooflessness', then the scale of the problem will be relatively small, certainly smaller than if one defines homelessness as living in 'insecure' accommodation, which could include young people in a wide range of housing situations:

> **Obviously the further the line is drawn from the 'sleeping rough' end of the continuum, the larger the problem appears to be** (Watson and Austerberry 1986, p. 13).

With this in mind, let us consider the problem of measuring youth homelessness.

2.3 Homelessness statistics

Statistics play an important part in the description and analysis of any social problem. Statistics feature in most accounts of social issues – whether they be in the press, in Parliament or in the reports and publicity of involved agencies. The reaction of policy makers to a problem will depend in part on its size – on the number of people it is thought to affect and whether this is increasing, decreasing or remaining static. Decisions about the potential allocation of resources is clearly dependent on some notion of measurement. Similarly, when resources have been allocated to address a problem, the outcomes of these measures can often only be assessed by changes in the numbers involved. Rossi's comment from the USA is widely relevant. As he says:

> **to devise effective programs and policies and to allocate appropriate amounts and kinds of resources to them, it is essential to know with some confidence the total number of the homeless and how fast it is changing** (1989, p. 45).

In the field of homelessness, however, statistics are either absent or highly unreliable. The following report, focusing on London, points out that:

millions of words have been written about the scandal of bed-and-breakfast accommodation . . . the risks faced by young teenagers alone in the capital. . . . But almost all of this discussion takes place in a statistical and informational void (*The Sunday Times*, 11 December 1988).

It is important to understand just why there are so few agreed statistics on homelessness. There are two main reasons for this: practical difficulties with measuring homelessness, and the difficulties arising from the lack of any agreed definition of homelessness. Let us begin by considering some of the practical issues.

Practical difficulties with measuring homelessness

There are a number of practical reasons for the lack of accurate statistics on homelessness. Of particular importance are the methodological problems that researchers face in attempting to measure homelessness, which some have described as trying to 'count the uncountable' (Rossi 1989, p. 47). The first problem is actually locating a sample of homeless people. For example, people who do not live at conventional addresses are usually missed by conventional surveys, such as the census, because the sampling frames for these surveys are often drawn from lists of addresses. In the UK, for instance, the census figures of 2,700 sleeping rough in 1991 were greeted with derision by agencies who pointed scornfully at the nil returns by Birmingham and Cardiff (*Guardian*, 23 July 1991). Similarly, in the context of the USA, Rossi (1989, p. 49) points out that homeless people who sleep rough are not statistically numerous and can be difficult to locate. He suggests that just 1.5–0.10 per cent of the population fall into this extreme form of homelessness. This means that, in theory, 70–500 adults would probably have to be approached in order to encounter one such homeless person. Reaching such a 'statistically rare' category is both time-consuming and expensive. Yet even those homeless people who are more statistically numerous may still be difficult to locate and count for several reasons, in particular because they may be concealed or hidden. Young people who are staying temporarily with friends, for example, may not contact homelessness agencies. They may not even see themselves as homeless. In this way, their housing problem goes unrecorded. One of the most important problems with measuring homelessness, therefore, is actually locating the homeless.

However, this is only part of the practical difficulty with measurement. Even if one can contact all those who are homeless, one still has to address a number of additional problems, such as the time-scale of homelessness. Young people often move in and out of homelessness. Some are homeless for months or years, but others are homeless only for a night or two (Hutson and Liddiard 1991, pp. 36–40). Because of this, the number of people homeless on any one night will be considerably lower than the number of people who experience homelessness over the period of a month or a whole year. Rossi (1989, p. 65), for example, estimates that the number experiencing homelessness in Chicago over one year can be at least two to three times greater than on any one night. Subsequently, even if one could measure all those who are homeless on a specific night, one is still faced with the problem of estimating the number of people who are homeless over a longer period of time.

One is also faced with the problem of trying to estimate the number of people who are homeless in a particular area or region, from what is usually just a small sample. In many homelessness surveys, for example, national and regional figures are often arrived at by extrapolating from local figures. Yet, as Rossi (1989, pp. 66–70) notes, it is often difficult, in such extrapolations, to take account of regional, urban/rural and seasonal variations.

These represent just some of the practical problems with measuring homelessness. However, perhaps the most important problem is the lack of any agreed definition.

Definitions and measuring homelessness

We have already seen that the manner in which homelessness can be defined varies enormously, yet the way in which one defines homelessness is basic to measurement. For example, if one defines homelessness as simply sleeping rough, or 'rooflessness', then the scale of the problem will be relatively small, certainly smaller than if one adopted a broader definition of homelessness.

Because different professionals have different definitions of homelessness, so they also produce different statistics. In this way, statistics can tell us more about the organisation collecting them than about the phenomena that are being measured. Kitsuse and Cicourel (1963, p. 135), for instance, show that criminal statistics are produced not directly by the action of 'criminals', but rather by those people in agencies and courts who define, classify and record certain behaviour as criminal. In a similar way, Atkinson (1978) points out that suicide statistics reflect not so much the actions of the individual, but rather the decision of coroners to define a death as 'suicide' and then to place this verdict on the death certificate. Because statistics are dependent upon the way in which organisations define issues, statistics are clearly social constructs rather than empirical measurements (Miles and Irvine 1979). Homelessness statistics are no exception. They tell us very little about the actual problem of homelessness and much more about the organisation collecting them and how it defines homelessness. One of the most explicit examples of this are the 'official' homelessness statistics in the UK.

'Official' homelessness statistics

The homelessness figures that are most consistently cited in the UK are the 'official' homelessness statistics, which represent the number of households officially accepted and recorded as homeless by local authority housing departments.

In the UK, Part III of the 1985 Housing Act (previously the 1977 Housing (Homeless Persons) Act) laid down certain criteria that define someone as 'officially' homeless (see Box 2.2). Someone is deemed homeless if they, together with anyone normally resident with them, have no accommodation that they are entitled to occupy, or cannot secure entry into such accommodation. Yet they must also fulfil a number of other criteria before actually being *accepted* or defined as homeless by the local authority. Namely, they must have a local connection of some sort, they must not be intentionally homeless and, most importantly, they must show that they are in 'priority need' of accommodation or in some other special category.

It is fairly clear, therefore, that the UK official homelessness statistics are based upon a somewhat restrictive definition of homelessness, which in turn should imply fairly low statistics. On first consideration, however, these 'official' homelessness statistics appear to be high, which indeed they are. In England in 1992, for example, 141 860 households were accepted as homeless by local authorities. Official homelessness has virtually tripled since 1978 (see Figure 2.1). Yet because of the way in which official homelessness is defined, these figures are actually a significant underestimation of the problem. They tell us very little about homelessness in general and youth

Box 2.2 Local authorities' legal duties towards homeless people, Housing Act 1985

Applicants are homeless if any one of the following applies to them:

- they have no accommodation that they are legally entitled to occupy;
- they have accommodation, but are in danger of violence from someone who lives there, or it is not reasonable for them to continue to occupy it;
- they are living in accommodation intended only for an emergency or crisis;
- they are part of a family who are having to live separately and who normally live together;
- they live in mobile accommodation and have nowhere to place it.

If the authority is satisfied that the applicant is homeless or threatened with homelessness within 28 days, then it must make further enquiries to decide whether he or she comes into one of the priority groups; these are:

- people who have dependent children;
- pregnant women;
- people who are homeless because of fire, flood or similar emergency;
- people who are vulnerable because of old age, mental illness or handicap; physical disability or other special reason.

If the authority decides that the applicant is homeless and in priority need and did not become homeless intentionally, then the authority has to ensure that housing is available to them. This usually means the provision of council housing.

However, if the applicant has no local connection with that authority they can be referred for housing to an authority where they do have a local connection.

If the applicant is in priority need but is intentionally homeless, the duty is to provide only temporary accommodation for a limited period and advice and assistance in finding housing.

If the applicant is not in priority need, the authority only has a duty to provide advice and assistance to them in finding their own accommodation.

Source: Association of Metropolitan Authorities 1990, p. 27.

FIGURE 2.1 *Households accepted as homeless by local authorities in England, 1978–1992*

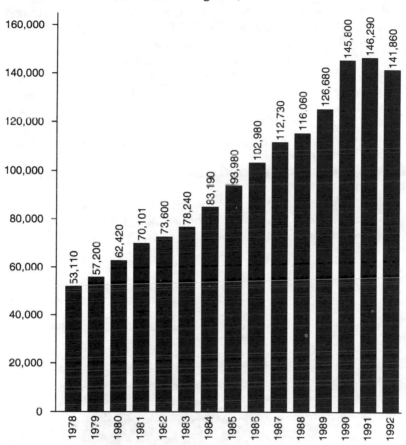

Source: Department of the Environment, *Homeless Households*; 1992 figures from the Department of the Environment, personal communication.

homelessness in particular. What they do tell us a lot about is the way in which housing departments define and record homelessness.

It should be noted that these 'official' figures, substantial as they are, only represent the number of officially homeless *households*, and not *individuals*. Because of the criteria that determine whether or not someone is in 'priority need' of accommodation, the majority of cases accepted by local authorities (two-thirds of acceptances in 1992) are households with dependent children. Subsequently, the number of

Youth Homelessness

individuals, as opposed to households, represented by the 'official' homelessness statistics are estimated as being three times as high, so that 142 000 households would be translated into some 412 000 people, including approximately 200 000 children (Burrows and Walentowicz 1992, p. 6; Greve and Currie 1990, p. 8).

Additionally, the number of people recorded in official statistics as homeless relate only to those *accepted* by local authorities as being homeless, as we have already seen. Yet as Figure 2.2 illustrates, approximately only a third of the people who *apply* to local authorities on grounds of homelessness are actually *accepted*. In 1992, for instance, only 36 per cent of those applying to local authorities in England were accepted as homeless. In some districts, the number of applicants accepted as homeless can be as low as 10 per cent (Thornton 1990, p. 4).

With the exception of pregnant women, very few homeless young single people are included in these official homelessness statistics. In

FIGURE 2.2 *Homeless applications and acceptances in England, 1992*

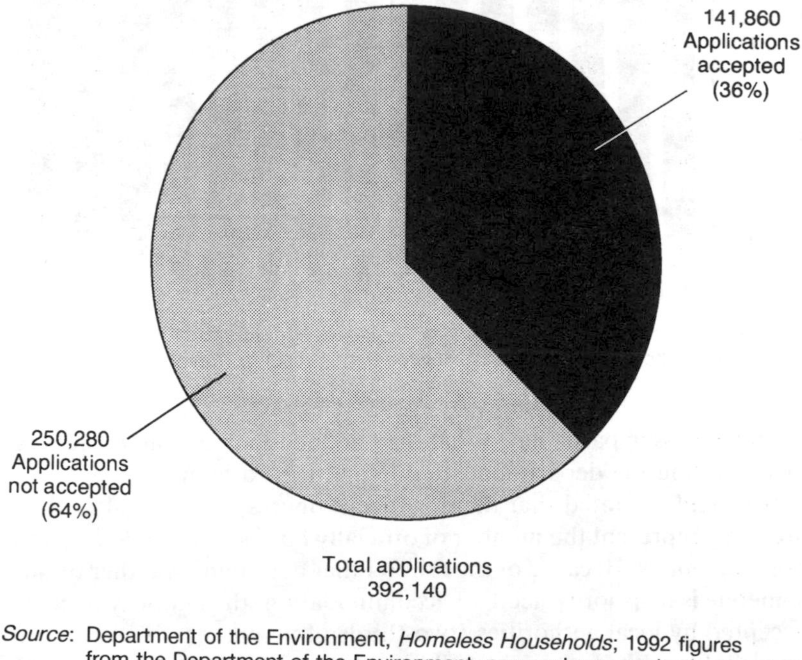

141,860
Applications
accepted
(36%)

250,280
Applications
not accepted
(64%)

Total applications
392,140

Source: Department of the Environment, *Homeless Households*; 1992 figures from the Department of the Environment, personal communication.

Box 2.2, we briefly discussed local authorities' legal duties to homeless people under Part III of the 1985 Housing Act. It is clear from this that young homeless people are not deemed to be in 'priority need' of accommodation purely on the basis of their age. However, people who are 'vulnerable as a result of old age, mental illness or handicap or physical disability or other special reason' are deemed to be a priority group, and the initial Code of Guidance indicated that 'other special reason' should include 'homeless young people who are at risk of sexual or financial exploitation'. In practice, however, the situation is not so clear and a survey of local housing authorities in England and Wales found that some 35 per cent would not accept as vulnerable young people 'at risk of sexual or financial exploitation' (Thornton 1990, pp. 50–7). It is clear, therefore, that only a small number of the young single homeless are ever accepted as officially homeless because local authorities differ widely in their interpretation of 'vulnerability', an issue that we discuss in more detail in Chapter 5 in the context of the 1989 Children Act.

Even the figures of those applying to local authorities underestimate the scale of homelessness among young single people, for the simple reason that many young people, aware that local authorities are unlikely to help them, may not even bother to apply. Ninety per cent of Randall's sample (1988, p. 25), for instance, had not been in touch with any local authority since becoming homeless. Indeed, it appears that some of those who do approach local authorities are turned away without their enquiry ever being recorded (Abrahams and Mungall 1989, pp. 31–3). It can be argued, therefore, that the UK official homelessness statistics seriously underestimate the true scale and complexity of homelessness. They certainly exclude almost all the young single homeless.

Statistics on the young single homeless

Statistics about the young single homeless are generally not easy to collect from official sources in any country. The statistics collected by the agencies and projects dealing with young homeless people are usually the main indicators that we possess, and even these are surrounded by problems:

> **It is commonly held that the numbers of the young homeless in London are rising significantly, but it is hard to prove this with effective statistics. There are no accurate data and the evidence that**

does exist is largely anecdotal and incomplete. It has been consistently argued, however, that the statistics that do exist underestimate very substantially the scale and complexity of actual homelessness (O'Mahony 1988, p. 13).

One problem is that many agencies do not keep figures. While some object in principle to the collection of information about their clients, seeing it as an invasion of privacy (O'Mahony 1988, pp. 13–14), many more simply do not have either the time or the resources to collect detailed information about their clients. Additionally, many young homeless people may initially be somewhat hesitant to impart too much information, while some informants may simply lie.

Because of the lack of national co-ordinating bodies, it is extremely difficult to combine existing agency figures to construct national pictures of the problem. Although there have been some attempts to address this issue (see Action on Housing Need 1991), double counting and other problems make it extremely difficult to obtain any kind of complete image. Moreover, as mentioned earlier, there are clear difficulties with actually contacting and counting many homeless people.

Nevertheless, campaigning agencies need to make estimates. If they cannot quantify the problem, they cannot hope for resources. Table 2.1 shows Shelter's estimate of those people living in homeless situations in England who are not included in the official homelessness figures. Their total estimate of 1.7 million 'unofficially' homeless people in England is evidently huge and a cause for substantial concern.

TABLE 2.1 *Estimate of 'unofficial homelessness': actual and potential, England, 1990s*

Description	Estimate of numbers
People sleeping rough	up to 8,000 (Shelter estimate)
Unauthorised tenants/ squatters	up to 50 000 (Shelter estimate)
Single people in hostels	up to 60 000 (1991, DoE)
Single people in lodgings	up to 77 000 (1989, DSS)
Insecure private tenants	up to 317 000 (1992, OPCS)
'Hidden homeless' people	up to 1 200 000 (Shelter estimate)
Total	1 712 000+

Source: Burrows and Walentowicz, 1992, p. 8.

The figures have been collected from a number of different sources. For example, the estimates of insecure private tenants and single people in hostels and lodgings have been obtained from official sources, 'although they are each collected in different ways for different purposes' (Burrows and Walentowicz 1992, p. 7). The figure for unauthorised tenants – or people who move into a property and pay rent although the tenancy has not been allocated to them – and squatters is an estimate that is subject to a large margin of error, although it is claimed that 'it is a figure which is generally accepted by a wide range of opinion' (ibid., p. 7).   However, it is clear that the basis for many of these estimates is the experience of homelessness hostels, agencies and projects. The estimate of 8,000 people sleeping rough in England, for example, is based upon reports from emergency night shelters. Subsequently, such statistics can often be seen as less a measurement of youth homelessness and more a reflection of the agencies themselves. Voluntary agencies, for instance, report seeing a rapidly rising number of young homeless people and these agency referrals are often cited as providing evidence of a growing problem. For example, the Piccadilly Advice Centre in London dealt with some 29 000 enquiries in 1986, compared to 21 000 the previous year and just 9,000 in 1983 (Randall 1988, p. 68). These figures indicate more than a threefold increase in the scale of youth homelessness in just three years! While these statistics probably do indicate a growth in youth homelessness which undoubtedly did occur between 1983 and 1986, they may also largely reflect the agency involved. The West End of London, for example, has a large number of homelessness agencies which constantly refer clients to one another. The apparently huge increase in the numbers of homeless young people that the Piccadilly Advice Centre experienced may have resulted, in part, from other agencies referring more and more young people to each other, as the agency established itself and its reputation. In this way, statistics on the young single homeless may say more about the agency providing them than they do about the problem of youth homelessness.

The strategic use of statistics

If statistics reflect the organisation collecting them and how it defines homelessness, then it is not surprising that there are large discrepancies between the different homelessness statistics used in the public arena.

For example, in the USA the figures produced by Rossi (1989, pp. 62–5) for those of all ages sleeping rough and using shelters in Chicago shocked the Chicago agencies with their low numbers. Rossi's survey estimated that there were some 2,000 street homeless nightly and 4,000 to 7,000 annually homeless in the city (ibid., p. 65). This contrasted with the annual estimates of 15 000 to 25 000 homeless people that the agencies had been using. From his Chicago figures, Rossi estimates a national figure of 300 000 to 500 000 street homeless in the USA each night. This is a great deal lower than the national estimate of 2–3 million by the Community on Creative Non-Violence (ibid., p. 70).

We have already seen that a large part of the difference in numbers rests upon how homelessness is defined. We saw earlier, for instance, that the official definition of homelessness in the UK is a narrow one, excluding almost all single young homeless people, and the 'official' homelessness statistics are correspondingly low. This is not surprising in light of the fact that local authorities have a responsibility to house homeless people. It is understandable that they apply fairly narrow definitions, which in turn minimise the scale of the problem with which they must deal (Liddiard and Hutson 1991, pp. 374–5). For example, housing departments exercise a degree of discretion in interpreting the 1985 Housing Act (Bramley 1988, p. 29). At a time when housing departments are facing increasing financial constraints and their supply of accommodation has dwindled dramatically, it is likely that they will become increasingly restrictive in who they define and accept as homeless. Certainly, it is interesting that in 1988 there were 242 470 homeless applications in England, of which 116 060 – or 48 per cent – were accepted. In 1992, however, there were 392 140 applications in England, of which 141 860 – or just 36 per cent – were accepted as homeless. Watson and Austerberry have written:

> **. . . definitions obviously serve a purpose. Priority need households and restrictive policies are necessary because local authorities cannot fulfil their responsibilities to all those who apply for housing as homeless . . . local authority housing departments adopt a gate keeping role between the homeless and the limited stock of council houses** (Watson and Austerberry 1986, p. 13).

In contrast, we have seen that many homelessness projects and agencies adopt broader definitions of homelessness, which may include all those living in unsatisfactory accommodation.

Consequently, their figures and estimates are higher. However, this is not surprising either. Campaigning bodies and those offering a service to young homeless people need to stress that the scale of homelessness is large, in order to attract publicity and media attention. At the same time, high numbers legitimate their existence and are important in obtaining funding. As Beresford (1979) points out:

> **The media are crucial to the agencies for the part their publicity can play in legitimising them and their version of the problem, gaining them resources and ensuring their survival. . . . It is always presented as a large and growing problem. It is not only that the larger the problem the more resources they can claim, but that size is a central news value** (pp. 152 3).

Because the problem of homelessness is largely concealed, it is essentially unquantifiable and any estimates of its scale can be neither proved nor disproved. As such, it is not surprising that while local authorities in England accepted 146 000 households – the equivalent of 420 000 individuals – as 'officially' homeless in 1991, Shelter, a campaigning agency, suggests that an *additional* 1.7 million individuals are 'unofficially' homeless in England (Burrows and Walentowicz 1992, p. 8).

2.4 Gender and ethnicity

Some of the difficulties with measuring youth homelessness are particularly highlighted by examining the scale of homelessness among women and black people. There is some consensus, for example, that both of these groups suffer disproportionately from homelessness. However, this is not always reflected in the homelessness statistics, of whichever country. In this section, we briefly examine why this is so.

In terms of their economic position, both women and black people are significantly disadvantaged in many countries. For instance, women have been heavily concentrated in low-paid and low-status employment (see Lonsdale 1992). In the UK, women's average earnings are two-thirds that of male earnings, as shown in Table 2.2. Similarly, black people in the UK and the USA have tended to hold unskilled, lower-paid and less secure jobs in manufacturing and

TABLE 2.2 *Gross weekly earnings of full-time employees in Great Britain: by sex and type of employment, 1990*

	Males	Females
Manual employees		
Mean	£237.2	£148.0
Median	£221.3	£137.3
Non-manual employees		
Mean	£354.9	£215.5
Median	£312.1	£191.8
All employees		
Mean	£295.6	£201.5
Median	£258.2	£177.5

Source: Social Trends, 1992, p. 92.

service industries, and thus have suffered disproportionately from unemployment (see Rhodes and Braham 1987). In 1991, for instance, the unemployment rate among West Indian and Guyanese males in Great Britain was 18 per cent, which is double the national average for males of 9.1 per cent. In terms of the UK housing market, households headed by women and black households are more likely to be living in poor physical conditions, to have fewer amenities and to live in unpopular areas (Dutta and Taylor 1989, pp. 25–6; Family Policy Studies Centre 1991, p. 6). Both categories are also over-represented in council housing and underrepresented in owner occupation, so they have been particularly affected by changes in the housing market (Sexty 1990, pp. 27–41; Thornton 1990, pp. 25–8).

In the light of these factors, it is not surprising that both women and black people are disproportionately represented among those accepted as 'officially' homeless in the UK (Miller 1990, p. 22). For example, in London, while only 10 per cent of households are black, they represent 32–40 per cent of the households 'accepted as homeless' (Doherty 1989, pp. 18–19; Shelter 1992a, p. 1). Similarly, women are well represented because the main category of people accepted as officially homeless are those with a responsibility for dependent children. However, even the official homelessness statistics fail to reveal the full scale of homelessness among women with dependants. For example, homeless women with children may still fail to qualify for housing and so are excluded from the official homelessness statistics. If they leave a partner, for instance, their homelessness can be deemed 'intentional'. Some young women may also find themselves in a vicious circle of losing their children to state care or to relatives because they are having problems with accommodation. Yet if they are without these children, they may then no longer qualify for council accommodation. Moreover, even if women are eligible for re-housing, they may prefer to remain in their existing accommodation rather than spend several months or years in bed and breakfast or other temporary accommodation. In this way, the homelessness of many women may remain unrecorded and unacknowledged.

The true scale of homelessness among young women and young black people is even more distorted when one examines the single homelessness statistics, which are usually collected by the agencies and projects dealing with young homeless people. All too often women and black people are underrepresented in these figures, which can give the misleading impression that homelessness is simply a white male problem (Sexty 1990, p. 52).

The key to understanding the relative invisibility of young women and young black people in such homelessness statistics is to understand more about the nature of their homelessness. For example, women tend to use hostels less than men. In the first place, there may be fewer beds available for them and, if there is provision, women may not feel safe in such accommodation (Gosling 1990, p. 5; Harman 1989, p. 52). Similarly, young people from ethnic minority groups are often unwilling to use hostels, which may be in white areas with predominantly white staff. In a study of applicants to a black housing advice centre, for instance, 85 per cent had never used a night shelter (O'Mahony and Ferguson 1991, p. 7).

Street homelessness is also less common among both women and black people. Women are particularly vulnerable to attack when sleeping in public places and young black men are especially concerned about being harassed or arrested by the police if they are on the street (O'Mahony and Ferguson 1991, p. 5). This explains why researchers and the media, heading for hostels or for the street, as they often do, tend to find more single white men and fewer women or black people.

While women and black people make less use of hostels, they tend to make more use of relatives and friends when faced with homelessness (see Cowen and Lording 1982). In adopting this

44 *Youth Homelessness*

strategy, their housing needs tend to go unrecorded and remain hidden:

> **When in urgent housing need, black people are more likely to turn to relatives or friends within their own communities than to make use of 'white' welfare agencies, so that their accommodation problems often remain hidden** (Thornton 1990, p. 27).

These strategies are illustrated by a study of young people in North Staffordshire (Smith and Gilford 1991), which showed that women tended to come to agencies dealing with housing need from a stay with parents or friends (see Figure 2.3). In contrast, young men more often came from 'no fixed abode' or hostels. One in three young men came from these situations compared with only one in twelve women.

It is for these reasons that young women and young black people are often largely absent from many youth homelessness statistics. Namely, these statistics are generally compiled by agencies working with young single homeless people, and young women and young

FIGURE 2.3 *Previous night's accommodation of young housing clients*

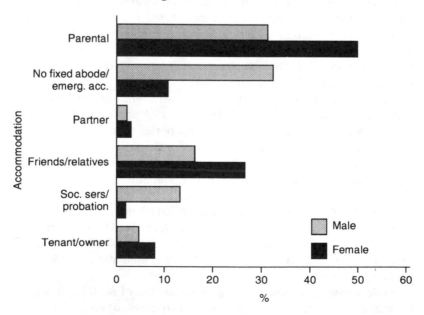

Source: Smith and Gilford, 1991, p. 3.

black people may not be in contact with these agencies. Subsequently, these groups do not appear to be experiencing a significant problem with youth homelessness, but in actual fact this is a false impression arising from the manner in which youth homelessness is measured.

The definition and measurement of homelessness are thus crucially important and yet highly problematic. The problematic nature of homelessness statistics is a particularly important point, because it is so frequently ignored. Frequently, statistics on the scale and nature of homelessness are treated as if they were objective facts, from which all manner of conclusions can be inferred. However, it can be seen that homelessness statistics may say little about homelessness as such and much more about the way in which the statistics have been collected and how the problem has been defined.

3

Explaining Youth Homelessness

3.1 Introduction

Once a social issue is defined, there is a need for it to be explained –
for the explanation of the problem will determine the solution. In all
countries, politicians, the media, homelessness agencies, academic
commentators and young homeless people all seek to explain youth
homelessness. Yet these categories of people do not always explain
the issue in the same way. This chapter examines these various
explanations. The first part of the chapter outlines the many issues
that are introduced to explain youth homelessness. The second
section looks beyond specific issues to the broader approaches taken
to explain youth homelessness. Basically, there are usually two
general perspectives adopted in explaining youth homelessness: a
'structural' approach and an 'individual' approach. However, this
dichotomy is probably too crude, and instead a wider range of
approaches has been suggested here. In summary, this chapter
attempts to address two questions:

- What are the main issues raised when youth homelessness is
  explained?
- What range of approaches can be identified in explaining youth
  homelessness?

3.2 Issues in explaining youth homelessness

The housing market

Homelessness is, by definition, a housing issue. Subsequently, it is
perhaps not surprising that the housing market is often cited as a key

to understanding the problem. Rossi (1989), speaking in the context of the US housing market, says:

That there are homeless people in fairly large numbers means that our housing market is not providing appropriate housing abundantly at prices the homeless can afford (p. 181).

It is often argued that the root of youth homelessness lies in a lack of affordable accommodation for young people. There is certainly evidence to support this claim. For example, in the UK it is fairly clear that recent years have seen a dramatic reduction in the availability of housing that most young people can afford. Public rented and private rented accommodation have both experienced a substantial decline, while, in contrast, the owner occupied sector has grown dramatically – as illustrated in Figure 3.1.

This sharp decline of affordable housing has not been confined to the UK. The USA, for example, has also witnessed a dramatic reduction in inexpensive housing, which has similarly been linked by commentators to the growth of homelessness (see Wright and Lam 1987). As Marcuse (1990) comments:

No wonder so many are homeless, with housing this hard to find. One might almost rephrase the question: 'Why are some of the poor homeless?' to 'How do so many of the poor manage to avoid being homeless?' (p. 149).

In the UK, the sharp reduction in public rented or 'council' housing is in large part a result of Conservative housing policies in the 1980s and 1990s. Local authority building programmes in England, for example, were cut by more than 93 per cent from 125 000 completed houses a year in 1969 to just 8,000 in 1991. Public-sector house building in the early 1990s is at its lowest peacetime level since the 1920s (Thornton 1990, p. 16). At the same time, this decline has been compounded by the sale of over a million council houses since 1980. Additionally, there are a number of restrictions upon local authorities, which prevent them from using much of the money they have raised from council house sales to replace these buildings with new housing (Ginsburg 1989, p. 65). The net result has been that public rented housing has declined from 32 per cent of Great Britain's total housing stock in 1978 to under 22 per cent in 1991. Yet, as we have already discussed, single people and childless couples are largely excluded from the priority groups for rehousing by the local authority. They

Youth Homelessness

FIGURE 3.1 *Stock of dwellings by tenure in Great Britain, 1971–1991*

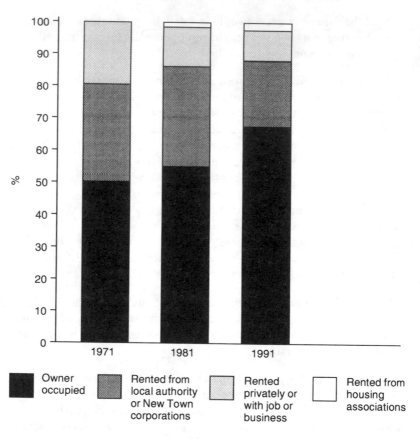

%

<table>
<tr><td>Owner occupied</td><td>Rented from local authority or New Town corporations</td><td>Rented privately or with job or business</td><td>Rented from housing associations</td></tr>
</table>

Source: Department of the Environment, *Housing and Construction Statistics: Great Britain*, June quarter 1992, Part 2, p. 27.

are instead expected to look towards owner occupation or the private rented sector for their accommodation.

In contrast to the decline in public rented housing, owner occupation in the UK has experienced a steady expansion, particularly since 1979 when it became a cornerstone of the government's housing policy. The 'Right to Buy' scheme, for instance, which was introduced in 1980 to empower council tenants to buy their house from the local authority – often at a reduced price – was an integral part of this attempt to expand home ownership (Malpass 1986b, p. 224). The owner-occupied sector in Great Britain has been increasing steadily from 50 per cent in 1971 to almost 68 per cent in 1991. However, the high entry costs of such accommodation make it an unrealistic option for most young people. In fact, under 25-year-olds account for only 4 per cent of owner-occupied households (Thornton 1990, p. 15). For most young people, therefore, the only viable accommodation option is the private rented sector.

The private rented sector has experienced long-term decline, which has been particularly marked in the UK. In 1939, private tenants easily outnumbered owner occupiers and tenants in the public rented sector. They still formed nearly a quarter of all households in 1966 (Emms 1990; Minford et al. 1987). By 1991, however, the private rented sector accounted for less than 8 per cent of the total housing stock. This decline is partly linked to state control of rents and security of tenure which made some landlords reluctant to rent or improve properties. In addition, many private rented properties were cleared in urban slum clearance programmes. In European countries such as France, Germany and the Netherlands, private rented properties have also been lost through urban renewal and gentrification, but the private rented sector is still a major provider for poor households. In the UK, many of these households are in local-authority housing (Emms 1990, p. 3).

Because young single people have generally not had access to council housing and because home ownership is seldom possible, they have necessarily used the private rented sector. However, the marked decline in this sector has removed a crucial source of affordable accommodation from this group. Additionally, the decline in properties available has intensified competition between tenants and has forced prices to rise. Because young single people are traditionally a low-income group and are often unpopular as potential tenants, they have been particularly badly affected by the declining supply and rising prices of private rented accommodation.

The large gap that this decline in private rented accommodation has left in the supply of affordable housing, particularly in the UK, has been recognised by almost everyone – including government and policy makers – although proposed solutions to the problem vary. In the UK, housing associations have been encouraged to fill this space, particularly by the Conservative government, which hopes to see the voluntary sector playing a more significant role in the housing market (Thornton 1990, p. 19). There is no doubt that housing associations have an important role to play in the provision of affordable accommodation for young people. Unlike local-authority housing, for example, they often concentrate on providing housing for single people and for special-needs groups – such as young homeless people – who fail to qualify for local-authority housing (Balchin 1989, pp. 150–2). However, scepticism surrounds the ability of housing associations to fill the enormous gaps left in the supply of affordable accommodation by the large decline in public rented and private rented housing. In 1991, for instance, housing associations only accounted for just over 3 per cent of the total housing market, clearly too small a contribution to properly address what Malpass (1986b, p. 228) calls Britain's 'deepening housing crisis' – the most obvious manifestation of which has been the rise in youth homelessness.

The labour market

It is important to understand that youth homelessness and the housing crisis for young people is not solely related to housing-market structures. It is often argued, for example, that it also has much to do with young people's economic weakness. As Donnison (1980) points out:

> **Most housing problems are really problems of unemployment, poverty and inequality** (p. 283).

Unemployment and low pay are often identified as integral to homelessness and housing problems and, since the early 1980s, both factors have increasingly affected young people in all western industrial countries (see Ashton 1986; Raffe 1987). The high incidence of unemployment among young people is illustrated in Figure 3.2. In January 1993, for example, 23 per cent of males aged 18–24 in the UK were unemployed, compared to a rate for all ages of 14.5 per cent. Similarly, throughout the countries of the European Economic Community (EEC) in 1990, unemployment in the 15–24-year age group accounted on average for over a third of all unemployment (Heddy 1990, p. 39).

It must also be remembered that national unemployment rates mask differences between regions and between different groups, be they ethnic, gender or religious groups. We saw in the previous chapter that the unemployment rate among West Indian and Guyanese males in Great Britain is double the national average, but

FIGURE 3.2 *Unemployment rates by age in the United Kingdom, January 1993*

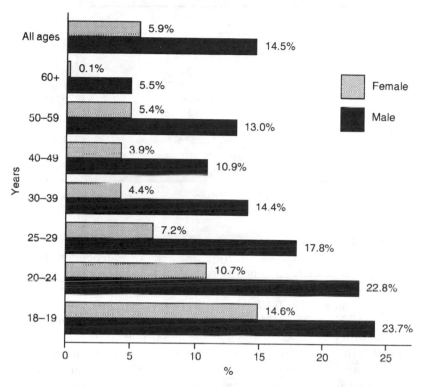

Source: Department of Employment, *Employment Gazette*, March 1993, p. 535.

regional differences can be just as stark. In the UK, for instance, unemployment varies considerably between geographical regions – in spring 1992 the unemployment rate in East Anglia was 7 1 per cent, compared to 12.1 per cent in Northern Ireland. Similarly, in France in April 1992, the unemployment rate among those aged under 25 was 23.5 per cent in the depressed Haute-Normandie region, compared with 10.7 per cent in the Alsace area. As Rossi (1989, p. 186) notes in the context of the USA, high rates of youth unemployment are closely linked to youth homelessness. Yet unemployment per se is not directly the issue – rather, it is more a question of the subsequent low income levels that unemployment incurs.

Youth Homelessness

TABLE 3.1 *Average gross weekly pay for full-time males and females, Great Britain, 1992*

	Male	Female
Under 18	£113.8	£108.8
18–20	£170.5	£149.3
21–24	£237.5	£196.9
25–29	£298.7	£251.6
30–39	£360.9	£275.0
40–49	£392.6	£256.1
50–59	£353.3	£237.8
60–64	£290.0	£211.4
All ages	£335.7	£238.8

Source: Department of Employment, *New Earnings Survey 1992* (London: HMSO) p. 13.

It is widely acknowledged that benefit levels for unemployed young people are inadequate for meeting the costs of independent living. Although in the UK large numbers of young people, particularly 16- and 17-year-olds, are now on training schemes, the income from Youth Training (£29.50–35.00 a week) is only marginally higher than benefit levels (£26.45–34.80 a week, 1993–4 rates). Even young people with jobs have traditionally been poorly paid (see Table 3.1). In Great Britain in 1992, for instance, full-time male employees of 16 and 17 earned only one-third of the average full-time male wage.

With such rates of pay, benefit or training allowance, the only affordable option is to remain in the parental home. However, many young people who become homeless do not have this choice. They must find independent accommodation, which is not only increasingly scarce but, critically, is increasingly beyond their financial reach. As Doogan (1988) points out:

> **youth homelessness is but one symptom of the deteriorating economic position of young people that has its roots in the dramatic restructuring of the world of work** (p. 91).

Benefit issues

Since the mid-1980s the UK has witnessed widescale cuts and restrictions in benefit payments, particularly to young people under

25. Although the details given in the account below relate to changes in UK legislation, similar restrictions in benefits can be found in the USA and many European countries. These changes in the UK have been closely linked to fears that increasing unemployment, particularly high among young people, would escalate welfare costs. The rationale behind many of these benefit changes has thus been to discourage young people from leaving home and subsequently claiming additional money for rent and living expenses (Thornton 1990, p. 31). However, the direct result has been a rise in youth homelessness, for young people who are unable to live at home have increasingly been unable to obtain or keep accommodation or live on the benefits available (see Hutson and Liddiard 1991). These benefit restrictions have taken a number of forms.

One of the earliest developments was the government's changes to the regulations relating to payments for board and lodgings, which specifically penalised unemployed young people. In 1985, following a growing concern about the increasing numbers of unemployed young people living in bed and breakfast accommodation, fuelled by media reports of young unemployed people living on the 'Costa del Dole' in seaside towns (see Brynin 1987), limits were set on these payments. Additionally, under the 1985 Board and Lodging Regulations, claimants under 26 (with some exceptions) could only claim full board and lodging allowances for short periods of time – varying from eight weeks in Greater London, Birmingham, Manchester and Glasgow to just two weeks in coastal areas and four weeks elsewhere. When this time period expired, the board and lodging benefit dropped dramatically and they had to leave the area and not return to claim benefit for six months in order to obtain the full rate again (Saunders 1986, pp. 76–8). Not only did these regulations largely fail in their intention of encouraging young people to return to their parental home, but there is also evidence that they created very considerable hardship for young unemployed people (Thornton 1990, pp. 28–30). Although these regulations were later abolished in 1989, they were just the first of many restrictions on benefit for the young unemployed.

The most widespread and important change to the benefit system was the 1986 Social Security Act, which came into effect in April 1988. One of its main features was the establishment of an age-related system of benefit entitlement. Personal allowances to cover food, bills and other living expenses were generally no longer based on *need*, but instead on *age* (Thornton 1990, p. 31). Young people under 25 now receive just 80 per cent of the Income Support that their contemporaries of 25 or over receive, while those youngsters under 18 who are eligible receive just 60 per cent – even if all are in identical situations. This age differential is illustrated by the weekly Income Support rates for single people (April 1993–April 1994):

Aged under 18 (usual rate): £26.45 a week
Aged under 18 (in certain circumstances): £34.80 a week
Aged 18–24: £34.80 a week
Aged 25 or over: £44.00 a week

In fact, the 1988 Social Security Act saw the end of benefit eligibility for most 16- and 17-year-olds, with only a small number of exceptions. Young people under 18 who are unemployed either have to enlist on a youth training scheme or usually go without any money at all (see Lunn 1988). This has resulted in particularly severe difficulties for unemployed 16- and 17-year-olds. In 1992, for example, three-quarters of 16- and 17-year-olds at one London night shelter had no income, compared to half of those over 18 (Strathdee 1992, p. 9).

The rationale behind these changes has been to encourage unemployed young people under 25, and particularly those under 18, to live with their parents by making it increasingly difficult to live independently, at least in terms of finance (Thornton 1990, p. 31). Prior to the changes of 1988, unemployed young people living away from home were entitled to higher rates of benefit than their contemporaries still living in the parental home, because of the greater expenses involved in independent living. Since the implementation of the Social Security Act, however, both groups receive the same rates of benefit. Additionally, unemployed young people who are living independently now have to pay an increased proportion of their housing costs from their benefit, which often leaves them with a much reduced income.

Before the Social Security Act, for example, everyone living on state benefits could receive Housing Benefit to pay for rent or mortgage interest payments and rates and some claimants could receive up to 100 per cent of their accommodation costs, consisting of rent, general rates and water rates. From April 1988, however, while people on maximum benefit could still receive 100 per cent of their rent through Housing Benefit, *all* claimants still had to pay at least 20 per cent of their general rates (later the Poll Tax) and all their water rates. Tenants have to meet these costs out of their other benefit, such as Income Support. Because those under 25 are already on lower rates of benefit than their older contemporaries, these changes have particularly affected young people. This disparity between Housing Benefit and the full accommodation costs has meant that young people often cannot afford to pay the full rent and are frequently being evicted. In addition, because of these problems, private landlords/ladies are increasingly unwilling to take tenants on benefits (Hutson and Liddiard 1991, pp. 13–15; Sharp 1991).

Similar difficulties have resulted from various changes to board and lodging payments in 1989. Before 1989, board and lodging payments for hostel residents and 'commercial boarders', or people living in bed and breakfast hotels, lodgings, in adult placement schemes and supported lodgings, covered the cost of 'services', such as rates, fuel, cooking and food, cleaning, laundry and furniture as well as basic rent. From 1989, however, all hostel residents and 'commercial boarders' had their board and lodging payments replaced by Housing Benefit and Income Support, and full charges for meals, heating and other services were no longer included in rent payments. Subsequently, rates and service charges now had to be paid from the resident's other benefit, despite the fact that service charges are particularly high in bed and breakfast accommodation and hostels. These changes in board and lodging payments have meant that bed and breakfast accommodation has generally become too expensive for most young people. The changes have also caused difficulties for homelessness hostels in so far as they now have to collect these charges directly from their tenants.

These changes mean that unemployed young people who leave home are considerably worse off financially than those still living with their parents. However, as many young homeless people either come from care or leave a situation of conflict at home, they have little choice but to live away from parents. These benefit changes force many of these young people into an even more precarious financial situation (Killeen 1988, p. 2).

In addition to the fact that many unemployed young people cannot afford to maintain independent housing, the 1986 Social Security Act also made it more difficult for unemployed young people to actually obtain accommodation in the first place. In particular, it is now extremely difficult for young unemployed people to receive any help with their initial housing costs. Before April 1988, single payments were available for one-off items such as furniture, a deposit, or rent in advance. The Social Security Act, however, replaced this old system of single payments with the Social Fund. Through the Social Fund, grants are generally no longer available and instead have been replaced by loans, which are consequently repayable from benefits. However, no one has a legal right to a payment from the Social Fund, as was the case with the previous regulations. Priority groups are set out and young homeless people are not a priority group as such when considering such loans (O'Mahony 1988, p. 127). Moreover, loans are only made if the benefit office concerned has enough money in its budget, if officials approve them, and if the claimants can afford to make the repayments (Central London Social Security Advisers Forum 1988). While grants are still available in a few cases, they are only made if they help re-establish someone in the community, and even these are discretionary. In any case, deposits to secure rented accommodation are specifically excluded from the Social Fund.

Because it is generally no longer possible to get a grant to pay initial housing costs and even loans are difficult to obtain, those unemployed youngsters fortunate enough to find themselves accommodation are often unable to take up their tenancy because landlords are, understandably enough, unwilling to accept potential tenants if they are unable to pay a deposit, or even rent in advance, which can sometimes be up to £200. However, even when the deposit demanded by a landlord/lady is a fairly small one – just £25 for example – this can be as much as a week's benefit. Thus it is effectively beyond the reach of many unemployed youngsters, particularly if those young people do not have family support to rely on. The already substantial problems that unemployed young people face in their search for affordable accommodation are thus dramatically compounded by these various benefit changes.

The importance of benefit restrictions in explaining youth homelessness is not confined to the UK. In the USA, benefit levels have also declined:

> **income support programs that cover unattached people below retirement age have undergone a severe deterioration in value over the past decade and a half, exacerbating the erosion of the life chances of the poor caused by labour and housing market trends** (Rossi 1989, p. 190).

Demographic changes

All these difficulties have been further compounded in many western industrial countries by a number of demographic changes. While there has been a huge reduction in the *supply* of suitable and affordable accommodation for young people, there has been a corresponding increase in demand for such accommodation. This increase in demand is closely linked to the peaking of the birth rate in the 1960s and the resulting demographic bulge of young people. Yet the nature of recent demographic changes is considerably more complex than this. The key issue is the formation of separate households. As Malpass notes:

Demand for housing can increase even within a static or falling total population if new households are forming faster than old ones dissolve (1986a, p. 12).

For example, although the overall population of England and Wales increased by only 0.5 per cent between 1971 and 1981, Britain nevertheless saw an estimated increase of over 10 per cent in the number of households in this period (Brynin 1987, p. 26) and this increase seems set to continue. Government estimates show that, although the overall population is likely to remain static, by the year 2001 the total number of households in Britain will have increased by 10 per cent and the number of single-person households by 34 per cent (Thornton 1990, p. 7).

There are several reasons for this increase in households, particularly single-person households. In part, it is linked to the numbers of young people now attempting to begin an independent housing career. However, the greater longevity of the elderly, combined with their preference for separate households, is also important (Malpass 1986a, pp. 12–13), while the growth in divorce further increases the number of single-person households (Lipsey 1987). Whatever the cause, the growing number of households increases the pressure on available housing.

Explanations of youth homelessness in terms of the housing market, the labour market, benefit issues or demography are all 'structural' explanations. These are explanations that specifically relate youth homelessness and its increase to the structure of society. However, the issue is frequently explained in more personal terms. Youth homelessness is often linked, for example, to the individual behaviour of young homeless people themselves. The rest of this section outlines some of these individually based explanations.

Leaving home

When discussing individually based explanations of youth homelessness, or explanations that are specifically related to an individual's
behaviour, commentators usually concentrate on the idea that young
homeless people, through their behaviour, are somehow directly
responsible for their homelessness:

> **There is a view often expressed that it is the fault of the young
> people if they find themselves without anywhere to live. This
> argument stresses that the young do not have to leave home**
> (O'Mahony 1988, p. 2).

The issue of young people leaving home is certainly central to this
idea. Young people, the argument goes, take the decision to leave
home and thus they must accept responsibility for any difficulties they
subsequently encounter. This is certainly a common view and one
that is popular among some politicians. In a UK context, for
example, the then Prime Minister, Margaret Thatcher, replied to
evidence of increasing homelessness in London as follows:

> **There is a number of young people who choose voluntarily to leave
> home; I do not think that we can be expected, no matter how many
> there are, to provide units for them** (*Hansard*, 7 June 1988, vol.
> 134, p. 713).

Similarly, as Nicholas Ridley said in Parliament, when he was
Secretary of State for the Environment:

> **we should do nothing to tempt young people to leave home,
> particularly when they do not have a home of their own to which to
> go. That is half the problem that we already face** (*Hansard*, 22
> March 1989, vol. 149, p. 1075).

These quotes raise a number of interesting issues, some of which
will be discussed later in this chapter. However, it is clear that both
these quotes explain youth homelessness specifically by reference to
the behaviour of young people – in particular, by their actions in
leaving home. For some commentators, leaving home per se is seen
to be one of the keys to understanding and explaining youth homelessness, and one for which young people must accept responsibility.
  Other commentators, including ourselves, have responded to these

arguments by making a number of observations. It is pointed out that many of the young people who become homeless have no real choice over whether or not to leave home (Killeen 1988, p. 2). As we will shortly discuss, many homeless young people come from care, which means that they have to leave their care accommodation at a certain date. Similarly, for those young people who do leave a parental home, significant numbers have been evicted by their parents and, as such, have had no choice but to leave. The situation in the USA is very similar (Rossi 1989, p. 189). Indeed, of the young people who do appear to have made the decision to leave, the degree of choice often appears to be a minimal one. Family conflict can be instrumental in forcing the young person to leave (O'Mahony 1988, p. 5), as can physical or sexual abuse (Thornton 1990, pp. 23 4). These points, however, do not necessarily deny that young people leaving home early is relevant in explaining youth homelessness. They simply question the apportioning of blame to young people themselves.

There is another viewpoint that also sees leaving home as important in explaining youth homelessness, but from a different perspective. Many homelessness agencies, for example, do not doubt the link between leaving home early and homelessness. Indeed, educating young people into the realities of leaving home – while at the same time not denying that their desire to leave home is a valid one – is seen to be an integral part of measures aimed at preventing homelessness (O'Mahony 1988, p. 141). However, their argument is that by leaving home – for whatever reason – young people are subjected to the vagaries of the housing and labour markets in a way that they are not when they remain with their parents. In this way, the individual behaviour of young people – in the form of leaving home – is crucial to explaining youth homelessness, but only when it is viewed in conjunction with structural factors. This view would argue, for instance, that large numbers of young people have always chosen to leave home and, indeed, this is often perceived to be a central part of the transition to adulthood (see Willis 1984). However, this has not always been translated into homelessness. That increasing numbers of young people are now finding themselves homeless is not, therefore, a simple result of their choosing to leave home. Indeed, it would appear that in the UK the government has been fairly successful in discouraging many unemployed young people from leaving home (Jones, G. 1990, p. 15) and yet youth homelessness continues to rise. Instead, leaving home is an important element in explaining youth homelessness, but only because of the

nature of the housing and labour markets that young people are
entering when they leave home:

> **The problem is not that young people leave home but that when
> they do, there is often nowhere for them to go** (Gosling 1990, p. 5).

Leaving care

If it is generally accepted that there is a link between leaving home
early and homelessness, there is no doubt at all about the close
connection between leaving state child care and homelessness. This
link is common to all western industrial countries. In the light of the
fact that in the UK under 1 per cent of young people are ever taken
into care, the proportion of young homeless people with a care
background is enormous. Randall (1988, p. 22), for instance,
discovered that 23 per cent of his sample group had been in care at
some stage, while 22 per cent of our own sample had a care
background (Hutson and Liddiard 1991, p. 25). Similarly, O'Mahony
(1988, p. 10) estimates that 30–40 per cent of the young people using
homeless facilities in London have had experience of care. Thus there
is no doubt that leaving care has a strong link with homelessness.
Again, however, there are a number of differing approaches to
explaining why this should be so.

One perspective tends to see the experience of care, per se, as
making young people additionally vulnerable to homelessness.
Namely, young people in care, by the very nature of care, have often
experienced disrupted childhoods and may well have been subjected
to a range of abuse – emotional, physical and sexual – that in itself
may create significant difficulties in terms of coping with independence.
Additionally, family support – financial or otherwise – has been
shown to be central in the negotiation of independence (Hutson and
Jenkins 1987, pp. 49–50), and yet many young people from care
invariably lack this. This can have a number of important implications:

> **care leavers setting up home on their own for the first time require
> advice and emotional support which may not be available from
> family and informal networks. . . . Care leavers – notwithstanding
> the difficulties and disruption, and even psychological damage
> which they may have experienced in their early lives – are expected
> to cope on their own from a much earlier age than other young
> people** (Watson 1988, p. 124).

This quote raises a slightly different point, which sees an experience of care as being important in explaining youth homelessness – not so much because of the problems of young people in care, but rather because of inadequacies in the care system itself. Young people from care, for example, are expected to be capable of independent living at a younger age than their contemporaries from a parental home. Many young people remain in the parental home until their early twenties (Jones, G. 1990, p. 6). However, most young people in care are expected to have left by the age of 18. Moreover, financial and accommodation support for care leavers after they have left care is often inadequate (O'Mahony 1988, p. 10).

The two explanations about the link between a care experience and homelessness can be combined. It is possible, for example, to suggest that the key to the influence of care on youth homelessness is the inadequacy of the support services available for young people leaving care. Yet, simultaneously, one can also concede that these support services are only inadequate because young people from care have a number of additional problems, such as a disrupted childhood and inadequate family support.

Physical and sexual abuse

The link between youth homelessness and abuse is being increasingly realised, particularly as the extent and effect of sexual abuse is becoming more widely recognised. The rates of abuse reported by young people who use homelessness hostels are high. For example, in one Scottish study, 17 per cent of the residents had experienced sexual or physical abuse from their parents (Killeen 1988, p. 12). A more recent study of young women in English and Welsh hostels estimates that four in ten young women who become homeless have experienced sexual abuse in childhood or adolescence (see Hendessi 1992). This connection between sexual abuse and homelessness is not a new phenomena. Astonishingly, the same rate of incidence is found in the Salvation Army's 'Girls' Statements' in 1886 (ibid., p. 3). There certainly appears to be a direct link between abuse and young people running away from home before they are legally allowed to leave (see Newman 1989).

The connection between sexual and physical abuse and homelessness has several strands. On the one hand, disclosure and discovery of abuse may result in the breakdown of the family and the child or

young person being taken into care. As we have just seen, this can
have a number of implications for the move to independent living.
On the other hand, an abusive situation may mean that the young
person leaves home at the very earliest opportunity. The situation is
often particularly difficult for young women because of their relative
economic weakness and the lack of facilities available to them on
leaving a situation of abuse (Akilu 1991). One should also not
underestimate the devastating psychological effects that physical and
sexual abuse can have upon young people (see Kenward and Hevey
1989; Hevey and Kenward 1989). Survivors often report low self-
esteem and lack of confidence, depression, severe mood disturbance
and suicide attempts (Hendessi 1992, p. 19). These effects can leave
abuse victims particularly prone to an array of problems, such as
prostitution.

While youth homelessness and prostitution are often linked in
media reports (see Chapter 4), there is little hard evidence on the
extent to which homeless young people are involved in prostitution.
However, two surveys from the USA suggest that it is a minority.
Price (1990, pp. 9–13) points out that many young people working as
prostitutes work from home and that most homeless young people
(80 per cent of those surveyed) did not use prostitution as a source of
income. Another study of young people living on the streets in
Hollywood, USA, found that less than a third had traded sex for
money, food, shelter or drugs (Robertson 1990, p. 4).

What is far less ambiguous, however, is the strong link between
prostitution and earlier sexual abuse. For example, a study in Boston
compared street youth involved in prostitution with those who were
not involved in prostitution. Interestingly, it was discovered that of
the prostituting group, 85 per cent of the males and 88 per cent of the
females reported child molestation, incest or rape prior to their
introduction to prostitution, while there was virtually no such
reporting among non-prostituting street youth (Price 1990, p. 11). In
his work on boys involved in prostitution in the UK, and specifically
London, McMullen (1988, p. 37) similarly outlines the strong link
between previous sexual abuse and involvement in prostitution.

Because the UK benefit system expects young people under 25 –
and particularly under 18 – to be living with their parents (which is
clearly inappropriate for many of these young people) the difficulties
of abuse victims are often compounded by financial problems. While
there has been some acknowledgement of this problem in the benefit
regulations, for a young person to be exempt from the usual

requirements for age-related benefits they must first disclose their abuse, which many are unwilling to do (Thornton 1990, p. 34). There is no doubt, therefore, that young people who have been subjected to sexual or physical abuse are, as a group, particularly prone to homelessness and other problems such as prostitution.

Mental illness

There also appears to be a link between homelessness and mental illness. A study of homelessness in the USA, for example, discovered that 23 per cent of the sample group had experienced at least one stay in a psychiatric institution. As Rossi (1989, pp. 146–7) notes, when these figures are compared to the overall adult population, of whom less than 5 per cent are ever hospitalised in a psychiatric institution, the rates of mental illness are high. These figures certainly reflect mental health problems among the older homeless population, who have traditionally been identified with such problems in both the USA and the UK (National Assistance Board 1966, p. 139). There is, however, evidence to suggest that some young homeless people in both countries are also suffering from psychiatric problems of some kind. Brandon et al. (1980, p. 87), for example, in a study of young homeless people in London, discovered that 17 per cent of the males had experienced mental illness serious enough to warrant hospitalisation.

There are two slightly different, yet interrelated, explanations for a link between homelessness and mental illness. The first explanation focuses on why mental health problems make young people more prone to homelessness, the second emphasises that homelessness itself can lead to mental health problems.

In terms of explaining just why mental illness makes young people more vulnerable to homelessness, the most obvious explanation is that mental health difficulties dramatically affect the ability to cope and live independently. There is also evidence that the problems created by mental illness are exacerbated by a lack of support services. The reasoning is similar to that used with the situation of care – the problem is less that young people are mentally ill and more that the support services available to them are inadequate.

The connection between the deinstitutionalisation of mental care services and the increase in homelessness has been a focus of particular attention, in both the UK and the USA (Caton 1990, pp. 15–17). The *principle* behind deinstitutionalisation or 'community care' – namely, the replacement of institutional care for mentally ill people with treatment in people's own homes – has been broadly welcomed. However, the main controversy arises from the inadequacy of community care in *practice*. It is estimated that some 10 per cent of residents being discharged from psychiatric hospitals in the UK do not have a home to which to return (Watson 1988, p. 125). The relative failure of the community care system is indicated by the high percentage of psychiatric patients readmitted into hospital care. Since 1979, for example, readmissions in the UK have persistently accounted for more than 70 per cent of admissions into mental hospital each year:

> **A pattern of repeated admission and discharge may lead to housing being lost; poor or unsettled housing conditions in their turn may lead to a deterioration in a person's mental health** (Thornton 1990, p. 25).

This quote raises a second theme in explaining the relationship between mental illness and homelessness – namely, homelessness is itself seen to cause and exacerbate mental illness. There is little doubt that the experience of homelessness is a highly disruptive one for many young people and it is consequently of little surprise that some of these youngsters begin to exhibit signs of mental disturbance (O'Mahony 1988, p. 40).

Of particular interest is the cause and effect issue. While it is undoubtedly the case that some young people become homeless as a direct or indirect consequence of their mental illness, it is equally apparent that mental illness can be a consequence of living without secure accommodation and being homeless. There is a subtle relationship between the two. This is highlighted by the hostel issue. Many homelessness hostels, which represent a safety net for young people, are often unable or unwilling to accept young people with mental health problems (Liddiard and Hutson 1991, pp. 378–9). Subsequently, these youngsters are forced to remain in a situation that exacerbates their mental health problem. Mental illness is undoubtedly linked to youth homelessness. Again, however, it is difficult to determine the exact nature of the relationship. This is also the case with crime.

Crime

The issue of crime and its relationship to homelessness is an intriguing one. Although there is some debate about the exact nature of the relationship between crime and homelessness, the connection is not doubted. In the USA, for instance, Rossi (1989, p. 164) notes that 41 per cent of the Chicago homeless have served jail sentences. Similarly, Randall (1988, pp. 33–4) found that 38 per cent of his sample group of homeless young people in London had been charged with or convicted of a criminal offence at some time. Brandon et al. (1980, pp. 164–5) also found that, from their total sample, 64 per cent of the males and 23 per cent of the females had received a conviction of some kind prior to the initial interview. It was interesting that in a follow-up interview and after a longer experience of homelessness, 83 per cent of the males and 31 per cent of the females were found to have been convicted of an offence of some kind.

Just why there is such a link between homelessness and offending is less than clear. There is some evidence to suggest that insecure accommodation and homelessness can increase involvement in crime. Undoubtedly, 'survival' offending is a significant problem for many young homeless people, whereby they resort to shoplifting and petty theft simply to feed themselves or to raise money for accommodation (Liddiard and Hutson 1990, p. 173). However, once apprehended, homeless young people – because of their lack of a fixed address – are far less likely to be offered bail than their housed contemporaries (Watson 1988, p. 129). Instead, they are frequently remanded in custody, which has significant implications for their housing opportunities.

This brings us to the second theme in explaining the link between crime and homelessness – namely, an involvement in the criminal justice system can increase the risk of homelessness for young people. Being taken into custody can directly affect one's housing situation. Accommodation can easily be lost while the tenant is in custody. Moreover, accommodation needs to be found again on release. A known criminal record can certainly affect the chances of accessing private rented accommodation and some homelessness hostels are hesitant to accept some young offenders, particularly violent or sexual offenders (Liddiard and Hutson 1991, pp. 378–9). Indeed, this is one of the reasons why it is estimated that approximately one-third of young people leaving custody are either homeless or at risk of becoming homeless (Watson 1988, p. 129). The most disturbing aspect of crime and homelessness is its cyclical nature. Namely, homelessness appears to be linked to offending, which in turn can lead to apprehension and custody – which in turn increases the young person's potential housing problem.

Alcohol and drug abuse

If the relationship between crime and homelessness is unclear, so too is the relationship between alcohol and drug abuse. There is some evidence that suggests a strong link between homelessness and alcohol or drug problems, certainly among older homeless groups in the UK and the USA (Rossi 1989, p. 156). Among young homeless people, however, the situation is less clear. Young homeless people are often portrayed in the media as heavy users of alcohol, and particularly drugs. Yet, as we shall see in the next chapter, there are a number of reasons why the media concentrates on these issues. Many commentators, for example, argue that the level of alcohol and drug abuse among young homeless people is generally exaggerated. Randall (1988, pp. 32–3) found that the level of drinking among his sample of young homeless people was remarkably similar to that found among their housed contemporaries. Thirty nine per cent of his homeless sample consumed three and a half pints of beer or the equivalent once or more a week, which compares to a general figure for unemployed males, aged 18–24, of 40 per cent. Similarly, Randall discovered that 64 per cent of his group had taken drugs at some time in the past, although the majority had simply been casual users:

> **The general picture which emerges is one of a casual experimentation with drugs which is common to young people, but only a very few for whom use had been prolonged** (1988, p. 33).

However, as this quote illustrates, some young homeless people – albeit a minority – undoubtedly do have a significant problem with alcohol or drugs, or both.

As with other topics, the question is one of cause and effect. There is evidence to suggest that alcohol and drug abuse can be as much a consequence of homelessness as a cause. Homelessness is undoubtedly a highly stressful experience, such that the temptation to indulge in drink or drugs may be considerable (O'Mahony 1988, p. 99). However, an identifiable alcohol or drug problem can have significant consequences for a young person's prospects in the housing and labour markets. As with crime, accessing accommodation with a known alcohol or drug problem is difficult. Indeed, there is evidence to suggest that many homelessness hostels exclude young people with an alcohol or drug problem (Liddiard and Hutson 1991, pp. 378–9). Therefore once young people develop such problems, they may often become caught in a cyclical pattern of homelessness and substance abuse. Once they have a problem, they are increasingly likely to be homeless which, in turn, is likely to compound the problem.

We have briefly summarised a selection of individually based factors – or factors closely related to individual behaviour – that are often identified as being important in explaining youth homelessness. This is not a comprehensive list, but it does represent a broad outline of the main issues. There is no doubt that *all* explanations play a part in helping us to understand youth homelessness. Becoming homeless, for example, is a complex process, in which a number of factors appear to play a part. The controversy arises over the particular emphasis that is variously placed on them. There may be agreement over a link, between homelessness and crime for example, but exactly *why* there is a link and the direction of cause and effect is open to some debate.

3.3 Approaches in explaining youth homelessness

We have seen that there are a number of specific issues that have a close link with youth homelessness and we have also seen that these links can be interpreted in a number of ways. Moving on from this, we suggest that it is possible to identify a number of broad approaches to the way in which youth homelessness is explained and interpreted. As mentioned earlier, two main approaches are traditionally taken towards homelessness. The explanations of it are structurally based or individually based (see Greve and Currie 1990; Thorns 1989; Thornton 1990). Indeed, the first section of this chapter follows this division. What we now want to suggest, however, is that when looking at approaches to the explanation of youth homelessness, this dichotomy is perhaps too crude. Brandon et al. (1980), for instance, made a useful but underrated contribution by outlining five broad models for explaining homelessness:

- Political model

- Individual culpability model
- Pathological model
- Child model
- Spiritual/religious model

All these approaches are relevant to youth homelessness, whatever its national context, and each have something to add to our understanding of youth homelessness.

The political model

> Here the important factors are political, social and economic rather than personal. The emphasis is on the social context of actions rather than on the actor (Brandon et al. 1980, p. 63).

This approach generally coincides with what are usually described as 'structural' explanations. Homelessness is seen to stem from the structure of society rather than from an individual's actions or behaviour. The important factors, therefore, are seen to be issues such as the housing market, the labour market and the benefit system. This approach views individually based factors as important only because they make young people more vulnerable to the influence of structural issues, something that we discussed in relation to leaving home. This view also tends to emphasise that looking in detail at the characteristics of homeless people simply individualises youth homelessness and moves the emphasis away from the structural root of the problem.

Certainly, the 'political' model is a view widely adopted by many academic commentators on youth homelessness, such as Greve and Currie (1990, p. 16). There are, however, a number of criticisms of this approach. First, to suggest that looking at the characteristics of homeless youngsters is simply individualising the problem is perhaps too simplistic, although a valid point. Only by looking in detail at the individual features of the situation is it possible to assess the impact of these structural factors on young homeless people themselves and so identify appropriate provision. This closely relates to the second main criticism of this approach – namely, there is a tendency to treat homeless people as almost powerless victims of the structures of society, something that is both patronising and ignores the fact that young homeless people, like all social actors, are in some ways and to some extent capable of self-determination. In the words of Doogan (1988):

> **In the long run such a perspective is debilitating since the victim is essentially powerless, the object of circumstances and not its subject** (p. 114).

The individual culpability model

> **This image sees homeless young people as individually culpable for their condition and behaviour** (Brandon et al. 1980, p. 60).

Unlike the 'political' model, the 'individual culpability' model sees the key to youth homelessness as having little or nothing to do with society or societal structures. On the contrary, youth homelessness is seen to be a consequence of the individual behaviour of young homeless people themselves, to whom this model correspondingly apportions a degree of blame (Johnson et al. 1991, p. 11). Young homeless people, it is argued, do not have to leave home. They do not have to engage in crime or substance abuse. As individuals in a free society, the argument goes, they have a choice and they are responsible for whatever decision they make.

This approach is more common among some commentators than others. It was a central theme, for example, in many statements from the UK government in the 1980s and early 1990s, as was apparent in the discussion on leaving home. It was also often expressed by members of the public. For example, in a television documentary discussing a controversial homelessness night shelter in Swansea, a local resident said:

> **Homeless people choose to be homeless. . . . If I'm single, I look for somewhere to live, I find a job and I look for somewhere to live . . . 95 per cent of the people coming here don't want to help themselves** (*Wales This Week*, 18 April 1991).

The advantage of this perspective is that it gives some credibility to the self-determination of young homeless people. However, because such an approach introduces an individual allocation of blame, it also carries punitive implications. Crucially, it also fails to acknowledge the constraining role that structural factors can have on individual behaviour and individual opportunities.

The pathological model

> In this perspective homeless people are seen as socially inadequate, maladjusted and psychologically disturbed. . . . They are unemployable rather than unemployed, unhousable rather than unhoused (Brandon et al. 1980, p. 68).

This 'pathological' model also sees the causes of homelessness as individually based, but, unlike the 'individual culpability' perspective, it does not necessarily apportion individual blame or hold the individual as directly responsible (Johnson et al. 1991, p. 12). Rather, the individual's behaviour is perceived to be a consequence of individual pathologies that in turn may result from such factors as childhood abuse or an experience in care. One hostel worker, for instance, described young homeless people to us in the following terms:

> It's not necessarily that they're troublesome, it's just that they've got problems – that's why they are homeless.

Interestingly, this model does give some acknowledgement to the influence of structural factors – that is, a poor environment, such as a difficult housing or labour market, will simply compound existing pathological problems. As such, this approach offers something of a compromise between the 'political' and 'individual culpability' models. There is, however, a major criticism of this perspective, which revolves around the issue of stigma. According to this model, young homeless people are an innately special group with a number of specific problems and, by implication, they require specialist support. Consequently, this approach can stigmatise young people and present a misleading picture of the young homeless – many of whom have no problems other than one of accommodation (Hutson and Liddiard 1991, pp. 45–7).

The child model

> As in the pathology model, impotence, dependence and diminished responsibility are implied in contrast to the mature objectivity of the observer. However, it does this by reference to immaturity rather than pathology (Brandon et al. 1980, p. 74).

Like the 'individual culpability' and 'pathological' approaches, this perspective also identifies the key to youth homelessness as being an individually based one. However, in line with the 'pathological' category, the 'child' model similarly diminishes the responsibility of the individual, who is viewed as possessing childlike qualities and is naive, vulnerable and immature. Youth homelessness is subsequently seen to arise from the fact that many young homeless people are simply too immature to cope. One worker at an advice agency, for instance, described young homeless people to us in the following way:

Well, they're not prepared for leaving home, although they do so, you might say, very quickly and very young . . . they're not emotionally or psychologically prepared either.

Similarly, a press article described young homeless people as follows:

In fact many of the young people living rough . . . are too young to have learnt how to take charge of their own lives (*The Times*, 19 June 1990).

In theory, of course, this approach is not necessarily incompatible with a structural perspective. Problems with the housing market, for example, may make additional demands on a young person that some young homeless people may not be mature enough to cope with. Indeed, unlike the pathological model, this approach generally avoids the problem of stigma – the homeless young person is viewed as intrinsically 'normal', albeit somewhat immature. The main problem with this view, however, is that it is somewhat patronising. There is evidence to suggest that many homeless youngsters show considerable resilience and maturity in learning to cope with, and survive, youth homelessness (Randall 1988, p. 35).

The spiritual/religious model

Homelessness is seen as a fall from grace which the deviant shares, to a greater or lesser extent, with all human beings . . . he also lives in a sick, uncaring and spiritually bankrupt society which itself does not heed Christian values and directions (Brandon et al. 1980, p. 66).

According to this model, homelessness is related not so much to social or economic privation, but instead to the spiritual poverty of society. In this sense at least, the model is related to an individually based interpretation of homelessness. Yet as the above quote indicates, the 'spiritual/religious' approach also sees youth homelessness as stemming from society, which itself does not adopt the Christian values of compassion and caring. Improving the material provision for homelessness is deemed unlikely to have any great impact on the problem, unless the spiritual content of both society and homeless individuals is also improved. In many respects, this model is now largely out of fashion, although it can still be found in the approaches of some homelessness agencies.

Outlining these models and the various perspectives that they adopt is a useful exercise for understanding the many different approaches taken in explaining youth homelessness as a whole. But while these models contribute more to our understanding than the simpler 'structural' and 'individual' division, it is still necessary to be aware that the reality of homelessness situations is even more complex than the portrayal of five simple approaches would suggest. It will already be clear that certain categories of people are likely to favour certain types of explanation. However, it is also likely that commentators may make use of several different perspectives in any one account of youth homelessness. The next three chapters consider in more detail the ways in which those involved – the media, homelessness agencies and young homeless people themselves – variously interpret the issue of youth homelessness.

4

The Public Presentation of Youth Homelessness

4.1 Introduction

Homelessness has long featured in the media. Vagrancy, for instance, was a topic of regular media interest throughout the nineteenth century, both in the UK and the USA (see Hoch 1987; Jones 1982). More recently, the British public was shocked in 1966 by *Cathy Come Home*, a drama documentary about a family becoming homeless and spending time in temporary accommodation (Rose 1988, p. 178). The public outrage after the programme even led to the issue being raised in Parliament. Similarly, a later drama documentary in 1975, *Johnny Go Home*, set out the risks facing a young man coming to London with nowhere to stay; a government Working Group was set up as a result of this (Beacock 1979, p. 131). After a lull in media coverage, youth homelessness returned to the UK headlines in the 1980s and 1990s, with young homeless people featuring in documentaries and even appearing as characters in soap operas and comedy series.

The media presentation of a social problem like youth homelessness is important, not least because of the impact that such accounts have on public attitudes. For many people, the media is their main source of information about youth homelessness. This chapter examines a variety of material concerned with the public presentation of youth homelessness and attempts to answer two main questions.

- What patterns can be identified in the way in which youth homelessness is publicly presented?
- What is the interconnection between the media, public opinion and policy decisions?

4.2 Patterns in the presentation of homelessness

The public presentation of a social problem such as youth homelessness is complex. It is presented to the public in a number of different
ways and through a variety of different sources. To simplify this
section, we will deal separately with the press, television documentaries, agency reports and, finally, with academic commentators.

The press

The media, and particularly the press, do not give equal coverage to
every potentially newsworthy issue. Stories are more likely to be
selected if they exhibit, or can be made to exhibit, certain
characteristics. For example, the media are often attracted to
negative and problematic themes, such as sex, drugs and violence,
which can draw a ready audience (Curran et al. 1980; Galtung and
Ruge 1981). It was clear from a detailed analysis of 26 feature articles
in the UK and 41 in the Australian press[1] that youth homelessness
has many of the qualities sought by the media.

One press article entitled 'Little Beggars' (*Independent Magazine*,
3 December 1988) unashamedly acknowledged that youth homelessness is very much a media subject (see Figure 4.1). The standard
media coverage is described in the article as follows:

> **The cameras roll and, to a lachrymose, morally outraged comment-
> ary, the little beggars describe how they ran away from wretched
> home lives to become hard cases on the West End 'scene' in which
> all things arrive prematurely: drugs, prison, violence, warped sex,
> degradation.**

However, one must be careful in attributing these characteristics
directly to the social problem of youth homelessness. Although it
may appear that the media is describing reality, the media actually
plays an important part in creating this reality (Beresford 1979,
p. 141). While the press select items for news according to certain
rules, the news is written as if these rules do not exist. Galtung and
Ruge (1981, p. 61) note that the more an issue satisfies the media's
criteria for a good story, the more likely it is to be selected; however,
once it has been selected, the elements that made it newsworthy in
the first place will be accentuated. Certainly, particular methods of

presentation were evident in the coverage of youth homelessness that we examined. Let us look in more detail at the themes in this distinct press style.

The presentation of an unfamiliar problem

Homelessness is often presented in the press as an unfamiliar and mysterious problem, of which the public is largely unaware. Most obviously, it can be presented as an issue that is largely hidden from public view, which is why the public are unfamiliar with it. For example, in one article entitled 'Who Cares about the Homeless?' (*Sunday Correspondent*, 14 January 1990), we are told that the public is largely unaware of the homeless men and women who are 'huddled in draughty recesses'. In another feature article (*Sunday Express*, 24 June 1990) the hidden aspect of the problem is similarly emphasised. The headline 'The Lost Generation' is followed by the promise to launch a 'crusade to find a lost generation of children'. It is pointed out that 'Britain today is better equipped to find a missing car or a lost dog than a runaway child'. If the world of youth homelessness is hidden from public view, then the journalist has a good story by exposing this world to the public. The presentation of homelessness in hidden terms creates a need for it to be interpreted and explained.

Even if a social problem such as homelessness is quite visible and not physically hidden; if the public still feel that the problem is unfamiliar, then the need for the media to interpret it remains. For example, it is clear that the increasing media coverage of youth homelessness in the late 1980s and early 1990s rested, in part at least, on the growing visibility of youth homelessness in the UK, as the numbers of young homeless people living on the streets increased (see Liddiard 1990). As the problem of youth homelessness grew and became more visible, so too did the desire to understand more about the issue, which was still seen as part of an unknown and unfamiliar world.

Because youth homelessness is often presented as an unfamiliar problem, the public are made to feel that they do not have the experience against which to check the facts. In reality, however, the problem of homelessness may not be as mysterious or unfamiliar as the media often implies. Beresford (1979) suggests that the general public does have first-hand experience of homelessness in the visibility of street homelessness and because they themselves may

FIGURE 4.1 *Little beggars*

LITTLE BEGGARS

*Slouched in sleeping bags, dreaming of making it
in the capital, more and more children and teenagers are begging
on the streets of London. Photographs by* BRIAN MOODY

BY ANDREW TYLER

"I know it sounds stupid," says Darren, a 14-year-old Mancunian who has lived for 18 months on the capital's streets, "but with me being involved in numerous films and documentaries, what's getting me, like, is if they're all so bothered, why don't they find me somewhere to live?"

We used to look at footage of the Bowery bums of New York, watch the city's sober classes lift a leg over their crumpled bodies *en route* to Broadway a few blocks away. And we thought it could never happen here, but that if it did we would never get used to it. In this past year, however, we have become as accustomed as New Yorkers to the hard stuff: teenage beggars, like Darren, slouched in sleeping bags in the tunnels of London's West End Tube stations, hands cupped, heads bowed.

Darren thinks it is comic that he should have achieved celebrity for having joined the new army of bums. His plan, after his father hopped off to Spain with a younger woman and the relationship with his mother fell apart, was to join the gossip column set that he'd read about in the tabloids. He thought the streets of London were jumping with them. "From Manchester," he says, "London looked full of film stars walking around the West End...Emma Ridley, the wild child...just, like, full of yuppies all rich and famous. But it ain't. In fact, London's full of tramps, homeless like me. Hee hee."

If *he* was wrong about what London was paved with, he says, *we* have the wrong melodramatic notions about the scene he inhabits. It is not a case of round-the-clock close shaves and dramas. There is little street-corner camaraderie. In fact it is not even a "scene" at all, but largely solitary figures drifting from pavement to arcade, from day centre to pub to soup van.

Darren is under-age even among these young cohorts. As he is not yet 16, the law

*Left: Irish beggar Zach Doyle, aged 19, on the London Underground.
Right: Fourteen-year-old Darren has lived on London's streets for 18 months*

THE INDEPENDENT MAGAZINE 3 DECEMBER 1988

4.1

Source: Independent Magazine, 3 December 1988 (photos: Brian Moody).

states that he should be in council care or back home with his family. But he has proved resistant to both these settings, and since he cannot legally be provided with independent housing or income, it is bureaucratically more convenient to have him drift on, unseen.

His 15-year-old Scots friend Steph, probably the West End's highest-grossing beggar, is similarly placed. But things will not necessarily improve once they reach 16, the traditional age of independence. Following the April social security cuts, it seems there is now no legal income for the majority of 16- and 17-year-olds who are not in work or on YTS schemes.

And this, says Nick Hardwick, director of Centrepoint, the West End emergency youth shelter, is most of the explanation for the dozens of cupped-hand youths now haunting the Tube, the other factor being the increasing rarity of cheap accommodation. "The stereotype might be that they are lazy and idle, but these kids are often more enterprising and less apathetic than those who stay behind. The majority have come to the capital seeking work. They've taken Norman Tebbit's advice and got on their bikes." Their begging, he says will generally be short-term, aimed at acquiring the cash to afford somewhere to live. Without an address, many employers will not entertain a young applicant. Others get hooked and dragged down by their begging. What was a temporary expedient becomes a habit.

If the intention has been to cure these young people of any incipient benefit dependency, it seems to have worked. Many can no longer be bothered to claim now. "But instead of the benefits culture," notes Hardwick, "what is developing is a pretty degrading street culture that is actually much more damaging."

Drug-dealing, burglary, robbery and prostitution are the more extreme stratagems for survival. Hanging around the back of supermarkets at garbage time will usually provide something useful. Or those with a special thirst might act the

4.1

have been temporarily homeless, spending time on a friend's floor, or in temporary accommodation. As Beresford suggests:

What actually seems to happen is that the mass media divorce us from our own experience by imposing their own meaning on the phenomena (p. 143).

This is one way in which the press coverage of social problems such as youth homelessness is not strictly objective, although it gives the impression that it is reflecting reality.

The presentation of negative themes

The manner in which the press present a social problem is partly determined and mediated by the desire for a good story. Negative news is more likely to be selected by the media for several reasons (Galtung and Ruge 1981, pp. 58–9). For example, the public response to negative news is more likely to be consensual than is the public response to positive news. Negative events are more likely to be unexpected, shocking and less frequent than positive events and, as such, they make good stories. A number of negative themes can be identified in the media's treatment of youth homelessness – in particular, the problematic lifestyle of some homeless people.

Sex, drugs and violence are common currency of the press throughout the world. Prostitution, involving both young women and young men, sexual abuse, drug addiction and violence are all alluded to in the press articles under review. In many articles there is direct reporting of the problematic aspects of youth homelessness. For example, in Australia, drug deaths among young homeless people hit the headlines in 1990 (*Sydney Morning Herald*, 23 June and 12 July). However, on closer inspection, it is surprising that press articles rarely report first-hand evidence of either prostitution or hard drugs. Rather these topics are only introduced indirectly. For example, in an article headlined 'Lambs to the Slaughter' (*Sunday Express*, 24 June 1990), it is admitted that nothing actually happened to the two runaway girls described in the feature (see Figure 4.2). However, we are told that the father *thinks about* stories of teenage girls being dredged from the Thames and of 'young girls lured into prostitution and pornography' and, in this way, these topics are introduced. In another article headlined 'Street Couple Resigned to a Life Without Hope' (*Independent*, 8 January 1990), violence and prostitution are introduced in a similarly indirect way (see Figure 4.2). The reader is told that Michelle prefers the street, 'despite the risk of physical and sexual attack', and John says:

Many times I have been asked to sell my arse . . . I haven't, but I know lots of kids who have.

This is not to deny that prostitution, drugs and violence are significant problems potentially facing young homeless people. What is interesting, however, is the manner in which the press feel compelled to introduce these negative themes even when they may lack any direct evidence to support their claims.

The presentation of contrasts

The negative aspects of youth homelessness are sometimes exaggerated by the use of contrasts, which is a common journalistic technique. For example, the 'huddled masses' of the homeless under Waterloo Bridge are contrasted with the 'elegant concert goers' on their way home (*Sunday Correspondent*, 14 January 1990). One newspaper headline similarly emphasises a contrast: 'There's No Place Like Home: Just an Empty Pavement after the City Has Gone off to Bed' (*Observer*, 17 September 1989). Even in one local newspaper, 'home sweet home' is contrasted with 'a coffin cold concrete passage in a bleak underground car-park' (*South Wales Evening Post*, 21 December 1990).

The presentation of human interest stories

There has long been a tendency to personalise news, because a reader can more easily identify with an event or situation when it has been personalised. Such stories can 'cross barriers of sex, class and age' and thus they are likely to appeal to a wide audience (see Curran et al. 1980). The attraction of the human interest story can also be understood in relation to news-gathering techniques. Where news must be gathered quickly, interviews with individuals will often be relied upon. For example, we were told by a national television reporter in the UK that the standard procedure for a television editor is to check the story from its originator, usually an agency; to take a minister's statement; and then to contact relevant agencies to find 'victims' to interview.

Homelessness is thus personalised, as is often the case with social problems, by using the stories of such victims. In this way, 'the people

FIGURE 4.2 *Street homelessness in London*

SUNDAY EXPRESS

JUNE 24 1990   WEATHER: Rain reaching the South — See Page 3   PRICE 50p

LAMBS TO THE SLAUGHTER

Youngsters who seek a future but find only squalor

🏃 CRUSADER

TODAY the Sunday Express launches a crusade to find a lost generation of children.

Every year 100,000 youngsters go missing in Britain. Many flee to big cities like London expecting to find shelter and jobs but discover only squalor.

They sink into a quagmire of sordid streetlife. Adrift in an adult world, they are lured into degradation, easy prey for any urban predator.

The runaways are a danger to themselves and a temptation to the unscrupulous, a blight on our city streets, a source of anguish to their families and a reproach to our civilised society. They sleep rough in doorways and squats, beg money from tourists, steal from shops and even resort to prostituting themselves in back alleys. Many, like a 16-year-old girl who was dragged from the Thames recently, find death.

Yet Britain today is better equipped to find a missing car or a lost dog than a runaway child.

Some flee abuse at home, or institutional care and foster parents. Some are abducted by strangers or family members but many run away from caring families to satisfy an adolescent wanderlust.

For the parents there is little help; police forces are under-resourced and have no facilities to do more than take details of a missing child and search their locality.

In London, where thousands of missing children roam the streets, there are only four policemen in the Juvenile Protection Squad and many forces admit they do not even pass on details of missing children to Scotland Yard.

If your child goes missing in Yorkshire there is no guarantee that the Metropolitan force will ever be informed, even though they are likely to head for the capital.

Unless foul play is suspected most runaways become just another statistic in a log book at

THE LOST GENERATION
Page 11

local police stations. Some children see sense and return home, others are picked up by suspicious bobbies on the beat but too many vanish without trace.

What is happening to our children has been kicked under the carpet for too long. We need to uncover the roots of a scandal which shames us.

The Government must set up an inquiry taking evidence from police, volunteer groups, social services, parents and children to learn more about the problem.

It must formulate a national policy to tackle the problem at its roots so that:
□ Children are educated in schools and through public information campaigns to the consequences of running away, just as they are to the consequences of drug abuse.
□ Children who suffer abuse at home, are kicked out by uncaring parents or run away from institutions have an alternative to the streets.

But first the Government must immediately announce a centralised Register of Missing Persons. It would cost little to add a facility to the new national police computer allowing forces access to a central bank of information and photographs of missing people.

This would enable city police forces and transport police to be immediately alerted to look out for runaways as they arrive at mainline railway or coach stations, and it would better equip officers to find missing children on city streets.

The police have been asking for such a facility for some time, the Council of Europe recommended that member nations provide a central register as far back as 1979.

The Sunday Express urges the government to act now. In the meantime we are taking action ourselves.

On page 11 we announce details of a Helpline for parents who feel nobody cares and for the children who would like to go home but are afraid to make the first move.

CHRIS SCHWARZ

Lonely sorrow of a girl on the run

IN tears, a 15-year-old runaway realises the streets of London are not paved with gold.

The Sunday Express found Becky with a friend, penniless and hungry, in Piccadilly Circus.

Within hours of arriving in London's West End from the Midlands, the schoolgirl who ran away from her foster mother, had been picked up by older boys and found room on the floor of an East End squat.

Within days, she had been put to work — begging pennies from tourists because "she looked cute".

Within a week, she was wearing stolen clothes and shoes and stealing food.

But she was lucky.

A police officer tackled her outside Buckingham Palace as she scrounged from tourists, and this weekend she and her friend were back home again.

On page 11, we detail the runaways' week on the streets and the anguish of the parents who searched for them.

For these two runaways, the story did not end in disaster, but for many more, it does.

4.2 a

Source: (a) *Sunday Express*, 24 June 1990 (photo: Chris Scharz);
(b) *Independent*, 8 January 1990 (photo: John Voos).

THE INDEPENDENT Monday 8 January 1990   ...HOI

Benefit cuts 'force more teenagers to sleep rough'

Street couple resigned to a life without hope

4.2 b

change from being muffled, needy shapes into individuals' (*Sunday Correspondent*, 14 January 1990). In the articles under review, news items were usually personalised through the use of interview material with photographs, life histories and personal observations of homeless people themselves. For example, a middle-page spread on homelessness in one local UK paper is dominated by a personal account and photo of Shayne: 'My Nightmare in Cardboard City with Rats 'n Roaches' (*Llanelli Star*, 24 May 1990). A headline in *Sydney Morning Herald* (25 November 1989 – 'Homeless Girls Ask PM for Shelter' – personalises the issue in a similar way.

The presentation of stereotypes

Stereotyping indicates that a simplified view is presented that hides the complexity of the subject. It is clear that a stereotypical view of youth homelessness arises in part from the journalistic desire to exaggerate those aspects of a social problem that are deemed to be most newsworthy, such as sex and drugs. Perhaps one of the most obvious stereotypes presented by the press is the way in which they portray youth homelessness as almost exclusively *street homelessness*. The vast majority of young people featured in the articles we reviewed were, or had been, sleeping rough. In effect, the large numbers of homeless young people staying temporarily with friends or in other temporary accommodation are largely ignored by the press. This is not to suggest that the media deliberately create or endorse stereotypes. The emphasis on street homelessness is easily explained: it most effortlessly fills the requirements of a good story. It is easily understood by the public and, most importantly, the street homeless are relatively easy to find and to interview. As the manager of one homelessness advice centre explained to us:

It's when they become roofless . . . that they become an image that can be understood by most people, because the image of a young person living in a squalid bedsit would be difficult to film . . . but with these young people (the street homeless), you just send the cameras down.

Even when less extreme examples of homelessness are dealt with, the stark image of sleeping rough still appears. For example, one article that we reviewed (*Guardian*, 3 March 1987) was concerned with young people in the UK who were trapped in their parents' homes because of increasing property prices. However, to illustrate the article, which had featured young career couples, there was a picture of someone sleeping on a pavement with the caption: 'Out in the cold: for some who escape the streets are paved only with the meanest bedclothes'. Although the press were dealing with the less extreme images of homelessness, it was still deemed necessary to illustrate the article with a more familiar image of street homelessness.

In a similar way, it is clear that the press often stereotype youth homelessness as an experience bordering on the anarchic, where one is continually forced to hustle to survive and there is constant drama. The reality of homelessness, however, is quite different, and one of its most disagreeable features – boredom – is also one of the most mundane, and thus generally ignored by the press. This is illustrated in the following quote where, interestingly, the journalist is aware of press stereotypes and directly critical of them:

. . . we have the wrong melodramatic notions about the scene he [homeless young man] inhabits. It is not a case of round-the-clock

close shaves and dramas. There is little street-corner camaraderie. In fact it is not even a 'scene' at all, but largely solitary figures drifting from pavement to arcade, from day centre to pub to soup van (*Independent Magazine*, 3 December 1988).

The presentation of ambiguity

Recent research on the impact of the media has shown that the way in which an audience interprets media messages is determined less by the content of the media and more by the initial viewpoint of the audience (see Morley 1980). In other words, the public tend to adopt and endorse only those media messages that are compatible with their existing viewpoints. Certainly, few academic commentators now hold that the media present consistent ideological messages.

The diverse media portrayal of social problems is most obvious in the way in which the same problem can be treated in different newspapers. For example, two contrasting views of youth homelessness in Britain – in particular, begging in London – can be seen in two articles from different national newspapers (see Figure 4.3). In one, with a sympathetic main headline 'Destitute Teenagers Face Jail Penalty' (*Guardian*, 3 January 1990), the public is told of Tracy, who goes begging for a few pounds simply to buy herself and her dog some food. However, in another article, headlined 'The Wild West End' (*Mail on Sunday*, 26 May 1991), the issue of begging is described to the public as 'a sinister and violent new phenomena which threatens to engulf the capital and . . . could break out into open warfare as the tourist season reaches its peak', and of beggars being abusive, spitting and threatening to infect members of the public with AIDS.

The difference between the two articles arises from a number of sources. On the one hand, it obviously reflects the different political stances and different audiences of the two newspapers. It also indicates the obvious fact that homeless beggars, like homeless young people, are heterogeneous. It may also reflect the change in public opinion over a year or the different source of information used by the journalist – the police in the later article and probably agencies in the first. Whatever the source of the difference, these articles illustrate the diverse way in which similar problems can be dealt with by the press.

What is more interesting, however, is the way in which there are often contrasts and ambiguities within the same article. It is from

FIGURE 4.3 *Two views on young beggars*

4 **HOME NEWS**
THE GUARDIAN
Wednesday January 3 1990

Probation officers alarmed at big rise in arrests under 1824 law aimed at ridding London streets of Napoleonic war casualties

Destitute teenagers face jail penalty

Waterloo sunset ... Mark and Tracy can only pay fines by begging. 'The CID are warning everybody's time,' says Tracy

Young beggars governed by law of the Bullring

4.3 a

Source: (a) *Guardian*, 3 January 1990 (photo: Martin Argles); (b) *Mail on Sunday*, 26 May 1991 (photos: Ian McIlgorm).

these contrasts and ambiguities that different readings and interpretations can be constructed by the audience. Although their tenor was generally sympathetic to the homeless, many of the articles we looked at contained elements that could be interpreted in quite different ways. Referring again to the article 'Destitute Teenagers Face Jail Penalty' (*Guardian*, 3 January 1990), the tone of the feature is largely sympathetic. However, the fact that the central character,

4.3 b

Tracy, has a dog allows a quite different interpretation. For example, the dog confirms the views of those readers who believe that beggars cannot be living below the poverty line if they have enough money to keep a pet. Similarly, in the article entitled 'Little Beggars' (*Independent Magazine*, 3 December 1988), the chief characters can be seen as either innocent or 'working the system'. They are ambiguously portrayed as both victims and victimisers. For example, this description of a young beggar allows readers to take whatever angle suits their existing viewpoints:

His voice has an appealing tone and when he's sober he is tender, clever and a masterful break dancer. When he is unsure of himself or drunk – 'I need a little drink just to carry on the day' – he can be verbally and physically savage. A quarrel with a man over a pint of beer ended with Darren kicking the man's nose into an unrecognisable pulp.

Likewise, in the article entitled 'Caught in a Teenage Trap' (*Guardian*, 23 November 1989), the main tenor of the piece is concern about the removal of state benefit from youngsters who fail to go on youth training schemes. However, a careful reading shows that Chris simply refuses to join such a scheme, seeing it as 'slave labour', while 'employers will not take him because they dislike his punky clothes and hair gelled into the shape of a trident'. Thus the reader who sees the young homeless as work-shy has their views confirmed, as does another reader worried about the persecution of youth by government regulations.

The presentation of structural issues and statistics

We have seen that the press often describe youth homelessness in personal terms. Yet, simultaneously, the serious and the popular press may also discuss youth homelessness in structural terms, examining issues such as the housing market, unemployment and changes in welfare benefits, although human-interest stories are often used to illustrate these points. Use is also made of statistics.

The way in which the press focus on structural explanations and statistics is surprising. Many structural issues, for example, are highly complex. One journalist said of recent benefit changes: 'Experts have had to call in experts to understand the new arrangements' (*Observer*, 17 September 1989). Similarly, we have already seen that the use of statistics in the field of youth homelessness is laden with difficulties, as some journalists illustrate (see Levy 1989). Nevertheless, the press consistently refer to structural themes and statistics, despite these problems. This emphasis arises in part from the media's reliance on homelessness agencies for their stories and for their information. It is clear that the statistics and structural information used by the press often comes directly from these agencies who, as we shall see, play an important part in informing the media of social problems like youth homelessness.

Television documentaries

The use of television documentaries is an important means by which social problems are presented to the public. The British drama documentaries *Cathy Come Home* (1966) and *Johnny Go Home* (1975) were nationally known exposures of homelessness in their time.[2] It can be seen from Box 4.1 that documentaries often use a similar style to the press. They tend to focus on street homelessness, with an emphasis on the more negative aspects of homelessness, such as prostitution and drugs, and the story is invariably personal. However, in some respects, documentaries are distinctive. For instance, because they usually last for half an hour or more, documentaries frequently look at a problem through time – following an individual or giving an historical account. This gives documentaries an additional depth which is often missing from press accounts.

In both of these drama documentaries, the emphasis is clearly on the negative and more sensational aspects of homelessness, with problems accumulating through time. The newcomer succumbs to drugs, prostitution and other dangers of the streets. The road is downwards. The message is to warn others not to take the same route. The viewer is led to imagine that the film cameras were following these characters over a period of weeks or months, and has charted their gradual decline. The importance of following a story through time, or at least appearing to, is that it gives more authority to the media's message. The reality, however, may be somewhat different. Beresford (1979, pp. 156–7), for example, wonders if the cameras waited all night to see the cardboard box stir as Tommy woke up and if Tommy's family did not notice the film cameras and crew as they opened the door on his surprise return. Clearly, these scenes have been reconstructed, although this is not to deny that the cameras often follow a character for weeks or months, as Wilkinson's (1981) filmed experience of being homeless for a month illustrates.

While these documentaries clearly emphasise the more problematic aspects of youth homelessness, it is also important to remember that the risks and dangers highlighted by *Johnny Go Home* were not necessarily exaggerated. It was later discovered that Roger Gleaves, who ran the charity hostel used by Tommy, had a history of sexual

---

Box 4.1 Two drama documentaries

Johnny Go Home 1975
Annie, who ran away from home when she was 12, has lived rough
ever since. She is a drug addict and, at 16, lives by begging in
Piccadilly. Tommy ran away several times from his home in
Glasgow, but is new to London. He is drawn by the bright lights
and excitement of the capital. The audience is told:

> **Tommy's new found friends rapidly introduce him to the
> twilight world of Piccadilly. . . . In the heat of an improvised
> bonfire in the old Covent Garden, the kids, the drifters and the
> down-and-outs gather in a way that's hardly changed since
> Dickens's time** (cited in Beresford 1979, p. 156).

Street Kids 1988
Three young men arrive at Centrepoint hostel, London. One
'hopes to get a place of his own, a job and a girlfriend'. They meet
'Ferret' from Glasgow, who has been living on the street for 10
years and is involved in the rent boy scene. The audience is also
introduced to two young girls, dirty and barefoot, who speak of
'trying any drugs that are going' and being pestered and beaten
up by pimps. We see young men with extreme mohican hair cuts
reeling around in underground stations and other boys giggling
in squats. By this time, one of the main characters tells us that
he'll take 'any drug . . . I'm shaking for a drink'. Another says that
he is not looking for a job. By the end of the documentary, one of
the main characters has won £4,000 in a competition and has a
flat, a suit and a job. Another has returned home. The third tells
us, as he freshens up in a public toilet, that he 'can't handle
London'. He concludes:

> **I'm just popping every night to get high. I've pulled knives on
> people because I don't know what I'm doing . . . I'm going to
> end up floating down the Thames.**

---

perversion and had made money from working rent boys. In 1975
he was arrested for the murder of a former lodger (Rose 1988,
pp. 199–200). Similarly, the confession by Dennis Nilsen in 1983 to
the murder of 15 young men, many of them homeless, is further
evidence of the real risks facing some young homeless people (ibid.,
p. 200).

Interestingly, the despair of the subject is often reinforced in documentaries by beginning and ending on the same note. In *Street Kids*, the boys meet 'Ferret' at the beginning of the film. At the end of the film, the viewer sees 'Ferret' greet another newcomer, full of expectations and wearing a new anorak. 'Ferret' asks him if he has 'seen the kids on the square' (our original heroes). 'They're junkies,' 'Ferret' remarks, 'you'll be like them.' The tale has come full circle. *Cathy Come Home* similarly opens with Cathy and her husband in their own house resisting the bailiffs' hammers. At the end of the film, we see the bailiffs again. This time the door of a squat is broken down and Cathy comes out.

In the two documentaries featured, the structural causes of homelessness are not explicitly mentioned. They are overshadowed by the more emotive subjects of drugs, prostitution and sexual abuse. In fact, Beresford (1979, p. 157) complains that in *Johnny Go Home* complex issues such as young people's desire for independence, social and regional inequalities in employment, the nature of the family and the extension of childhood are merely reduced to 'a matter of runaway kids and the dangers awaiting them in the big city' However, it is interesting that, although the legal complexities of homelessness and welfare legislation are often difficult to explain (as discussed earlier), a number of documentaries do directly illustrate the structural basis of youth homelessness. This is again partly because of the role of agencies – and, to a lesser extent, academic commentators – in informing the media of social problems such as youth homelessness.

Agency reports and publicity

Much of what is written about youth homelessness has its origins in the agencies that are variously involved with young homeless people. Not only do agencies produce large amounts of publicity material and reports, but the media often rely on these for their own features. In this way, agency reports and publicity have an important impact, both directly and indirectly, upon the public presentation of social problems such as youth homelessness. This agency material can be diverse and can include research reports, publicity or campaigning reports, briefing papers, annual reports and leaflets.[3] This kind of material can be easily collected in any country by the student of a social problem and can then be used to help construct a picture of any issue. Unsurprisingly, this material also tells us a great deal about the agencies themselves.

In a number of ways, the presentation of youth homelessness found in agency material tends to differ from its presentation in the press. Over all, greater stress is laid on the structural factors behind youth homelessness – the housing market, unemployment and, above all, benefit policies. Similarly, while many agencies use a mixture of human interest stories and statistics, a pattern so typical of press presentations, agency reports also exhibit themes that are quite specific to agencies, such as messages of their own work and progress. Nevertheless, agency reports may still emphasise the more sensational aspects of homelessness, because it allows them to justify their intervention and to outline the important nature of their services, which in turn helps them to attract resources.

Box 4.2 succinctly illustrates this emphasis on the value of the agency's work, which the account accentuates by its stress on the

---

Box 4.2 An agency account

A volunteer talks of his encounter with Julian, a 16-year-old from Blackpool. At first he would only speak in 'surly monosyllables'. Then, over a cup of tea, 'he took a deep breath and began his story':

> He'd moved in with his grandmother after a series of rows with his parents, but after a month Gran said he'd have to go, so, three weeks ago he'd come to London. . . . We sat drinking coffee and chatting, then, out of the blue he admitted that since arriving in London he'd been involved in the rent scene [male prostitution]. . . . We discussed the legal angle, the chances of being attacked again, the risks to his health and self-esteem, then we got onto the reason why he was selling himself. After a bit of hedging, he came out with it – fruit machines. Julian is one of the small number of young people addicted to gambling; an addiction so intense they are unable to generate an interest in anything else.
>
> Now we could view the crisis in its true proportions. I was able to tell him of the great work that the advice projects do, the importance of getting him into a supportive hostel and the possibility of his attending a self-help group specialising in his problem (Centrepoint Soho 1988, p. 6).

sensational. For example, a teenager reveals the serious problems behind his situation – male prostitution and addictive gambling. The style in this account is particularly journalistic and dramatic. The focus on the problems of the young person in question allows the agency to then highlight the value of their services.

In large part, the content of agency reports, like the content of press reports, is determined by the reports' perceived audience. Yet the audience for agency reports is varied. For instance, it is clear that many agency reports, with the emphasis on their practical work and their attempts to resolve the problem, are designed for potential funding bodies. However, many reports also attempt to address policy makers either directly or through the press. For this reason, agency accounts contain detailed illustrations of policy problems and policy recommendations. In fact, agency presentations are strongly influenced by the demands of the press (Beresford 1979, p. 152). While agencies hope to affect the press, journalists also rely on agency material for their articles. Many aspects of agency reports, such as the use of sensational examples, are there to attract press interest. Certainly, there are many similarities between the press and agency styles. A similarity can be seen in the following quote from an annual report of a London-based homelessness hostel, which shows the narrative style, the contrasts and the stereotypes one would expect in a press account:

> **All the bright lights and the bunches of people stepping from the clubs, hailing cabs or laughing in strolling groups may confuse you; you may feel you're in heaven. But, no, you're in crisis; you don't have a home, you don't have money, you don't have a job, you don't have a friend and you don't have much hope** (Centrepoint Soho 1988, p. 4).

In a similar way, the Soho Project's diary of nightly street work reads like a press list of the stereotypical images of youth homelessness:

> **. . . taking a suicidal young man to the nearest casualty department to get emergency treatment for a drug overdose. Or explaining to a young woman that we can help her to get identification so that she can claim social security and no longer have to rely on the dubious generosity of her newly found boyfriend. Or talking to a group of male prostitutes about the dangers of AIDS. Or finding a young couple sleeping in cardboard boxes and getting them a bed for the night** (Soho Project 1988, p. 4).

This similarity is not surprising in a situation where agencies write directly for the press. Often, the main objective of a report or publication is to gain press coverage and so publicity. Agencies, for instance, need to engage the public not only for publicity, but also for donations. Many voluntary agencies are increasingly dependent on the public and sponsors for their revenue and this clearly determines how they present the problem. Similarly, publicity can be seen to be important for influencing policy makers. It is not surprising, therefore, that agencies often adopt journalistic tactics – simplifying, stereotyping, personalising and photographing – in order to reach their audience.

Academic commentators

In theory, the academic stands aside from the media, the agency, the politician and the public. In reality, the distance between the academic and the press is not so great. Academic researchers are now being made more aware of the need to make their material accessible to the public and to the politician. With this in mind, they are now often encouraged and instructed by their funding bodies to write directly for the press. Yet there are other connections between media coverage and academic interest. Academics have often sought to examine the issues that have assumed prominence in the media. For example, the delinquent gangs and the teddy boys who featured in the media of the 1950s and 1960s led in part to the academic interest in 'style' (see Brake 1980; Hebdige 1979). Similarly, the examination of the Mods and Rockers phenomenon in the 1960s, and its treatment by the media, led to important developments in the field of labelling theory (see Cohen 1972). Social problems often march through the sociological textbooks in much the same way as they march through the headlines – with a time lag of several years reflecting the time it takes to produce academic texts.

4.3 The media, public opinion and policy making

Media images are public images. Whatever 'public opinion' may be, it is certainly connected in some way with the media. Moreover, in a democracy at least, there is often a belief that policy makers are somehow influenced by this 'public opinion' and media coverage.

However, the precise linkage between the media, public opinion and policy making is far from clear. For example, do the media simply reflect public opinion or do the media actually play an important part in determining public opinion? Similarly, is there a close link between public opinion and policy making, or is the relationship between them only a tenuous, even symbolic, one? In this section, we consider in some detail the connection between the media, public opinion and policy making. We begin with a specific case study from the UK of media coverage in the field of homelessness, which is summarised in Box 4.3 overleaf.

In many respects, these accounts are typical examples of press coverage, with the use of negative themes, ambiguity, human interest stories and a stress on street homelessness. It is interesting, however, that the way in which the events were treated by the press assumed that the interconnection between the media, public opinion and policy decisions was a straightforward one. The articles explicitly suggested that the government was goaded into action by public opinion, which in turn was voiced by the media. Certainly, it was interesting that this package coincided with the clearing of the 'cardboard city' in the Bullring near Waterloo Station, London which had been the source of many of the preceding press reports and photographs of homeless people, and 'a growing embarrassment for the Government' (*The Daily Telegraph*, 18 June 1990). However, if we take a wider look at the situation, the interconnections between the media, public opinion and policy making may not be so simple.

The media and public opinion

Few would disagree with the following observation by C. Wright Mills:

> **Men and women live in second hand worlds. . . . The quality of their lives is determined by meanings they have received from others. . . . The mass media is now even more central in the creation of their images in our heads of the world outside** (cited in Negrine 1989, p. 4).

Few would disagree that, with the advent of television, the public are exposed to the media more than ever before, such that the mass media have become fundamental to the way we understand the

---

Box 4.3 Press coverage of a government homelessness package

On 18 June 1990, a £15 million package was announced by the British government to clear the homeless from the streets of London and other cities. The most widely reported item in this 'Church Halls to Hostels' package was a programme to provide emergency hostel shelter for the estimated 1–3,000 people sleeping rough in London.

The financial package was covered by all the quality UK newspapers, with front page headlines, editorial comment and feature articles. The story was represented in a consistent way and very much in line with the press style we have outlined. Personal stories and photos of young people sleeping rough were found alongside estimated statistics of the numbers. The images of the young people were also ambiguous. Young homeless people were presented with pity as 'shivering in the rain' (*The Times*, 19 June 1990) or having been 'propositioned for sex' (*Guardian*, 19 June 1990). However, more negative references were made to a 'deeply entrenched lifestyle' and to the bullying of the elderly homeless by younger ones (*The Daily Telegraph*, 18 June 1990).

Even within one article, the images were ambiguous. For example, sympathy is expressed in the description: '. . . many of the young people living rough are scarcely more than children whose parents have failed them'. However, simultaneously, the notion that many young homeless people simply do not want to help themselves is also presented: '. . . empty beds exist every night in shelters and hostels run by voluntary agencies, often not far from these illicit encampments and well known to those living there' (*The Times*, 19 June 1990).

This initial package was extended in the autumn of 1990 to £96 million over three years and named 'The Rough Sleeper's Initiative' (Strathdee 1992, p. 28). Money was allocated to develop the following accommodation – direct access (£23 million); permanent move-on (£70 million) and private-sector leasing (£3 million).

---

outside world. What is more contentious, however, is the precise impact of the media upon the public.

The effect of the media upon the public and public opinion has long concerned academic commentators in the UK and the USA, and there have been marked shifts in how they have approached the issue (Barrat 1986, pp. 16–18; Curran and Seaton 1991, pp. 249–76). One view – the so-called 'hypodermic syringe' model – perceives the media as having a direct effect upon the public and society. This view claims that media images are adopted in a straightforward and wholesale manner by the public. Certainly, this direct-effect model has had some impact upon studies of the media, such as the effect of media violence, particularly on young audiences (Belson 1978), and the effect of media images of women and sexuality (Ferguson 1983; Tuchman 1981). However, this model is now largely discredited because of the way in which it simplistically assumes that the audience passively and uniformly absorb whatever media messages are presented to them.

Researchers in this area have instead shown that the impact of the media upon the public is more complex than the simple hypodermic syringe model assumes and is actually mediated by a number of factors. For example, the influence of neighbours and particularly 'opinion leaders' has been shown to be important in determining how media messages should be interpreted (Katz and Lazarsfeld 1956). Similarly, Trenaman and McQuail (1961) showed that the public select and interpret the media according to their existing viewpoints. Morley (1980) illustrated that only those media messages that reinforced what individuals already believed were selected by the audience. In a well-known UK study concerning the media exposure of welfare fraud (Golding and Middleton 1982), the authors show how news reporting of the luxurious lifestyle of social security claimants whipped up a moral panic of 'scroungerphobia'. The authors suggest that the media represented the interests of those in positions of power and that the media were used to raise public anxiety. However, a later commentator (Negrine 1989) suggests that the success of the media campaign rested on existing misgivings about the welfare state already held by the public. He speaks of the press *resonating* with rather than *affecting* the public. For this reason, the same media item can be interpreted differently by different categories of people. Cumberbatch et al. (1986), for example, found that after wide media coverage of the 1984–5 miners' strike in Britain, audience views as to what the strike was about varied considerably. The authors conclude that:

While the public may have all watched the same news, they didn't all see it in the same way (p. 5).

Whatever the interconnection between the media and public opinion, it is clear that the public at large does not play much of a role in communicating directly with the media (Best 1973, p. 207). Of course, homeless people themselves can and do enter into the media and the political arena, albeit in a minor way, in the verbatim interviews reported in the press and on television. But Beresford (1979, p. 161) suggests that the homeless in these accounts are simply extras designed to give some authenticity to media accounts. The media, like the politicians, need to get their information from accredited and easily accessible sources. They turn to experts – such as agency workers dealing with the problem or, to a lesser extent, the academic commentator. The general public and the homeless do not usually enter into this exchange between the media, agencies and policy makers, although the term 'public opinion' is often used.

Public opinion, the media and policy making

The feeling that the government somehow directly responds to public opinion was expressed in several remarks from the press coverage of the British government's 1990 homelessness package (see Box 4.3):

> **[Young homeless people have become] a talking point for visitors and a deep political embarrassment to the Government** (*The Times*, 18 June 1990).

> **The alarm and pity this [youth homelessness] causes to the populace has at last communicated itself to the Government, which has responded with a mixture of proposals** (*The Times*, 19 June 1990).

However, it is difficult to locate this 'alarm of the populace'. As Beresford (1979) says:

> **The 'public' is involved only as an abstract and unreal entity. There is no way of summoning it, of hearing its views, or of being restrained by it** (p. 160).

While 'the public' melts away, statements about the effect of the media on government and policy makers are more concrete. There is general agreement that wide media coverage can lead to an issue being taken up by policy makers (Best 1973). With many issues competing for the time and resources of Parliament, media exposure may lead to one issue taking precedence over another. In choosing to report items in a certain way and to omit others, the press can set the agenda for action. Whether it is the media who set these agendas or whether they are manipulated by others is under dispute (Barrat 1986, pp. 51–7). There is certainly agreement that agencies, and increasingly academic commentators, use and even manipulate the media. By knowing what events and personalities are likely to be newsworthy, they are able to present their material in a way that is likely to attract media coverage.

We have already seen that it is difficult to elicit the precise impact of the media upon public opinion. Similarly, it is difficult to identify and measure accurately the influence of media coverage on policy making. For example, the two documentaries *Cathy Come Home* (1966) and *Johnny Go Home* (1975) both shocked the British public and led to homelessness being taken up in Parliament directly after their screenings. However, in terms of legislative change, it is difficult to pinpoint the effect of these two documentaries. It must be remembered that policies are made in response to a variety of pressures, of which agenda setting by the media is only one. For example, a problem must be acknowledged by those in power. Even if it is recognised, a problem will usually only be addressed if a politically effective solution is apparent (Best 1973, pp. 224–55).

Detailed examination of how topics such as deviancy and crime are reported (Chibnall 1977; Cohen and Young 1981) has certainly led to a consideration of the impact of media messages upon both the public and policy makers. In particular, it has been suggested that the media can play an important part in stirring up a 'moral panic' in the audience, which can lead to creating and then controlling a scapegoat category. This has been analysed in relation to the crime of 'mugging' (Hall et al. 1978) and in terms of 'welfare scroungers' (Golding and Middleton 1982). Indeed, there was clearly an element of 'moral panic' in the media coverage of homelessness, the clearing of the Bullring, and the announcement of a funding package in 1990 (see Box 4.3). However, the classic study of the media and 'moral panics' must remain Cohen's *Folk Devils and Moral Panics* (1972).

Cohen examined the British Mods and Rockers phenomenon of the 1960s and particularly the manner in which they were treated by the media. He illustrated how deviant behaviour can be given a particular identity by the media, and how those involved – in this case the Mods and the Rockers – become 'folk devils', epitomising everything that is wrong with society. As a consequence, public concern about the issue escalates into what Cohen calls a 'moral panic', whereby the public, the justice system and policy makers dramatically overreact to what were initially only minor forms of deviant behaviour. Cohen's work is considerably more complex than this brief summary would indicate, but in this context his work and that of subsequent writers (such as Hall et al. 1978) is important because it identifies the mass media as important factors influencing both public opinion and policy making.

In conclusion, the media are fundamentally important for portraying a social problem like youth homelessness, and yet how they do this, and the effect that they have, is complex. Equally important are the agencies that deal with young homeless people. They are crucial for informing the media and others of the problem and yet they also provide many services for young homeless people. In the next chapter, we look in more detail at homelessness agencies and how they perform both of these roles.

Notes

1. The analysis in this section is based on a review of 26 feature articles in the press about homeless people in London and South Wales. Most, but not all, of the articles were about young people. The majority came from 'quality' daily and Sunday papers. These press articles, documentary videos and agency material were collected between 1987 and 1991. Their collection was incidental to the authors' research on young homeless people in Wales. This section is also informed by 41 articles in the Australian press between 1987 and 1990. The majority, but not all, came from the *Sydney Morning Herald*. The authors are grateful to Kristina Downing-Orr for this collection of articles.
2. The analysis in this section is based on the viewing by the authors of six documentary programmes presented on British television between 1988 and 1991, and the comments by Beresford (1979) on *Johnny Go Home*.
3. The analysis in this section is based on seven research reports, twelve publicity and campaigning reports, five information sheets and seventeen annual reports. In addition, two research reports and material from five agencies in Boston, USA, were used.

5

Agency Viewpoints

5.1 Introduction

Homelessness agencies are central to the issue of youth homelessness in the western industrial world. The importance of agencies is signified by their inclusion in almost every chapter of this book. However, until now, we have presented agencies as largely undifferentiated – in their policies and in their style of presentation. In this chapter we show their diversity.

We begin by illustrating the wide range of organisations that deal with young homeless people – housing and social services departments, accommodation and information agencies. These organisations differ in their resources, their particular histories and objectives, as well as their legal responsibilities.

We have just seen that the agencies involved in youth homelessness play a central role in presenting the problem to the press and, in turn, to the wider audience of politicians and the public (see Chapter 4). In this chapter, we look in detail at how agencies present the problem of youth homelessness to an outside audience. We show how different organisations can interpret the same problem in quite different ways and how the accounts they give often reflect the structure, purpose and resources of the agency itself.

Most agencies do more than just talk about the problem. Many provide direct services for young homeless people – in terms of accommodation, day services or advice – and it is this provision of services that usually justifies their funding. It is often assumed that homelessness agencies are indiscriminate and accept anyone who is homeless and with whom they are in contact. In reality, this is not the case. They must make choices as to who will be included and excluded in line with their particular resources and expertise. In the final part of the chapter, therefore, we look at the ways in which agency workers categorise their clients and potential clients in terms of whom they can and cannot help.

In summary, this chapter focuses upon three broad questions:

- What kinds of agencies are involved with young homeless people?
- How do agencies present the problem of youth homelessness and their homeless clients to an outside audience?
- How do agencies select and categorise their clients and potential clients?

5.2 The range of agencies

Before looking at the ways in which agencies talk about youth homelessness and their clients, it is necessary to appreciate the different types of agencies involved with young homeless people. Even within one city, there can be a range of agencies working. On a national and international level, the number of agencies involved is even higher. However, within this diversity there is a basic distinction between *statutory* and *voluntary* agencies.

Statutory agencies

Statutory agencies carry out the state's responsibilities to its citizens – in terms of education, housing, health, welfare and justice. These responsibilities are laid down in law. Statutory agencies are usually funded by central government and their working is centrally controlled by statute, although planning and funding decisions can be carried out at a local level. In the UK, as in most countries, the response of the statutory sector to single homeless people has been limited. While the details that follow are specific to the UK in the 1990s, the account illustrates the way in which much of the political debate about youth homelessness takes place over legislation and statutory obligations. In whatever country, the present context of a social issue can only be understood against its historical development whereby particular pieces of legislation form crucial landmarks.

The statutory responsibility for homeless people in the UK has shifted somewhat over time (Karn 1990, p. 11). The National Assistance Board, renamed the Supplementary Benefits Commission in 1966, had responsibility for running the old workhouses. The Welfare and Children's Department, renamed social services in 1970, had responsibility for providing residential care or temporary accommodation, where appropriate, for children and families.

However, in the 1977 Housing (Homeless Persons) Act this responsibility for providing temporary and permanent accommodation for homeless families was moved from social services to housing departments. For the first time, those accepted as 'homeless' were given priority over those on waiting lists for council houses. Since this date, the debate over the statutory responsibility for young single homeless people has continued between housing and social services departments. The two pieces of legislation over which the debate has taken place are the Housing Act and the Children Act.

Housing departments

Under the Housing (Homeless Persons) Act 1977, since replaced by Part III of the Housing Act 1985, housing departments in the UK must house those people who are deemed 'unintentionally homeless', have a local connection and, most importantly, fall into a priority category (see Chapter 2). Young homeless people are not included in the priority categories by virtue of their age alone. Whether they are in priority need or 'vulnerable' for other reasons is a matter of discretion, and resources are limited. The only duty housing departments have towards the majority of young homeless people without dependants is to offer them 'advice and assistance'. As youth homelessness became an issue through the 1980s, a few housing authorities – such as Sheffield, Glasgow, Newcastle and some London boroughs – began to house 16- and 17-year-olds and care leavers automatically, considering them as 'vulnerable', but the majority did not. A survey in 1987 showed that:

> **Half of the responding housing authorities said that they would not deem as vulnerable a young homeless person with 'no parents and no support'. One in eight authorities said they would** (Abrahams and Mungall 1989, p. 7).

Similarly, the 1991 Homelessness Code of Guidance for Local Authorities sets out the conditions under which a homeless young person could be considered 'at risk' and therefore vulnerable. Note that young age is not sufficient in itself:

> **Local authorities should consider the extent to which a young person is 'at risk' and therefore vulnerable by virtue of being homeless. Young people (16 or over) should not automatically be treated as vulnerable on the basis of age alone. Young people should**

be 'at risk' in a variety of ways. Risks could arise from violence or sexual abuse at home, the likelihood of drug or alcohol abuse or prostitution. Some groups of young people will be less able to fend for themselves than others, particularly for example: those leaving local authority care; juvenile offenders (including those discharges from young offender institutions); those who have been physically or sexually abused; those with learning difficulties and those who have been subject of statements of special educational need. These examples are not meant to constitute a complete list (para 6.13).

For many of the young single homeless, therefore, housing departments have little to offer other than 'advice and assistance', although, in theory at least, this situation has been modified somewhat by the implementation of the 1989 Children Act.

Social services departments

Part III of the Children Act 1989 (implemented in 1991) brought social services departments directly into the area of provision for young people aged over 16. Their most direct responsibilities are in relation to those young people leaving a variety of forms of care when aged 16 or over. These responsibilities continue until the young person reaches the age of 21:

> Where a child is being looked after by the local authority, it shall be the duty of the authority to advise, assist and befriend him with a view to promoting his welfare when he ceases to be looked after by them (section 24 (1)).

In fact, section 20 of the Children Act also extends the responsibility of social services beyond those who have been in care to other young people 'whose welfare would be seriously prejudiced' without such help:

> Every local authority shall provide accommodation for any child in need in the area who has reached the age of 16 and whose welfare the authority consider is likely to be seriously prejudiced if they do not provide him with accommodation (section 20 (3)).

'A child in need' is defined as follows:

> a) he is unlikely to achieve or maintain, or to have the opportunity of achieving or maintaining a reasonable standard of health or development without the provision for him;

b) **his health or development is likely to be significantly impaired or further impaired without the provision for him of such services; or** c) **he is disabled** (section 17 (10)).

The implications for young homeless people are interesting and the Guidance to the Children Act actually acknowledges the 'over-representation of care leavers amongst young homeless people, including those who sleep rough' (para 9.84). Throughout the Children Act, responsibilities towards children and young people lie with the local authority as a whole (housing, education, health, the police). However, the Guidance to the Children Act also sets out that, in terms of housing, 'the primary responsibility lies with the housing department of the local authority' (para 9.82). This responsibility is acknowledged in the Homelessness Code of Guidance:

Thus, while there is not formal correlation between the definition of vulnerability in the Housing Act 1985 and 'serious prejudice' (or 'need') in S.20 of the Children Act 1989, the two might be expected to arise in similar circumstances and housing authorities will need to have regard to a social services authority's or department's assessment that it has an obligation to provide a child with accommodation under 20 (1) or (3) of the Children's Act 1989 (para 6.15).

There are, however, two let-out clauses for housing departments:

... the Children Act 1989 requires the housing authority to respond to that request if it is compatible with its own statutory duties and obligations and does not unduly prejudice the discharge of its functions

and

The priority afforded to providing housing for young people leaving care is a matter for consideration locally (para 9.82).

Subsequently, it is not altogether surprising that despite the potential of the Children Act to provide statutory services and housing for young homeless people, relatively little was achieved in the first year of implementation. Only 62 per cent of social services departments surveyed stated that they accepted homeless 16- and 17-year-olds as 'children in need'. Eighty per cent of authorities said that a section 20 (3) assessment as 'welfare seriously prejudiced' did not automatically trigger acceptance as 'vulnerable' under the Housing

Act (CHAR 1993). Certainly, appeals and subsequent case law can alter practice. Crucially, however, it is evident that without a resolution of the acute shortage of housing and local authority funding that lies behind the interpretations of the Housing Act and the Children Act, they are unlikely to have a significant impact upon the youth homelessness problem in the UK.

The probation service

The link between offending and homelessness has long been recognised (NACRO 1981), and we discussed this in some detail in Chapter 3. In the UK, USA and Australia, juvenile justice agencies have responsibilities for runaways and young homeless people. In the UK, the importance of good-quality non-custodial accommodation in the lives of offenders and those at risk of offending was acknowledged and Area Accommodation Forums were set up in all probation areas (Home Office 1988). These Accommodation Forums were multi-agency groups with statutory and voluntary representation. Their objectives were to identify need and produce co-ordinated accommodation strategies (Fraser et al. 1992). However, despite these moves, a survey carried out in 1992 (personal communication from Housing Co-ordinators Group) indicated that between one-quarter and one-third of all people under supervision were still in housing need.

Probation addresses the accommodation needs of offenders, ex-offenders and those at risk of offending in a number of ways. One example is when the Home Office funds a specific number of beds in a scheme run by a partnership between a voluntary agency and a housing association (Watson 1988, p. 130). In such a case, probation may be represented on the management committee. Some probation areas also run supported lodgings schemes, often in partnership with social services. The landlord/landlady will provide a degree of support to the tenant in return for some financial guarantees and support from the agencies. These schemes are not funded from the Home Office, but are budgeted for at an area level. Many probation areas also have designated accommodation officers and some areas produce an index of local accommodation resources. In short, a great deal of probation officers' time is spent addressing individual clients' accommodation needs, often against a background of limited resources.

The Benefits Agency (formally the Department of Social Security)

Welfare benefits, in terms of level and ease of claiming, have an important effect on the lives of many young homeless people of whatever country. The student of youth homelessness, the agency worker and young people themselves need to understand the details. In the UK, the Benefits Agency is the government agency that young people must contact when claiming benefits. Income Support is an income-related benefit that provides financial help for people who are not in full-time work and whose income is below a minimum level set by parliament. In 1988 Income Support replaced Supplementary Benefit and rates for claimants under 25 were reduced, while most 16- and 17-year-olds lost their entitlement to Income Support altogether (see Chapter 3). For the first time, benefit levels were related to age and not need, and the economic weakness of young people significantly increased.

There are certain conditions under which a young person of 16 or 17 can claim Income Support – for example, if they are sick, a single parent, or obliged to live away from parents because of estrangement or a risk of physical or sexual abuse (Benefits Agency 1991). If a young person does not fall into one of these categories then Income Support may be paid if it is the only way to prevent severe hardship. There are no rules to say what severe hardship is, but homelessness or threatened homelessness is one of the factors considered. In all these claims for Income Support, each case is looked into separately and payments are often for a short period before employment or, more usually, a Youth Training place is found.

Housing Benefit is a social security benefit to help pay for rent for people living on a low income (Benefits Agency 1992). Payments are assessed and paid by the local authority. Housing Benefit is also age related and does not cover service charges such as heating or food. Once net income reaches Income Support levels then, for every extra pound earned, 65p of housing benefit is withdrawn. As Income Support levels are lower for those under 25, this taper particularly affects young people (Strathdee 1992, p. 13).

There are many problems even when a young person qualifies for these benefits (Social Security Advisory Committee 1992). The process of claiming benefits involves visits to many different agencies and the ensuing bureaucratic delays can result in eviction from accommodation or destitution. For example, in order to claim a

Severe Hardship Payment, a young person must visit the Careers Office, register as unemployed at the Unemployment Office, and then visit the Benefits Agency. Benefits may not be paid if the information from the Careers Office shows that the young person has not attended Youth Training regularly. Moreover, when young people move into accommodation in another area they must submit new claims for Income Support and Housing Benefit that are administered at different offices. They must then wait for their claim to be reprocessed. In any event, Housing Benefit and Income Support are both paid in arrears. It is not surprising that one survey found that 75 per cent of 16- and 17-year-olds using a London hostel had no income whatsoever (Strathdee 1992, p. 26).

The Careers Service and the Youth Service often have first-hand contact with young people in the UK who have accommodation difficulties, as do the Training and Enterprise Councils. The latter administer Youth Training, which is effectively compulsory for 16- and 17-year-olds who are without employment and not in education. They also administer Employment Training, which is vocational training for those people on benefit aged over 18. Although managers on these schemes may advise or refer young people asking for help with accommodation, there are no resources within the budgets of these services for such a task nor a formal recognition of the role they could play in terms of accommodation advice or support. Moreover, there is evidence that the government's guarantee that a training place be available for every 16- and 17-year-old who needs it is not being kept, that training is poor (Social Security Advisory Committee 1992), and that such training very often does not lead on to employment.

Voluntary agencies

While young homeless people come into contact with statutory agencies such as those detailed above, much of the day-to-day services are left to the voluntary sector in most western industrial countries (Beacock 1979, pp. 132–3). This is because young single homeless people usually still lie outside the direct responsibility of housing and welfare agencies. Although some voluntary agencies rely on donations from the public, many voluntary agencies also gain funds, directly or indirectly, from government sources. Traditionally, the voluntary sector provides innovatory services that fall outside the responsibilities of statutory agencies – such as women's refuges (see Pizzey 1974). However, as state welfare funding has become more limited, so voluntary agencies have increasingly been used as partners by statutory agencies to carry out statutory duties such as child protection. It is important to realise that although these agencies are described as 'voluntary', their staff qualifications and pay often differ little from the statutory sector (see Johnson 1981).

In the UK, some voluntary organisations, such as Centrepoint and Alone in London, were set up specifically to help with the problem of youth homelessness in the 1970s, while the Soho Project, set up in the late 1960s as a generalist youth advisory service, became increasingly involved with young homeless people in the 1970s. In addition, organisations traditionally catering for older homeless groups, such as the Salvation Army and the Cyreneans, have responded to an increasing number of young clients. However, the main source of voluntary-sector activity in this area since the mid-1980s has been the traditional 'children's charities' – Barnardos, National Children's Home, the Children's Society. The closure of the many residential homes for children, following a general move towards more community-based care, meant that some properties and staff could be redirected to services for the increasing numbers of young homeless people.

Although in some areas of the UK, particularly London, there is day-centre provision, advice, counselling and outreach work, voluntary agency provision for young homeless people has focused upon hostel provision. A similar mix of hostels and other provision can be found in the USA and many Northern European countries (Burton et al. 1989b). Certainly, in the UK, much of the money given by the government – through Urban Aid grants, through special-needs management money to housing associations, and through the Department of the Environment's hostels initiative (see Chapter 4) – is spent on hostel provision by voluntary agencies.

There has been a marked change in the provision of hostel accommodation for the single homeless in the UK. While many of the traditional homelessness hostels are being closed, new projects are opening. There are important differences between the type of provision offered in the two types of hostel.

Traditional homelessness hostels represent the stereotypical hostel provision most often associated with homelessness and vagrancy (Leach 1979). Most are institutional in character, in that they are large – often with over 30 bed spaces – and usually provide meals.

Some, known as resettlement units, are run by the state. Others are run by voluntary organisations such as the Salvation Army. They cater for a wide range of single homeless people, although their clients have traditionally been male, middle aged and white (Randall 1988, p. 38). These hostels generally prefer not to take younger people because of the institutional nature of their provision and because of the mental health and alcohol problems that some of their older clients present with. Despite this, these hostels are increasingly being used by homeless youngsters with nowhere else to go (see Steele 1989).

Youth residential projects were set up from the late 1970s specifically to cater for the younger single homeless person for whom traditional hostels were felt to be inappropriate. These residential projects usually only accept young people aged under 25 and often considerably younger (O'Mahony 1988, p. 50). In these projects, women frequently make up 50 per cent or more of the clients and the units are small, catering for less than 15 people (Pollitt et al. 1989, p. 40). Some form of support and independence training is normally offered and clients tend to stay for several months or even longer. Because of the acknowledged difficulties of communal living in hostels, moves are increasingly being made to offer young people single units scattered in general-purpose housing. Agencies are able to offer support to young people in these units, which they can then withdraw over time.

There is also a difference between direct-access hostels, where the client can simply arrive and request accommodation, and those hostels where clients can usually only gain a place through referral by agencies. In general, traditional homelessness hostels and resettle-ment units offer direct-access accommodation, whereas youth residential projects tend to take clients through referral from social services, probation or advice centres. The Resettlement Agency, a branch of the Department of Social Security, has since 1989, been closing resettlement units, handing them over to voluntary agencies, or giving grants for their replacement, because the services they offered were felt to be inappropriate. By 1992, 15 resettlement units remained open, accommodating 1,400 single homeless people, mostly men. The closure programme has led to an overall reduction in beds for single homeless people. In addition, the National Audit Commission criticised the Resettlement Agency for under-spending replacement grants and a lack of monitoring to ensure minimum standards in replacement units. The closure of this type of accommodation can lead particularly to a shortage or complete lack of direct-access emergency accommodation (Drake 1989, p. 124). There is also evidence that difficult clients can find themselves excluded from the newer, higher-quality and often smaller hostels (Liddiard and Hutson 1991).

Youth homelessness and agencies in the USA

State involvement in homelessness in the USA is even more limited than in the UK, partly because there are few statutory responsibilities to provide permanent housing for homeless people. Provision for homeless people is focused on the supply of free meals and shelter for the homeless (Sullivan and Damrosch 1987, p. 85). Funds may also be used from federal programmes concerned with health care for the homeless, substance abusers and homeless veterans (see Chapter 1). However, much welfare provision is carried out by charities and non-profit-making bodies (Cooper 1987) and based within the city or state (Ritzdorf and Sharpe 1987). In fact, many cities have homelessness programmes with a mixture of federal and charity funding (City of Boston 1990).

Some larger cities have private projects dealing with runaways and the young homeless such as The Bridge in Boston and Covenant House in New York. These are similar to voluntary projects and hostels in the UK. However, the services they provide differ in some interesting ways. Free health care often features in the USA because of the difficulties in obtaining treatment faced by those without jobs and lacking health insurance. There is also a much greater use of counselling in the USA, which in part is related to its wider use by the general population. This emphasis on counselling also tends to be associated with more personalised explanations of homelessness in the USA (see Price 1990), rather than the stress on structural factors found in the agency literature in the UK.

It is clear, therefore, that a diverse range of agencies work with young homeless people and provide an array of different services. As researchers, our first information about youth homelessness came from agency workers.[1] This interviewing of 'key' individuals or agency personnel is a common way of beginning to investigate any social problem (Hakim 1987, p. 26). Agencies have a public face and are accessible in a way that those directly affected by a problem are usually not. It is our analysis of these interviews with agency workers that forms the basis for the rest of this chapter.

5.3 Agency presentations to an outside audience

When we conducted our interviews with agency workers we quickly became aware that we were being given contradictory accounts of youth homelessness and that there were identifiable patterns in these contradictions. It became increasingly apparent that these differences largely reflected the nature of the agency from which the speaker came. Although this account is drawn from interviews largely from Wales (UK), there is no reason to believe that the findings are specific to this geographical area. A number of authors in the UK and the USA, like Scott (1970) and Lipsky (1980), have noted that the ways in which agencies may present social issues are often less than objective and that they have considerable scope for interpreting the problems with which they deal. However, this does not explain why the portrayal of youth homelessness and young homeless people should differ so widely between agencies.

'Ordinary' or 'problematic' young people

As we talked to agency workers, we became aware of a clear dichotomy running throughout much of what they said. Agencies were presenting homeless youngsters to us as somehow being either *ordinary* or somehow *problematic*. The difference rested on whether or not the young people were seen as having problems in addition to their immediate one of accommodation. This first viewpoint, whereby clients were generally referred to as 'ordinary', can be seen as a 'normalising' approach in which the client was not seen as being particularly different from their housed contemporaries. The following two agency managers expressed this viewpoint:

> **Homelessness is a temporary phase in a lot of people's lives . . . it's a necessary stage of their lives and they're not homeless for ever** (Advice Agency).

> **it doesn't matter to them where they sleep. . . . It's not classed as homelessness. I see it as natural – like living with your sister because your mother's giving you gyp** (Youth Club).

It is clear from these statements that these two managers saw the homelessness of their clients as essentially ordinary and unproblematic – something arising from the normal process of growing up and leaving home.

According to the second viewpoint, however, young people were generally referred to as 'problematic', although the term 'vulnerable' was more often used. This point of view – that is, young homeless clients being seen as having additional or special problems not widely experienced by their contemporaries living at home – can be termed a 'social pathology' approach. As two agency managers told us:

> **they're not the ordinary, able-bodied, able-minded person** (Youth Residential Project)

> **. . . really, homelessness is only *one* of their problems** (Advice Agency).

Obviously, this dichotomy between being ordinary and being problematic is a theoretical one and, in practical terms, a continuum should logically run between the two. There is certainly widespread agreement among commentators in this field that homeless youngsters represent a truly heterogeneous group (see Randall 1988). However, when we looked carefully at our interview material, we found that agency workers were presenting the problem and the condition of their clients not along a continuum, but at one end or the other. This is illustrated in the following quotations, where workers divide clients into just two types:

> **The majority are *ordinary*. You recognise if they are *vulnerable*** (Housing Department).

> **Really, there's two things going on – two sets of a problem really. . . . There are those people who are simply homeless for a period and when they find reasonable accommodation . . . will then stay there . . . and then there are other clients with recurrent homelessness and homelessness is *one* of their problems** (Advice Agency).

This simple polarisation is not surprising. A number of commentators on welfare organisations acknowledge that, for practical purposes, service providers often operate relatively simple classifications in highly complex situations. As Lipsky (1980) points out:

> **People come to street-level bureaucracies as unique individuals with different life experiences, personalities, and current circumstances. In their encounters with bureaucracies they are transformed into clients, identifiably located in a very small number of categories** (p. 59).

It is clear that agency workers tend to assign clients to a limited number of categories in order to facilitate the everyday work of the organisation by simplifying and standardising people before processing them (Prottas 1979, p. 3). What is less clear is why agencies, often dealing with very similar problems and similar young people, should present such markedly different accounts of the problem. There are a number of potential explanations.

Different kinds of clientele

It is to be expected that workers dealing with different kinds of clientele should talk about them differently. There are often very real differences between the types of clients a particular agency attracts since young people do not come into contact with agencies at random. They usually come through a variety of referral processes that are themselves selective (Randall 1988, p. 23). It is obvious that youngsters in a youth club, for instance, are likely to differ significantly from their contemporaries in a traditional homelessness hostel. In this way, differences in the portrayal of youth homelessness and young homeless people reflect differences on the ground. However, this is only part of the explanation. We have just seen, for example, that two workers from advice agencies, and ostensibly dealing with very similar client groups, gave very different accounts of the same problem.

Presenting to an audience

A second explanation is that the difference in statements is a reflection of the interaction between us, as researchers, and the agency informant. The respondent often carries a perception – false or otherwise – of the interviewer's views on the topic under discussion and this can necessarily affect their response (Hammersley and Atkinson 1983, p. 110). Because of its media exposure, most members of the public have views on youth homelessness and on looking carefully at our interview material we feel that agency workers were, on occasions, attempting to dispel the stereotypes that they felt we might be holding. It was likely, for example, that the youth club worker quoted above was attempting to present his community to us in a positive and unproblematic way, while the manager of the youth residential project was keen to emphasise the everyday problems of his work with a difficult clientele. When two people are consciously or unconsciously in debate, viewpoints and definitions tend to become polarised (Billig et al. 1988, p. 144), such that, as in this context, the acknowledged heterogeneity of young homeless people can disappear. They are presented publicly as either ordinary or problematic.

Agency type

The third and most crucial point is that the particular viewpoint of the agency worker depends, in part at least, on the nature of the agency or project that they represent. Here the nature of service provision, the basic aims, and the funding base of the organisation are important. Statements and definitions do not therefore depend solely on the characteristics of the clients. Instead, they can reflect the structure, purpose and resources of the involved organisation. As Scott notes, agency presentations of social problems are:

> **only partly determined by empirical knowledge. . . . Their content is also determined by, and reflects, certain social, cultural and political forces in the environments in which experts are immersed and on which they depend for economic support** (1970, p. 269).

Because agency accounts of the problem permeate almost every statement concerning youth homelessness, the implications are important. It is, after all, a belief in their objectivity that empowers homelessness agencies to talk with such conviction about the problem of youth homelessness. In reality, though, agency statements about youth homelessness do not simply reflect the characteristics of their homeless clients. They also reflect the structure, purpose and resources of the agency itself.

It is difficult to outline any kind of pattern between agency type and the presentation of young homeless people as ordinary or problematic. Nevertheless, two factors appear to have an influence – whether or not the agency is offering a universal or a selective service, and whether or not the agency is a statutory or voluntary body. In general terms, it appears that agencies that are offering something of a 'universal' service, and campaigning for better access to mainstream services such as employment, housing and benefits, tend to adopt a normalising approach and stress the ordinariness of their clients. If the problem affects ordinary people, then it must by definition be widespread and can affect anyone in the population. This legitimates the need for such a broad-based service. In addition, such a normalising approach is linked to an unwillingness to intervene in people's lives, thereby marginalising and stigmatising them. This approach is well expressed by an advice agency manager:

> **I think there's a danger of giving a social work label to something that's a normal life experience, and it's a way of saying that there's a problem with these young people, when there isn't.**

On the other hand, it appears that those agencies offering a more 'selective' service and who have a history of dealing with special-problem groups, such as social services and certain residential projects, tend to stress the problematic nature of their clients. By stressing the difficulties of such young people, these agencies justify intervention and legitimate their own special role and existence. As one advice agency worker explains:

> **It's part of the way social services and agencies categorise people – these people have problems and have to have specialist services and specialist accommodation . . . which isn't always the case.**

Importantly, however, such an approach also serves to minimise the scale of the problem with which these agencies are often legally obliged to deal. If the problem affects only people with 'problems', then it must by definition be small in scale. It is not surprising, therefore, that this approach is more often adopted by the statutory agencies such as social services and housing departments who have a legal responsibility to deal with such problems – a responsibility that many of their voluntary counterparts, who more often adopt a normalising approach, do not have. We have already seen this dichotomy in the statistics produced by voluntary and statutory organisations (see Chapter 2.)

The structure of funding and resources also plays a crucial role in how an agency defines and presents the problem, particularly in light of the financial insecurity that so many of these organisations find themselves in (Killeen 1988, pp. 80–81). Indeed, Wells (1980, p. 216) has even gone so far as to suggest that some homelessness agencies may, in their search for resources, consciously exaggerate the problem of homelessness and reduce every facet of the young homeless to a social problem. This implies that such agencies are in some way consciously manipulative in their portrayal of the problems with which they deal. Our evidence, however, suggests that definitions often evolve in an unconscious, implicit and ad hoc way. This view is shared by commentators such as Howe (1985); he stresses that welfare models have often

> **evolved gradually by the accretion of numerous decisions taken in the context of resource constraints, peer group pressures and purported claimant categories, themselves determined by internal working requirements and external social values and influences** (p. 53).

The role and position of the speaker

The differing viewpoints we were given also seemed to be connected with the role and position of the speaker within the organisation (Katz and Kahn 1978). The following statement about running away, for example, which particularly stresses the normality of runaways, came from a publicity officer of a children's agency whose responsibility was for publicity and funding:

> **An awful lot needs to be done to raise public awareness. Joe Public still tends to see it as youngsters from particularly inadequate families, or youngsters with severe behavioural problems, rather than it could be *their* kid.**

In contrast, workers on the ground and in close contact with homeless youngsters and runaways appeared to find it hard to maintain this view of ordinariness, often emphasised in publicity (De'Ath 1987), when the control of crime, drug use or violent behaviour is often part of their day-to-day work. As Wills (1978) says:

> **Organisations may incorporate several different goals, and hence, persons functioning within an organisational context may face the task of satisfying several different constituencies whose wishes may be conflicting** (p. 990).

It certainly appeared to us that this discrepancy between public images and the private reality was one factor in the job stress clearly experienced by many of the residential project workers we met.

Strategies

Although we have suggested that certain types of agencies or agency
workers tend to stress either the ordinary or the problematic status of
young homeless people, the correlation between the type of agency
and the viewpoint presented is not a consistent one. This is partly
because workers are using these definitions strategically and there are
difficulties and contradictions with both approaches – problems that
agency workers are often well aware of (Billig et al. 1988, p. 5). For
example, by defining young homeless people as essentially ordinary,
doubt is thrown on the need for special funding and intervention. On
the other hand, an approach that defines these young people as
problematic, while it may attract sympathy and both charity and state
funding, carries with it the inherent danger of stigmatising these
clients (Beresford 1979, p. 162). A stress on the vulnerability of the
client may also demonstrate that homelessness is not a general
problem, but one that somehow affects only a few and, by
implication, only those who are problematic or inadequate in some
way. A manager in a traditional hostel expressed the dilemma that
many organisations find themselves in:

> **It's a bit of a problem in the voluntary sector in that our main
> philosophy tends to be that homelessness is caused by lack of
> housing, which it is, but then we do deal with people with other
> problems as well.**

The paradox expressed above – of advocating a normalising approach
to such social problems, while, at the same time defining them as
problematic in order to achieve and maintain intervention – has been
recognised by some commentators (Moses 1978, p. 238), while others
have shown dilemmas such as these to be commonplace in many
areas of life (Billig et al. 1988). The existence of such dilemmas
certainly helps to explain why there is not a simple relationship
between agency type and the viewpoint taken. It can also help to
explain why the worker above, and others, explicitly switched from
one approach to another in the course of an interview. Since
definitions can be used strategically and, since each approach has
certain advantages and disadvantages, it is not surprising that
respondents sometimes adopted different approaches at different
points in the interview, as in the following account:

Of the homeless population, we meet a high percentage of people with special needs – it's the norm within that group. . . . The majority would be O.K. in ordinary mainstream accommodation (Manager of Traditional Hostel).

Outcomes of different definitions

Interestingly, these diverse presentations of youth homelessness and young homeless people can actually have a number of practical outcomes. For example, it is obvious that competing conceptions of an issue can potentially hinder co-operation and co-ordination between agencies (Handy 1976, pp. 212–13). However, it must be said that, in the field of homelessness, such difficulties appear to arise more from diverse aims or methods and long-standing rivalries between agencies than simply from diverse presentations of the same issue (Saunders 1986, pp. 92–3). Indeed, different interpretations of a situation need not necessarily lead to difficulties (Pottier 1993). In one important respect, however, agency perceptions play a crucial practical role – by acting as gatekeepers and controlling who can and who cannot be assisted by the agency. This role will be examined in the following section.

5.4 Classifications within agencies

We have already seen how many agencies are engaged in presenting, to an outside audience, young homeless people as either ordinary or problematic, and we have suggested that the reasons for this relate in a complex way to the very nature of the agency itself. Yet agencies working on the ground with young people, in whatever country, are also operating a second set of classifications which are being applied internally to sort and sift clients and potential clients. Agencies involved with these young people usually have only limited resources and they often have to make decisions about who they can or cannot assist. This is particularly important when they are offering accommodation. To help make these decisions, we suggest that some of the agencies we interviewed in the UK were using a set of classifications linked to whether their clients are seen to be *deserving* or *undeserving*, although these particular terms are not usually used. These notions serve, crucially, to exclude some young people from the services on offer. In particular, two extreme groups were being outlined as undeserving – those potential clients defined as *low risk* and *high risk*.

Deserving/undeserving – high-risk/low-risk clients

The distinction between deserving and undeserving recipients of welfare provision is by no means a new one and has been the focus of considerable attention in the UK and the USA (Handler and Hollingsworth 1971; Means 1977; Howe 1985; Katz 1989). While this theme has been directed at homelessness before – towards both the traditional vagrant (Cook and Braithwaite 1979) and homeless families (Minns 1972) – the issue of deserving and undeserving clients remains relatively undeveloped in the context of homeless young people.

In relation to agency services, the term 'low risk' was given to those youngsters whose problems were deemed insufficient to warrant the resources and intervention of the particular agency. On the other hand, the term 'high risk' was given to those youngsters whose problems were so severe and so extreme that the hostel or project simply could not cope with them. In fact, it appeared that agencies tended to target their resources to the middle, deserving, group. As a manager in a youth residential project commented:

> **If you put someone in the project who can cope adequately, then they don't need it anyway, and yet if you put someone in there who needs a lot of support, you'll disrupt the whole house. It's getting the balance right.**

This classification of some potential clients into the undeserving category has important, and somewhat paradoxical, implications for the services being offered by many of these agencies (Holman 1973, p. 440).

Targeting client groups

Non-intervention in the low-risk category of young homeless people is not particularly surprising. In general, welfare agencies do not have sufficient resources to offer them to those who do not present with an explicit problem (O'Mahony 1988, p. 50). Moreover, many workers are aware of the concepts of labelling and stigmatisation and they may object to intervention where it is not imperative. This recognition that agency contact can be stigmatising may also lie behind the way in which the service is presented (Spicker 1984, pp. 179–80). For example, accommodation is normally very basic and house rules are restrictive – in part to discourage all but the most desperate of clients from moving in. What was more surprising, however, was that very few agencies dealt with what they classed as high-risk clients, or particularly problematic young people who had significant problems in addition to their homelessness. We found, for instance, that large numbers of projects, particularly youth residential projects, excluded drug users or young people with a history of violence – a pattern replicating the findings of other commentators (O'Mahony 1988, pp. 52–3). As one worker in a youth residential project said:

We cannot take anybody in with serious behavioural problems; alcohol abuse or drug abuse; or any psychiatric problems or violent behaviour. But we're actually finding that's what a lot of young people are!

The exclusion of such young people is often due to the practicalities of running a residential project. Few agencies have the 24-hour staff coverage necessary to deal with high-risk clients. Moreover, such clients can adversely affect a project by attracting the police, alienating neighbours and, ultimately, influencing tenancies and funding (Washton 1974, p. 183). It may also be felt that there are other specialist agencies, such as drug or alcohol projects or less selective hostels, who are better qualified to deal with these difficult young people (Saunders 1986, p. 36). It is clear, therefore, that one agency's high-risk/undeserving client is, for another agency, deemed to be deserving. For example, the high-risk clients in many of the youth residential projects we spoke to were viewed as middle-range or deserving clients in the traditional hostels, where one worker noted:

We take people who are really at the end of the line – who've got experiences of prostitution; care; mental illness, or whatever.

This is not of course to deny that most agency workers, because of their past training and obvious commitment, remain concerned about these high-risk and undeserving clients. As a worker in a youth residential project said:

> **One thing that does concern us is that we tend to have people who we have to evict, because their problems are too great for us to cope with and there's nowhere, no provision [for them].**

Indeed, the exclusion of these potential clients is a source of intense frustration for some agency workers who are often well aware that their classifications can lead to hostels having to turn away homeless clients who are, in many respects, the ones in most need of assistance. This paradox was highlighted by one homeless young man we interviewed. He had been excluded from a youth residential project because he was deemed to be too high-risk. His discussion with the manager about what had occurred was taped in the course of an interview:

> **So there I was, you know what I mean, I was homeless. I went to a homeless hostel and I was told I couldn't have a place in a homeless hostel! . . . you said that you didn't feel that I'd benefit from it! But if you're on the street, you've got nowhere to sleep right, how can you not benefit from a bed? I couldn't work that one out** (Wyn, 18).

It is thus evident that most agencies are applying the categories of high-risk and low-risk to help filter the deserving from the undeserving clients. It is relatively easy to see how the low-risk clients can be perceived as undeserving, for they are seen as using valuable resources that would otherwise go towards more deserving clients. The high-risk category, however, can be seen as corrupting and spoiling future provision for the deserving. What was worrying was that even many of these traditional hostels, which usually catered for the most difficult clients, were now becoming more selective simply because of the sheer numbers of people they were having to choose from (Shelter 1989, p. 14). As one worker in a traditional hostel said:

> **We're getting more select, and that's a situation we're being forced into, because there's so many people out there. We don't just take anybody.**

The actual way in which this categorisation and exclusion of undeserving clients takes place is interesting. While a number of projects have admission criteria that openly prevent certain categories of difficult youngsters from entering the agency (Saunders 1986, pp. 35–6), most projects also use house rules, explicitly or otherwise, to filter out undeserving clients. The prohibition of drugs, alcohol and sex from the premises is almost universal. However necessary these rules are for institutional living, they also tend to discourage many young people and certainly exclude the heavy drug user or the heavy drinker. House rules thus make projects workable, but they can also serve the purpose of distributing scarce resources to what are perceived to be the most deserving clients (Hutson and Liddiard 1990).

Gender has always been an important variable in gaining access to homeless accommodation in so far as many of the homeless people housed by local authorities in the UK are either pregnant women or women with children. They are one of the few groups for whom local authorities have a statutory responsibility to provide accommodation (see Chapter 2). Gender is also relevant in project workers' judgements about how deserving a client is. A number of workers, for instance, felt that young women were significantly more deserving of agency resources than young men in exactly the same situation. As the manager of one traditional hostel, where men predominate, commented:

There may be very loose discrimination, and it would be positive discrimination, in the sense that we're very concerned about them [women] if they come along.

The fact that many of the new youth residential projects we visited took up to 50 per cent or more women may reflect the fact that women with accommodation problems are often picked up as vulnerable, referred on to residential projects and treated as deserving by virtue of their gender. When asked why her project had more females, one youth residential worker replied:

I think it's because they're vulnerable. . . . They are more likely to be referred.

Similarly, ethnicity may play an important role in the classification of a client as deserving. For example, although young black people are often underrepresented in projects for homeless young people (see Chapter 2), some agencies are nevertheless attempting to target this group specifically (O'Mahony 1988, p. 52).

We have thus suggested that young homeless people are presented to an outside audience, be they the media, researchers or the public, as being either 'ordinary' or 'problematic'. Simultaneously, young homeless people are often classified within agencies as low risk and high risk when allocating resources to the deserving. However, young people are not fixed or immobile within these categories. The processes by which young people can move between these categories have been discussed in more detail elsewhere (see Liddiard and Hutson 1991). For the purposes of this chapter, it is simply enough to acknowledge that these categories are not fixed or static.

In conclusion, there is a danger in this chapter that by identifying simple categories such as ordinary or problematic, deserving or undeserving, we oversimplify a complex situation with heterogeneous young people and diverse agencies. This is not our intention. Nor do we, in looking carefully at the categories agencies use, want in any way to criticise or cast doubt on present projects catering for young people. Instead, we have focused on how agencies present a problem to an outside audience and how they select their clients, because they are crucial components in the construction of a social problem such as youth homelessness. In particular, this chapter has shown that agencies, like other groups, apply their own distinct interpretations to social issues such as youth homelessness. This will be illustrated further in the next chapter as we look in detail at the interpretations that young homeless people give of their homelessness and how and why these can differ from those given by agencies.

Note

1. The material for Chapters 5 and 6 comes from two studies carried out by the authors in the Department of Sociology and Anthropology, University College Swansea.
    The first study, of young homeless people and runaways in Wales, was carried out over four months in 1988. Eighty-one interviews were conducted with agencies and 23 with young people. The study was funded by the Children's Society (Hutson and Liddiard 1989a and 1989b). The second study of young homeless people in Wales was carried out over 15 months between 1989–91. Sixty-eight interviews were conducted with agencies and 115 with young people. The study was funded by the Joseph Rowntree Foundation (Hutson and Liddiard 1991). The names of all respondents in both studies are pseudonyms.
    Chapter 5 is based on an article written by the authors for the *Journal of Social Policy*, published by Cambridge University Press (see Liddiard and Hutson 1991).

6

Young People's Viewpoints

6.1 Introduction

It is in this chapter that we show what it is like to be young and homeless. Throughout the chapter we are particularly concerned with young people's own accounts of their homelessness. These are often used by the media and by agency workers, but are seldom considered in their own right. Moreover, young homeless people are often treated as an homogeneous group when, in reality, they have a wide range of experiences, which they express in a variety of ways. The aim of this chapter, therefore, is to illustrate the diverse experiences of young people when they are homeless.

However, this chapter is more than simply a description of youth homelessness. As in the rest of the book, we are interested in the different meanings that can be attached to the same social problem. So far, we have focused on the ways in which youth homelessness can be interpreted by the media and by agencies. Young homeless people are a crucial group, but often a silent one. Because of their personal experience, they have particular viewpoints which can contrast with the interpretations of other groups such as agency workers.

In looking in detail at how young people describe and interpret their homelessness, we concentrate on three specific themes:

- How do young homeless people describe and interpret their experience of homelessness?
- How do young homeless people explain their homelessness?
- How do young homeless people define homelessness, and do they necessarily see themselves as being homeless?

As in the last chapter, the material on which we draw comes largely from our own research in Wales with young people coming from the large conurbations of Cardiff and Swansea, from small towns and rural areas (see note 1 on p. 122). We also draw on a study by Brandon et al. (1980), who interviewed over 100 homeless young

123

people using three emergency accommodation projects in central London in the mid-1970s. It is of course impossible to predict how other young people in the USA, Australia and Europe might speak about being homeless, but it is likely that there may be common themes in their experiences and viewpoints.

6.2 The experience of homelessness

Much of what is written and said about homeless young people implies that the experience of being homeless is both wholly negative and progressively problematic:

> **Although at the present time Britain does not have a large young, street-based population, there is a rapidly increasing number of homeless young people who find themselves trapped in a downward spiral of homelessness, unemployment and social deprivation which can end with life on the streets** (Saunders 1986, p. 6).

Similarly, Lord Scarman, at the opening of the International Year of Shelter for the Homeless in 1987, described homelessness as 'disintegrating and destroying human personality' and, ultimately, a threat to civilisation (Andrews 1987).

This negative view of homelessness is variously adopted by most homelessness agencies (Brandon et al. 1980, p. 76), although we also saw in the last chapter that agencies may suggest otherwise in certain circumstances. Most agency workers agree that young people face significant risks when they are living without secure accommodation – in particular, the risk of involvement in offending and entering the justice system (Hutson and Liddiard 1989a, p. 22). There was a consensus among the agency workers we interviewed that living without secure accommodation for any period of time can quickly lead to involvement in problematic behaviour, as this advice agency manager said:

> **whether it's prostitution, sweatshop labouring, stealing, drug dealing or whatever, . . . you've got to walk on the wild side in order to survive.**

A 'homeless career'?

Even at the beginning of our research, we were interested in this notion of homelessness as a downward spiral and an integral part of our research was a retrospective examination of young people's housing and employment careers. We wanted to see if the types of accommodation that homeless people used deteriorated over time and also whether there was evidence of problems increasing with the length of time that they were homeless. It should be noted that while introducing the notion of a 'homeless career' raises some interesting points, it requires simplifying what are actually very complex situations. This is why many academic commentators, with only a few exceptions (see Randall 1988), do not attempt to identify any kind of process in relation to youth homelessness. However, given the way in which many agencies present homelessness in these terms, we believed that it was important to try and elicit whether or not a process could be identified. In looking at our sample of young homeless people, we felt that it *was* possible to identify certain patterns that suggest that homelessness, for some youngsters, is a progressive decline – which would support the pessimism of many agencies (Hutson and Liddiard 1991, pp. 36–40). By analysing the accommodation histories of the young people that we interviewed, we were able to distinguish three phases.

Early phase

When our respondents initially left home or care, they used a range of accommodation strategies. Those young people who had left in a planned or semi-planned way often moved directly into private flats and bedsits. Their experience of homelessness usually began only when they subsequently found themselves being evicted from these flats and bedsits. However, most of our respondent group had left in an unplanned way, often after a crisis, and for these youngsters the initial strategy was to stay with friends or relatives, usually on a very short-term basis (Randall 1988, p. 21). A small proportion of young people were also forced to sleep rough at this stage, although it was usually very short term (Saunders 1986, p. 6).

It seems that the large numbers of young people who initially stay with friends and relatives often go on to do one of two things: they either return home or they may move into private bedsits and flats. We have evidence to suggest that for some of the 'hidden homeless' – those homeless young people not in contact with homelessness agencies – this is as far as they go. They either resolve their difficulties at home or they settle into a private bedsit or flat and may not necessarily experience accommodation difficulties again. This group is subsequently extremely difficult to identify and investigate (Austerberry et al. 1984, pp. 8–9). Most of our respondents, though, were those who had moved on from this situation and had either failed to resolve their difficulties at home or had been evicted from private flats or bedsits. These young people are at risk of moving into the next phase.

Middle phase

Of those young people who fail either to return home successfully or maintain secure accommodation, many appear to move into what we call the middle phase of a homeless career, where the types of accommodation change a little. In this phase, the use of relatives and friends declines in importance, as does the use of flats and bedsits, and other types of accommodation become more important. A small number of the young people we interviewed were using youth residential projects in the initial stages of homelessness, but the use of these hostels appears to be most significant at this middle phase. Similarly, other forms of accommodation – such as squatting or using traditional homelessness hostels – become more common, while the nature of sleeping rough begins to change somewhat. No longer is it simply short term, for a night or so. Instead, young people begin to sleep rough for longer periods of time – two weeks or more. It is also in this middle phase that young people begin to experience significant problems with obtaining and keeping employment.

It appears that a number of young people do manage to move out of this middle phase back to secure accommodation, often through the resettlement efforts of homelessness agencies. Yet we also found evidence to suggest that the longer young people live in unstable accommodation, the harder it becomes for them to move back into secure housing. Certainly, some young people move into what we call the late phase of homelessness.

Late phase

This is the stage in a 'homeless career' that seems to be the most problematic. By this phase, a significant number of young people are using traditional homelessness hostels and squats, while a high proportion are also sleeping rough. Many of those sleeping rough are doing so for considerable periods of time. Additionally, many of the young people who reach this stage have a number of other problems, such as involvement in crime and drugs. Not surprisingly, most are experiencing considerable difficulty in obtaining employment, particularly if they are sleeping rough (Drake et al. 1981, p. 65; Canter et al. 1990, p. 12). Many hostels – particularly youth residential projects – are also increasingly unwilling to accept these young people, often seeing them as too problematic for the services they have to offer (see Chapter 5). Young people are also more likely to be moving between towns or cities than at the earlier stages. For these young people, resolving their homeless situation becomes increasingly difficult.

Clearly, this model is very much an ideal-type. In reality, young people do not always progress through these stages in a systematic way and many young people do not proceed through these phases at all. Nevertheless, it is obvious that the longer young people remain homeless, the more difficult it may be for them to return to mainstream life (Saunders 1986, p. 8; O'Mahony 1988, p. 40). Early on, for example, young homeless people may return home or find private rented accommodation. In the middle phase, homelessness agencies may help their clients to find accommodation. Young people who have reached the late phase, however, may experience significant problems in obtaining both work and accommodation. This model would certainly endorse the notion of homelessness as a necessarily problematic and downward process. However, although we suggest that the experience of homelessness can be progressively problematic, an important issue is whether or not young people – rather than agency workers or even researchers – actually recognise it as such. Let us look at this in more detail.

What young people say

Investigating whether or not young people see the experience of homelessness in terms of a downward process is difficult. However, some youngsters undoubtedly do view their homelessness in these terms. Paul's (22) account, for instance, contains the idea that there is a downward spiral in homelessness:

> **I've gone from the streets up to where I am now. . . . If you go on the streets and then come back off the streets and like get to where I am at the moment, then you're doing pretty well . . . When most**

people hit the streets, that's it. They hit rock bottom, turn to drugs and stuff like that.

What is interesting is that Paul, although he is living in a traditional homelessness hostel, feels that *he* is on the up.

Nevertheless, many young people acknowledge that being homeless for any length of time is hazardous, specifically because it can make them vulnerable to other problems (O'Mahony 1988, p. 4). Many of our respondents, for example, linked difficulties with accommodation to difficulties with obtaining and keeping employment. For some, trying to secure accommodation, while simultaneously trying to hold down a job or training place, caused significant problems. For instance, Sara (23) found that the pressures of looking for somewhere to live made it impossible to keep her place on a training scheme:

I was doing Employment Training and quite happy with it – to be a secretary. Then the pressure of having to find somewhere to live was too much. I couldn't do both. . . . If I had found somewhere to live I probably would have finished the course.

There are also difficulties involved in actually obtaining employment when one has no fixed address. Anthony (21), for example, spoke of the way in which being unable to give a potential employer one's address created difficulties:

If I can get a job then I'll be able to sort out my homelessness . . . [but] you go for an interview, they turn round and say: 'Where can we get in touch with you to let you know whether or not you've got the job?' You've got nowhere.

Gareth (24) articulated what many young people and many commentators (Thornton 1990, p. 9) feel about the experience of homelessness when he pessimistically said:

Well, people won't employ you if you haven't got an address, so you've got to have an address before you can get employed. It's one big circle, you know. You've got to have an address to get employed and you can't get an address unless you've got the money to move in.

For all these reasons, many homeless young people find themselves moving from work into dependence on benefits. There can be little incentive to give up benefits because much of the work on offer is casual or low paid. If young people do take up casual work they risk problems and delays in reclaiming benefits when the job finishes. This is something that Robert (24) pointed out:

When you go through life and you get a bit of work here and a job there, it's very complicated. The DSS [Benefits Agency] run it as if it's simple – you're either working or you're not. . . . It's not like that. All you end up doing is full-time unemployment.

When talking about where they found a bed for the night, homeless young people also had few positive things to say. For many members of the public and the media, homelessness is equated with sleeping rough. It is believed that all homeless young people are, in fact, sleeping rough much of the time. For agencies and researchers, however, sleeping rough is only one facet of a much wider homelessness scene (Holmes 1986, pp. 210–11; Saunders 1986, pp. 5–8). In our research, nearly half the young people interviewed had slept rough at some time. From their accounts, it was evident that sleeping rough can vary enormously in context, a point made by other studies of homeless people (see Central London Outreach Team 1984).

On the one hand, many young people are often forced to sleep rough in an emergency, but only for a night or so. Sue (16), for instance, spent a night sleeping rough after an argument at home:

It was in the summer that we had the argument and I just couldn't handle it . . . the atmosphere in the house. So I just didn't even pack my bags. I just went . . . I had a thin jacket on and I thought I'd be all right, but it was freezing . . . I walked around and then I slept in the park.

On the other hand, some young people, particularly if they have spent some time in unstable accommodation, often have few accommodation options available to them and are frequently forced to sleep rough for considerable periods of time. As Stuart (21) commented, when asked where he had been living in the previous few months:

On the streets basically . . . I'd nip on the buses and sleep on there, and I'd get kicked off there at four in the morning. I'd just be wandering around. I was in a hell of a state like, rundown.

There was general agreement among young people that sleeping rough, whatever its nature, was wholly unsatisfactory and potentially very dangerous. Gaynor (24), when asked what the hardest thing about sleeping rough was, replied:

> **Not being able to have a wash and clean clothes, going without food, getting attacked and things like that . . . I mean, I got raped.**

Colin (18) also described the problems involved in sleeping rough:

> **In the nights, I'd be sitting there quietly and a few boys came out of the pub, drunk like, and they gave me a hard time, kicking hell out of me.**

Indeed, for some young people, such as Gareth (24), sleeping rough and homelessness were so problematic that even prison was preferable:

> **at least I've got my breakfast, dinner and tea like – three meals inside. I'll tell you, you're better off inside, right . . . even if you are banged up half the day.**

Staying with friends is a quite different, but equally common, form of homelessness. However, many of our respondents still spoke about it in quite negative terms. Half the young people interviewed had used friends as a source of accommodation, often in an emergency following eviction by parents or a landlord. In the words of Nick (17):

> **a night here, a night there, that's all. It's just like I'd go there and say: 'Can I stay tonight?' . . . Then I'd just go round all my friends then, seeing if they'd put me up . . . I didn't like doing it, but I had to.**

This heavy reliance on friends for emergency accommodation has been noted before by other commentators (Randall 1988, p. 21). Although friends were often an invaluable source of accommodation, we were nevertheless given many accounts of the problems of staying with friends. Phil (24) said:

> **going around my dwindling circle of friends, sleeping on floors and things like that . . . getting up in the morning not knowing where we'd be sleeping that night. We always managed but it was touch and go sometimes. . . . It caused a hell of a lot of stress.**

From these comments, it is clear that most young homeless people see the experience of being homeless as negative and often progressively problematic. This is not particularly surprising. It is, after all, how most agencies see the problem and some young people seemed to be drawing on media and agency images of homelessness when talking about their experiences. However, the situation is actually more complex than it may at first appear.

Homelessness as a positive experience?

Brandon et al. (1980) go to some lengths to question the view of homelessness as a negative experience usually held by agencies. First, Brandon and his team suggest that such a perspective is adopted partly because it justifies agency intervention:

> **The homeless are presented as more hapless and hopeless than our study would indicate. . . . The annual reports and campaign documents of the voluntary societies stress their own centrality in efforts to 'solve' homelessness. Apparently, without their work in counselling and residential provision, young people would drift wholesale into petty crime, prostitution and mental illness** (p. 192).

Secondly, Brandon et al. question the model of homelessness as a downward spiral by showing that many young people already had problems before they became homeless. They point out, for example, that nearly half of the young people they interviewed were 'already tangled up in a network of social processing' of care, penal and psychiatric institutions when they became homeless (p. 189). In view of this, it is difficult to extract the specific influence of homelessness on young people who already have difficulties.

Clearly, both these points are important. We discussed in the last chapter that it is in the interests of many agencies to emphasise the problematic nature of homelessness. At the same time, there is no doubt that some young people have a number of additional problems before they become homeless. However, there is a third point that helps to explain why agencies often present homelessness in such a negative way. Many of the young people who become homeless undoubtedly move back into secure accommodation and mainstream life quickly and without experiencing problems. However, very little is known of the numbers achieving this, or of the means by which they do it, because agencies usually have very little contact with this group. Instead, agencies are more likely to come into contact with those young people who are experiencing problems. It is not surprising, therefore, that agencies see homelessness as a negative experience, as they only tend to be in touch with the more problematic young people.

Interestingly, Brandon et al. also question the negative interpretation of homelessness by using the views of young homeless people themselves, who have both negative and positive things to say about their situation. As they point out:

> **Compared with the voluntary societies' and statutory bodies' conception of homelessness as mostly negative, our subjects had more complex views. . . . This minority seeing homelessness in a positive light contrasted starkly with the fire and brimstone views of the projects** (1980, pp. 56–7).

The extent to which young people can interpret their experience of homelessness in a positive way is indicated by Figure 6.1.

From our own research, we would also suggest that many young homeless people do not always speak of their homelessness in wholly

FIGURE 6.1 *Feelings about the total experience in London whilst homeless*

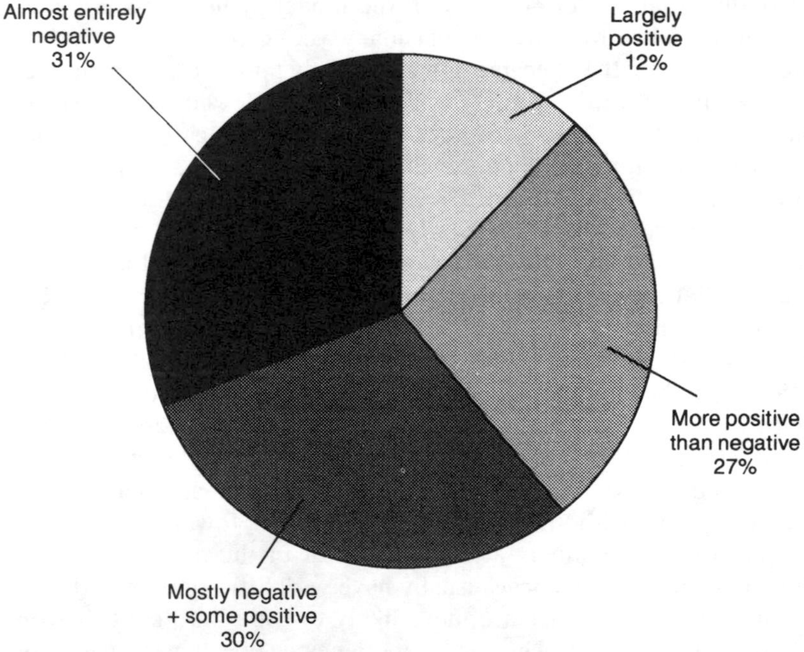

Source: Brandon *et al.*, 1980, p. 57.

negative terms. Certainly, some young people were keen to emphasise the positive elements of their homelessness, such as gaining new experience and new skills. Anthony (21), for instance, spoke of learning the skills of survival:

I lived on the streets for four months. . . . Well, the way I look at it now it's just part of life. I've learnt to survive.

Other young people, like those interviewed by Brandon and his team, emphasised the relative freedom that homelessness can entail. This freedom was expressed by Richard (24), although the experience of sleeping rough still came as a shock:

The first thought in my brain when I first started out was 'Oh, I can stay out as long as I want!' But it came as a bit of a shock – it hit me like a hammer!

It is clear from this quote that young people's positive viewpoints are often tempered by their experiences. The feelings of freedom, for example, are often a short-term emotion present in the first few days of a homeless experience, before the harsh realities of the situation become fully apparent. Certainly, very few of our respondents had anything positive to say about the virtues of sleeping rough, although a few who had slept rough for long periods of time tended to view it with some ambivalence. Nevertheless, there is clearly some disparity between the negative viewpoints of agencies and the more mixed accounts of young homeless people themselves.

By making this point, there is a danger of suggesting that homelessness necessarily has some positive features, which is what Brandon et al. (1980) imply. On the contrary, we suggest that there are a number of explanations for the more positive viewpoints of some young people. For some youngsters, their situation when homeless is an improvement on their previous situation. We have already seen that many young homeless people leave home situations of abuse and conflict. It is indicative of the problems they have left behind, that even homelessness can be preferable to remaining at home.

It is also important to recognise that the favourable views of some young people towards their own homelessness do not necessarily contradict a view that homelessness in general is problematic. While young people may concede that the experience of homelessness is often negative and even dangerous, they may acknowledge at the same time that *their own personal negotiation of homelessness* includes some positive elements.

6.3 Explaining homelessness

We saw in Chapter 3, that youth homelessness can be explained in many different ways. In this section, we examine the ways in which young people explain or account for their homelessness, which often contrast with the approach of homelessness agencies.

What young people say

It is difficult to generalise about how any category of people explain youth homelessness and young homeless people are no exception. They are an heterogeneous category who adopt a wide range of attitudes towards their homelessness and its causes. Let us begin, however, by considering how Brandon et al. (1980, pp. 59–75) claim that young homeless people view the problem. Using the five models of homelessness explanation outlined in Chapter 3, they suggest that very few young people have an explicitly structural or 'political' approach to the problem, and even fewer subscribe to a 'spiritual' approach. Rather, young people's interpretations tend to be more individually based. The majority of Brandon's sample, for instance, viewed their homelessness in terms of an 'individual culpability' model – seeing their homelessness as arising directly from their own irresponsible behaviour. Other young people adopted a more 'pathological' approach, seeing themselves as having a number of problems, such as family conflict and abuse, which made them particularly susceptible to homelessness. A few also subscribed to a 'child' approach, conceding that their immaturity represented a key to the problem.

To a certain extent, the views of the young people we interviewed in Wales echoed those interviewed by Brandon's team. The majority of our young informants adopted an 'individualistic' viewpoint, which can be described as 'a way of looking at the world which explains and interprets events and circumstances mainly in terms of the decisions, actions and attitudes of the individuals involved' (Jenkins 1982, p. 88). For example, some young people blamed themselves, and their own behaviour, for their present homeless situation. As Stuart (21) said:

> **I'm a fool to myself as well like. I've got to admit that. I have had some problems and some I've brought on myself because I'm stupid.**

A few young people stressed their immaturity, while others emphasised a number of problems, particularly family difficulties, as contributory factors. The clear majority of our respondents thus identified individual behaviour, be it their own or that of others, as central to the explanation of their homelessness. Even where responsibility was directed at more structural factors, such as the economy or government policies, blame was often personalised and directed towards particular individuals, such as the Prime Minister. Interestingly, a similar pattern is echoed in what young people are reported to say about their long-term unemployment (Coffield et al. 1986, pp. 83–4; Hutson and Jenkins 1989, pp. 114–26). However, understanding why young people tend to explain their homelessness or unemployment in individual terms is complex, although a number of factors appear to be important.

Certainly, the adoption of more individually based interpretations of a social problem may be related to the degree to which the person is isolated in their experience. For example, Hutson and Jenkins (1989, p. 124) noted that in a community where unemployment is widespread and commonplace, it was less usual for a young person to personalise the problem and adopt self-blame. Yet in an area where unemployment was not common and the experience was atypical, this often happened. The fact that homelessness is generally an atypical experience may help to account for the predominance of individualised explanations among young homeless people.

Similarly, the way in which young people explain their homelessness may directly relate to the way in which homelessness is often experienced. There is evidence to suggest that many young homeless people move in and out of homelessness. For some, being homeless may simply take the form of having to stay on a friend's floor for a few nights after an argument at home, before resolving their difficulties (Hutson and Liddiard 1991, pp. 36–7). Clearly, for some of these young people such a situation may not be seen as particularly problematic and there is an argument that this form of temporary homelessness is likely to persist regardless of the structure of the housing and labour markets. Where the experience of homelessness for some young people is so spasmodic, it is unlikely to be explained in terms of broader structural issues.

Interestingly, despite an emphasis on individual explanations, some of our respondents did identify their homelessness as being closely linked to the housing and labour market situations. However, these explanations were usually expressed in practical terms – such as being homeless because they could not find anywhere to live and because they could not find a job. The reasons for the practical emphasis of many young homeless people are fairly clear. Certainly, they may lack the political language of 'structural' approaches, although there is evidence that young people can and do pick up this language from agency and media arguments. More importantly, young homeless people are clearly in a 'practical' situation – they need accommodation quickly and they need help on a practical level to resolve their homelessness. Agencies and commentators, on the other hand, often have the freedom to adopt a more structural and theoretical approach to the explanation of youth homelessness.

Powerless victims or active decision-makers?

In explaining youth homelessness in structural terms, agencies and academic commentators often stress the lack of choice that young people have in leaving home, in leaving accommodation and in making a living. They tend to present young homeless people as powerless victims at the mercy of structural factors, such as housing and labour market trends. In contrast, though, we have just seen that young homeless people tend to adopt more individually based explanations that can in fact empower them. Certainly, running through the young people's accounts there is a much greater emphasis on their role as active individuals, with a degree of control over their lives.

When talking about leaving home, for example, many of those interviewed were keen to emphasise that they had taken the decision to leave. However, as researchers, we felt that many of these young people had actually exercised little real choice. Adrian (19), for example, told us that he left home through choice. Later, however, it became apparent that his decision to leave was imposed upon him:

> **I took a lot of bashing, because my mother split from my father, yeah, and I stuck with my father. He used to do what he did to my mother to me. . . . I thought 'I don't want to go through what she's been through! I'm off!'**

In the same way that agencies were often keen to emphasise young homeless people's relative powerlessness in the face of structural factors, it seemed clear to us that some young people were keen to emphasise the opposite. While we wish to point out that young homeless people can and do exercise some control over their situation, we must also concede that some young people tended to exaggerate – consciously or unconsciously – their degree of control over events. Of course, this exaggeration and the positive viewpoints identified above may be connected with the fact that their accounts of homelessness were often retrospective. Even if they had little choice but to leave home, young people may attach a more positive rationale to their situation in hindsight and feel that they left to become more independent. Without wishing to venture too far into the realms of psychology, there is a considerable body of work that discusses the ways in which threatening situations, such as unemployment and homelessness, can be reinterpreted by individuals. For example, Breakwell (1986, pp. 80–93) describes 'creative redefinition' when a situation imposed upon a subject may be reinterpreted to give the impression that the subject was actually imposing their will upon the situation.

It must be remembered that, in talking about their experiences, young people are presenting a picture of themselves and their lives. It is not surprising that this picture is often a positive one. Agency workers, on the other hand, are not talking about themselves when describing homelessness. They are talking about and justifying their work. Herein lies some of the difference.

6.4 Defining homelessness

It is clear by now that defining homelessness is a source of much disagreement (see Watson 1984; Watson and Austerberry 1986). We discussed this in detail in Chapter 2. However, it is interesting that, despite the difficulties surrounding any definition of homelessness, it is often assumed that young homeless people themselves accept whichever definition of homelessness is attached to them. In this section, we suggest that this is not the case. According to our broad criteria of '. . . not being in, nor having immediate or easy access to, secure accommodation' (Liddiard and Hutson 1990, p. 165), all our sample were, or had recently been, in a 'homeless' situation. However, when we asked the young people whether or not they considered themselves to be homeless, a number of our respondents did not, despite the fact that their accommodation situation was often as poor, if not worse, than those who did. In all, 58 per cent of our respondents saw themselves as homeless, 29 per cent did not see

FIGURE 6.2 *Responses to the question 'Do you see yourself as
homeless?'*

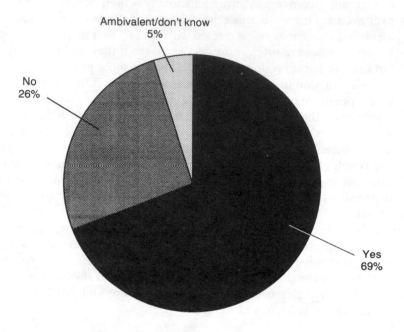

Source: Brandon *et al.*, 1980, p. 52.

themselves as homeless, and 13 per cent saw themselves as 'half and
half' or unsure. It is interesting that a similar pattern was identified by
Brandon et al. (1980) when they examined the self-perceptions of
homeless young people, illustrated in Figure 6.2.

Let us now look in more detail at why young people do or do not
consider themselves to homeless.

Why young people did see themselves as homeless

The complexity of the concept of homelessness is illustrated by Jude
(17). He said he felt 'homeless':

**the main time when I got kicked out. Not the other times because I
always went to friends. . . . But the main time, when I had to go to**

the City Council and there was a big sign saying 'Homeless' and an arrow. When I saw that, I knew that I was homeless. It struck home.

It is clear from these comments that Jude did not identify staying with friends as homelessness and this attitude seems to be fairly common. Sleeping rough, however, was often given as a reason for defining one's experiences as homelessness. This largely reflects the relative severity of the accommodation problem, although it may also indicate the importance of the stereotype, so often presented in the media, that simply equates homelessness with sleeping rough.

Certainly, many young people judged their homelessness in relation to accommodation criteria. However, it was more often the insecure and temporary nature of the accommodation that was stressed rather than simply the physical conditions. For example, Richard (24), moving from one traditional homeless hostel to another, felt homeless:

because it's not a permanent address, is it? In a place like this, you're settling down and you think to yourself: 'Well I can't really class this as a home', because you see other blokes coming and going left, right and centre like.'

Even Johnnie (18), in better-quality accommodation in a youth residential project, also felt homeless because he felt insecure:

because it's just temporary and, under the licence, if we're out of line, we're out instantly – back out on the streets again. That's what it [homelessness] means for me.

This is not to deny, though, that poor housing conditions in themselves were sometimes cited as a reason for being homeless. Jane (21), for instance, felt homeless when staying with her parents because:

We were so overcrowded. . . . There were five of us in a two bedroom house and they were pulling down those houses anyway.

Nevertheless, it is clear that housing conditions are only part of the picture. We found that emotional or psychological factors, such as loneliness, can also play a part in determining whether or not someone perceives themselves as homeless, a point noted elsewhere (Brandon et al. 1980, p. 53). Indeed, authors such as Canter et al.

(1990) have attempted to address the psychological factors often implicit in the definition of homelessness, by referring to the notion of 'hearthlessness'. This refers to the lack of any 'home-like identity within a place of abode' (p. 8). Because of the way in which it moves the definition of homelessness beyond simple accommodation issues, this concept is certainly helpful for considering why some young people in good-quality accommodation may still see themselves as homeless, while others in very poor-quality accommodation may not perceive themselves as being homeless.

Why young people did not see themselves as homeless

Nearly 30 per cent of the young people we interviewed did not see themselves as homeless. The reasons they gave are interesting. Some young people did not want to identify themselves with the stereotypical images of homelessness. Although Dave (19) was living in a resettlement unit, he did not see himself as homeless because 'I don't class myself as a tramp, or a dosser'. Similarly, although Alan (19) was staying in a traditional homelessness hostel, he said with pride, indicating his recent hair cut: 'No-one would think we're homeless. We're presentable.'

Some young people did not feel that they were homeless because they had family or friends around them. Although it might not be possible to live with them at the time, it was felt that they would be available in a future emergency. As Martin (17), living in a hostel, said about his family: 'They wouldn't see me on the streets.' Some young people certainly felt that, although they were not living at home, the existence of a parental home meant that they were not homeless, a point replicating the findings of Brandon et al. (1980, p. 54). June (17), for instance, was unsure about whether or not she was homeless. In answer to the question 'Do you see yourself as homeless?', she replied:

> **Well, no, because I've got a home to go to, and yes, because I can't go there.**

Again, the security and permanency of the accommodation is an important factor. For example, Hugh (21) was living in bed and breakfast accommodation. He states clearly the value of settled accommodation for young people. Because of his background in care, he was exempt from the time limits on board and lodging accommodation introduced by the government in 1985 (see Chapter 3). Settled accommodation, albeit not with his family, had made all the difference to Hugh and this is why he did not see himself as homeless:

> **because, as I say, I've been here three years, I treat this like my own house. I mean if I was moving like my mates are, just moving from one house to another – 'cos there's a law out, isn't there, you're only allowed to stay in one place for six weeks or something – forget that. Then I'd be classed 'homeless' but, because I'm settled here, I've got no worries.**

Of particular interest, however, were the young people who were living in very poor accommodation and yet had exercised some choice – albeit a restricted choice   over where they were living. Some of these young people were in squats. It seemed that those who had in some way chosen to live in poor accommodation often did not see themselves as being homeless. The most vivid expression of this point came from a 'New Age Traveller' interviewed at a summer solstice festival (Hill 1989; Jones, R. 1990). He was a particularly good example of a young person in what would generally be described as a homeless situation, and yet who did not see himself as homeless because of the degree of choice he had exercised over where he was living. When asked why he did not see himself as homeless, he replied:

> **I mean, look at this [car and tarpaulin sheet] – it's not much, is it? But it's my home. It's the home that I've chosen. I've chosen to live like this. That's why I'm not homeless** (Jack, 24).

This small group particularly illustrates the importance of criteria other than housing conditions in defining homelessness. However, almost by way of a footnote, the degree of choice that this tiny minority exercise in choosing to live in problematic accommodation perhaps distinguishes them from homeless young people in general. Consequently, we have suggested elsewhere that it may be more appropriate to describe these young people as 'homefree', rather than 'homeless' (see Liddiard 1991a).

In conclusion, young homeless people, like all social actors, bring a variety of different meanings to social situations. The distinctiveness of these interpretations are particularly apparent when they are contrasted with the meanings that other groups, such as agency workers, attach to the same issue or problem. Similar disparities can be identified in the way in which different groups, including young people, variously interpret the solutions to youth homelessness, which is what we examine in the next chapter.

7

Solutions to Youth Homelessness

7.1 Introduction

The solutions that are proposed to the problem of youth homelessness are varied. This is to be expected since the nature of the solution will depend on how youth homelessness is interpreted and by whom. We have seen throughout the book that different groups and individuals can perceive the same social issue in quite different ways, and thus it is not surprising that solutions should vary. For example, the solution offered will be closely linked with the explanation given, and in Chapter 3 we considered the variety of these explanations. At that stage, we did not link particular explanations with the different categories of people involved. In this chapter, though, we attempt to look more closely at how different groups perceive the solutions to youth homelessness. In particular, we address three broad questions:

- How do homelessness agencies perceive the solutions to youth homelessness?
- How do politicians perceive the solutions to youth homelessness?
- How do young homeless people perceive the solutions to youth homelessness?

7.2 Agency solutions

We saw in Chapter 5 that there are problems in talking about agencies as if they were homogeneous bodies. In reality, homelessness agencies represent a diversity of organisations and viewpoints on a national scene, let alone an international one. Nevertheless, it is still possible to talk in general terms about an 'agency' viewpoint – in contrast, perhaps, to 'young people's' or 'media' viewpoints. In terms of proposing solutions to youth homelessness, there is a significant difference between statutory and voluntary agencies. First, statutory agencies are generally precluded from campaigning and usually cannot make political statements. Secondly, lack of resources means that statutory agencies – such as housing and welfare services – often hesitate to accept responsibility for anyone that they are not legally obliged to deal with. Single homeless people tend to fall outside their statutory responsibility, although in the UK the Children Act (1989) has opened up the debate (see Chapter 5). For these reasons, statutory agencies usually only have a somewhat muted voice in campaigning for solutions to youth homelessness. Consequently, the agency solutions considered in this chapter come largely from voluntary agencies. Nevertheless, there are marked differences in the aims and objectives of voluntary agencies, and what one organisation might consider important, another agency might ignore. Moreover, there are important differences in homelessness legislation between different countries.

When looking at agency solutions in general, a useful distinction can be made between *campaigning* and *practical* solutions, although the distinction between the two is often blurred. Campaigning solutions aim to change social and economic structures. By their nature, they tend to be broad. Agencies generally agree that there are three basic causes of homelessness – a lack of suitable housing, a lack of employment, and an inadequate benefit system (see Chapter 3). The solution lies, therefore, in bringing about public policy changes in these three areas. Academic commentators often join with agencies in putting forward these broad solutions. For example, Rossi (1989, p. 211) makes the following point in relation to the USA, but its relevance is wider:

> **public policy decisions have in large measure created the problem of homelessness. They can solve the problem as well.**

The advantage of taking broad measures to solve youth homelessness is that many people benefit and no group is targeted, with the resulting stigmatisation or marginalisation. For example, if measures are taken to expand the supply of affordable accommodation or to increase the number of jobs, then a wide range of people will benefit. Young homeless people will gain both directly and indirectly by an overall reduction in the competition for jobs and accommodation.

However, it is difficult to bring about such broad policy changes. Changes in one area will have ramifications in many others. For example, changes in benefit policies in relation to young people are linked to national budgets, to basic ideas about the effect of welfare benefits on individual behaviour, and to notions of who is 'deserving' or 'undeserving'. Similarly, the reduction of unemployment among young people is connected with wider government moves against inflation and recession, both national and international. Because broad policies are complex and interlinked, there is often little that agencies and academic commentators can do except state these solutions in principle. Because broad solutions are both difficult to achieve and expensive to implement, campaigns are often run on more specific issues.

However, most agencies are more than simply campaigning bodies. They also provide practical services for their clients. Subsequently, agencies are also often concerned with more *practical* solutions to the problem of youth homelessness, such as providing their clients with a bed for the night. However, campaigning and practical solutions are interconnected. For example, if agencies can succeed in their campaigns for a more responsive benefit system, these changes will make it easier for them to resolve the problem of youth homelessness on a practical and day-to-day basis. We will now look in more detail at the specific solutions that agencies propose to the problem of youth homelessness, which are summarised in Box 7.1.

The housing market

The most obvious solution to homelessness is the increased provision of affordable housing. In most countries, the supply of housing can be divided into different sectors – owner occupation, the private rented sector, and state rented housing. We discussed in Chapter 3 the ways in which the supply of affordable housing in both the private rented sector and the state rented sector has dramatically declined in recent years, for a number of reasons. Given that homelessness is a housing problem, these factors have been identified as fundamental to the youth homelessness problem. Consequently, it is not surprising that most agencies, together with many academic commentators, perceive the provision of more affordable housing for young people as one of the keys to resolving the youth homelessness problem. Agencies make a number of specific suggestions about how this can be done.

In many countries, the state subsidises housing for its citizens in two ways – by building and renting state housing and by giving tax

Box 7.1 Agency solutions to youth homelessness

Housing market
- More local-authority housing should be built.
- The private rented sector should be expanded and improved.
- Housing association funding and involvement should be increased.
- The demand for single-person accommodation should be recognised.
- The need for emergency accommodation, transitional accommodation with support, and permanent accommodation should all be recognised.

Labour market
- Measures to tackle unemployment will in turn help to reduce homelessness.
- Accommodation, work and training can be combined in the Foyer model.
- Employment/training schemes should be useful and well administered.

Benefit issues
- The benefit situation of young people should be more generous. Those under 25 should not be discriminated against in terms of age.
- 16–17-year-olds should be better protected in terms of income.
- Measures should be taken to cover deposits and rent in advance, enabling young people to secure accommodation.
- Measures to encourage work without necessarily losing benefit will help young people leave unemployment.
- Financial measures to encourage friends and relatives to accommodate young people will help the situation.

Information and publicity
- Information and advice should be given so that young people can access benefits and accommodation for themselves.
- Accurate information, e.g. missing-person statistics and data on housing needs, is important for campaigning.
- Information can be part of a preventative campaign encouraging young people not to leave home unnecessarily.

Sources: See note 1 on p. 164.

relief to home owners (e.g. mortgage relief in the UK). It is particularly through state housing that low-cost rental accommodation is provided for those who cannot afford to buy their own property. However, we have already seen that in the UK the stock of state housing has declined as new public-sector house building has virtually come to a standstill and local authorities have sold off large numbers of council houses. At the same time, local authorities have been legally restrained from using the income from these house sales to build new homes. The result has been a dramatic rise in the competition for this housing resource, from which young single people are usually excluded. An increase in public-sector housing would clearly help to address the current homelessness problem. In order to achieve this, many agencies argue that a complete reversal in housing policy is required, with a move away from the Conservative government's emphasis on expanding owner occupation and reducing public-sector housing. Indeed, it is calculated that the building of permanent public-sector housing would be a cheaper solution than the present use of bed and breakfast accommodation for homeless families. In 1987 the government estimated that the first-year cost of building a family home to rent in London was £8,200 compared with the then average £15,540 bed and breakfast hotel bill. The government has refused to update these figures, but Shelter estimates that in 1992 re-housing all the homeless families in bed and breakfast into permanent housing would save around £68 million in the first year alone (Burrows and Walentowicz 1992, pp. 22–3). At the very least, agencies argue that the government must allow local authorities to spend the money that they have received from council house sales on building new properties. A report by the Association of Metropolitan Authorities (1990, p. 23) states that local authorities have some £7,300 million in accumulated receipts from the sale of properties. They suggest that less than a quarter of these funds would, if properly directed towards the area of greatest need, resolve the problem of homeless families in temporary accommodation and also enable councils to make a start in helping single homeless people.

An alternative to an increase in state housing is an expansion of the private rented sector. Young single people, who are generally ineligible for local-authority housing, have traditionally used private rented accommodation, although this sector has declined – particularly in the UK (see Chapter 3). Consequently, it is often argued that measures to increase this sector of the housing market will help young people. However, private landlords do not have a good reputation for providing accommodation of reasonable quality at reasonable rents. The main objective of most private landlords is to make a profit, which is not necessarily compatible with the provision of affordable housing. Certainly, there is evidence that the UK government's attempt to rejuvenate this sector by deregulation and by giving greater freedom to landlords has in fact led to a decrease in tenant security and increased evictions (see Sharp 1991). Agencies dealing with homeless young people often prefer to seek agreements with councils or housing associations where standards can be more easily controlled. This is not to deny, however, that an increase in the private rented sector, coupled with appropriate safeguards and security, could play a role in expanding the amount of affordable housing available to young people.

Although housing associations still only account for a tiny proportion of the UK housing market, they have nevertheless provided much of the special project and move-on accommodation for young homeless people. Moreover, in some parts of the UK, accommodation for some young single homeless people is eligible for Special Needs Management Allowance (SNMA) which, at between £2,000–4,000 a year per bed, can provide important revenue funding for accommodation projects. Subsequently, although their potential is limited, housing associations still have an important role to play in addressing the problem of youth homelessness in the UK, and many agencies would like to see them expand their involvement.

There is also a call for a more fundamental change in the housing market – namely, the need to acknowledge the increasing demand for housing from single-person households. In most countries the housing market has long been dominated by the demands of the nuclear family (Watson and Austerberry 1986, pp. 71–91) and yet, as discussed in Chapter 3, recent demographic changes have meant that the number of single-person households has risen considerably. It is interesting that, although the needs of the single elderly person are increasingly acknowledged by subsidised building programmes in the UK, the needs of some young single people to live separately from their parents has only been acknowledged for students. Yet, even here, restrictions on grants and housing benefit mean that students increasingly have to rely on parental support. However, models do exist for young single people's accommodation. The YMCA and the YWCA organisations in the UK and the USA, for example, provide some housing for young people (Rossi 1989, p. 203), although these organisations have not generally moved specifically to accommodate the young homeless (YWCA 1989). Similarly, in Denmark, flatlets are being built for young people that can be used for elderly people as the demographic structure of the population changes (Heddy 1990, p. 12), while a number of developments in France, and similar schemes in Germany and Belgium, offer accommodation for young workers and those on training schemes (Burton et al. 1989b).

While the basic solution to homelessness is seen to be a simple increase in affordable accommodation, agencies also acknowledge that some young homeless people have additional housing needs. For example, there is often a need for some kind of emergency accommodation when young people are evicted from home. Many young people who have been homeless may also need supported accommodation – either because of their age; because they need help to cope with factors that lie behind their homelessness, such as abuse; or because of the problems, such as offending or ill health, that may have arisen while homeless. Interestingly, the models for providing young homeless people with accommodation and support have changed considerably over time. For example, throughout the 1980s it was felt that care should be carried out 'in the community' rather than in large and isolated institutions. The kind of accommodation offered by traditional homelessness hostels – particularly resettlement units – was felt to be of poor quality and ineffective in resettling the individual and thus resolving their homeless situation (see Steele 1989). These units, which were once seen as a solution, themselves became identified as part of the homelessness problem and a cause of 'the revolving door' of homelessness (Beresford 1979, p. 142). Similarly, in the 1990s the model of youth residential projects, where accommodation and support are offered together for a transitional period, is being replaced by the provision of individual, permanent accommodation for young homeless people. In this way, the problems of communal living are avoided and young people remain in their own accommodation rather than having to make a disruptive move. As support and accommodation are separated, the support can be tapered off as it ceases to be required.

While the provision of affordable and appropriate housing is seen to represent the linch-pin of attempts to resolve the youth homelessness problem, the provision of jobs for young people, without which many youngsters cannot afford to access accommodation, is often seen to be equally important.

The labour market

The importance of *both* accommodation and employment for
resolving youth homelessness can be illustrated by the development
of 'foyers', or hostels for young working people. Foyers have been in
existence for many years in France, where they were developed to
help young people leave the countryside to seek work in the towns. A
recent Foyer Initiative in the UK, supported by Shelter and other
accommodation agencies, housing associations, training agencies and
central government, is developing under one roof affordable accommodation and help with training and finding work (see McKechnie
1991). The aim is to break the vicious circle of 'no job, no home, no
job', but foyers do not provide immediate accommodation for
homeless people. Instead, they are meant for young people aged
between 16 and 25 who are 'neither students, nor out of work but in
transition towards autonomy' (Shelter 1992b, p. 23). Subsequently,
foyers are not designed for young people with special needs. Their
style derives from good housing management rather than the social
support model, and the staffing (10 adults to 100 young people)
reflects this, although residents are required to enter into a personal
contract and agree to adhere to a programme. However, the strength
of the foyer model lies in bringing training and employment services
and local employers directly into an accommodation scheme.

Certainly, because unemployment can mean that young people are
unable to find or maintain accommodation, many agencies argue that
resolving youth unemployment will in turn have a dramatic effect
upon youth homelessness. However, large-scale reductions in unemployment rest on a number of factors, such as the performance of
national and even world markets. Ironically it has often been wars,
and the linked expansion of production, that have created jobs even
for the long-term unemployed (Axinn and Levin 1982, pp. 231–42).
Moreover, unemployment is often integrally linked to particular
economic policies, which are unlikely to be transformed by anything
other than a change in government. For all these reasons, while some
agencies campaign for broad changes in economic policy, the more
usual response is to demand more specific changes in the labour
market.

In particular, changes in education and training are seen to be
important, especially measures that enable young people who would
previously have looked for scarce unskilled jobs to gain a degree of

skill necessary to take up jobs in areas of expansion, such as technology. Certainly, state work programmes have been created in both the UK and the USA at times of unemployment. However, as many agencies are at pains to illustrate, there are often a number of problems with such schemes, some of which arise from conflicting goals (Katz 1986, pp. 230–4). On the one hand, for example, government work programmes should be useful and efficient. They should be able to employ qualified workers and offer incentives to those who work well. Yet, on the other hand, they should provide as many jobs as possible and the work should be less attractive than jobs elsewhere, otherwise they will attract workers from employment.

Homelessness agencies usually campaign for the more effective operation of these schemes rather than commenting on them in general, although many agencies believe that state work programmes by their very nature have little to offer. Interestingly, there is little evidence in the USA or the UK that training schemes markedly alter the recipient's chances of work on completion of the programme (see Rees et al. 1989). This is not surprising as the real problem is a shortage of jobs in the first place. However, many agencies also recognise that the crucial issue is not necessarily unemployment as such, but the very low incomes that unemployment usually incurs – which brings us to the issue of benefits.

Benefit issues

We discussed in Chapter 3 how the benefit levels for young people without work in many western industrial countries have been dramatically reduced in recent years. These reductions have led to a chorus of opposition from a variety of groups, but particularly homelessness agencies, who argue that these changes have led directly to the visible increase in homelessness in the UK since the late 1980s (see Young Homelessness Group 1988; Young Homelessness Group 1991). While it is clear that the key to resolving the current youth homelessness crisis must be the long-term provision of more affordable accommodation, the amount of benefit and the manner in which it is paid directly influences young people's ability to obtain and maintain accommodation. Moreover, in theory at least, benefit issues are more easily resolved than are housing market trends. In the UK, for instance, if the rights to benefit of those under 25 were restored to their position prior to the 1988 changes, the difficulties of many young homeless people would be effectively resolved (Hutson and Liddiard 1991, pp. 9–21). This would require relating benefit levels to need rather than age again, and restoring Income Support eligibility to 16- and 17-year-olds. Many agencies have also campaigned to make rent in advance and deposits available again to those drawing benefit. Some form of rent allowance for young people would enable them to compete effectively with older people, whose purchasing power is often greater (Burton et al. 1989b, p. 99). The importance attached to these issues has been highlighted in Cardiff, where a Bond Board has been set up by the local authority to enable tenants of approved private landlords to obtain a loan for a bond.

It is also argued that any measures that encourage unemployed people to work without automatically losing benefit could help young homeless people back into the labour market. Part-time working while on benefit, or a more revolutionary 'basic income' scheme to replace many benefits and tax allowances and give a basic income to all citizens irrespective of employment status, could achieve this objective, and both have been proposed (White 1991, pp. 211–15; 234–42).

It has also been suggested that benefit incentives for young people to remain in the parental household where appropriate could be helpful, so long as they did not discriminate against those who do leave home. In the USA, Rossi (1989, p. 208–9) estimates that the majority of the 5 million unattached (without spouse or dependants) aged between 22 and 59, who have incomes of below $4,000 a year, live with parents or siblings. He suggests that a benefit for such people to be shared with the host household would make many households more amenable to accommodating single people.

The potential importance of benefit measures for resolving homelessness can be seen in the USA. By the second half of the 1970s, for example, the proportion of Americans living beneath the poverty line had fallen from some 18 per cent in 1960 to less than 8 per cent. Schwarz (1988, pp. 24–36) and others largely attribute this to the success of government programmes, concluding that various welfare schemes reduced poverty at a rate five or six times faster than economic growth. The elderly were the main recipients of this welfare expansion. For example, the poverty rate for people over 65, who had earlier been overrepresented among the poor, was lower than that for the rest of the population. The rate dropped from 35 per cent to 16 per cent between 1959 and 1980 (Katz 1986, p. 270). More generous benefits also removed older people from the homelessness shelters. As Rossi points out:

How this was accomplished says a lot about how the problem of homelessness will have to be solved, if indeed it ever is (1989, p. 193).

Information and publicity

Information about benefits and housing rights can also be crucial in determining people's access to housing. In some cases, the simple claiming of benefits to which a person is entitled can be sufficient to avoid becoming homeless. For instance, welfare rights information was a keystone of civil-rights measures in the USA and led to the numbers of black families claiming the AFDC (Aid to Families with Dependent Children) benefits to which they were entitled rising from approximately 30 per cent in the early 1960s to over 90 per cent in the early 1970s (Handler and Hasenfeld 1991, p. 119). However, advice can be a second best to resources. Advice without accommodation can lead to young people circling a number of agencies with no results (O'Mahony 1988, pp. 47–8). It must also be remembered that the majority of young people gain information through family and friends. Nevertheless, many agencies emphasise the importance of appropriate information networks for resolving the problem of homelessness. In the Netherlands, for example, one agency, LOBW, has a telephone line for young people, runs supported accommodation, and gives access to independent housing. Interestingly, another agency, LOBH, provides information in a different direction – to developers, the government and housing associations (Heddy 1990, appendix).

Information about a social problem, particularly statistical information, is a powerful weapon in campaigning for solutions and bidding for resources. For this reason, agency recommendations often call for more and better co-ordinated information. An example of this would be the campaign in the UK for the central collection of missing-person statistics, which would give information about runaways (Newman 1989, p. 155).

Information can also be an important part of a preventative campaign to show young people the risks of leaving home or encourage them to return home. For example, one national poster

and leaflet campaign – 'Why not go to London?' – was funded by the
government in 1976 following the *Johnny Go Home* documentary,
although its impact was difficult to assess. However, there are a
number of problems with such preventative campaigns. We have
already seen that the majority of young people who become homeless
simply cannot return 'home', and that their leaving was usually far
from voluntary (Hutson and Liddiard 1991, pp. 23–5). Moreover,
because preventative work of this kind is relatively untargeted, it can
be expensive. Most significantly, because it has a largely long-term
and unquantifiable effect, preventative work is generally not seen to
be as important as the more immediate provision of services to the
homeless. This brings us to the more practical solutions outlined by
agencies.

Practical solutions

We have already seen that agencies often perform dual roles – on the
one hand, campaigning for general solutions to youth homelessness
and, on the other, providing day-to-day services for young homeless
people. The campaigning solutions outlined above are not easy to
achieve, even when they are fairly specific. This is one reason why
agencies delivering services often have to adopt more pragmatic and
practical solutions on a day-to-day basis; this can take many forms.

One practical solution is for agency workers to use their own
personal networks and expertise to short-cut the access routes to
housing, benefits and employment for their young clients. This can
certainly be an effective short-term solution to a situation, but it does
have a number of problems. For example, it can make young people
dependent on agencies, at the same time disempowering them. It also
puts at a disadvantage those young people who are not clients of
agencies.

Better co-ordination between agencies is also identified as an
element in resolving youth homelessness, at least in the short term.
'Co-ordination' can simply mean personnel from social services
informally talking to personnel from the housing department for the
first time, or it can involve the setting up of more formal local
planning groups with all relevant agencies. Co-ordination can lead to
the rationalisation of services, better use of resources and more
powerful campaigning. However, an evaluation of the multi-agency
accommodation forums set up by the probation service (see Chapter

5) queries the 'disproportionate cost of work involved' with the outcomes – in this case, only 30 per cent of the bids for additional bed spaces were accepted by the Home Office (see Fraser et al. 1992). Co-ordination can be difficult as well as time consuming, because of personal antagonisms and historical rivalries between different agencies. More co-ordination can also mean more bureaucracy and it can reduce the independence of smaller organisations and so affect the variety of services on offer (see Johnson 1981).

In general terms, the practical solutions that agencies identify are usually concerned in some way with improving their day-to-day running. As such, probably the most important practical solution identified by agencies is the need to increase agency activity. The expansion of agencies is clearly evident in their annual reports, where upward graphs and background motifs of bricks and mortar emphasise physical expansion (Centrepoint Soho 1986, p. 13; CHAR 1986, p. 1). Expansion does not always mean more of the same. Change and diversification in what agencies do makes further expansion possible. For example, in 1991 Centrepoint widened its coverage of youth homelessness by setting up a regional development unit to campaign and offer services throughout the UK. Similarly, the simple 'advice' that was offered by the Soho Project in the 1960s had by the end of the 1980s become 'counselling', 'liaison' and 'advocacy'. Homelessness agencies have also expanded their interests outside the field of homelessness. This widens the issues and also the solutions to campaign for. For example, the Young Homelessness Group in London now has members concerned not only with homelessness, but also with wider themes such as citizenship and education.

By way of a footnote, we have so far implicitly assumed that agencies want to solve the problem of youth homelessness. Yet, in theory at least, it may clearly be in the interests of agencies *not* to solve the problem. After all, the very existence of homelessness agencies is dependent on the existence of a homelessness problem. Indeed, the larger and more serious the problem can be shown to be, the more likely it is that additional funding and resources will become available. Homelessness agencies thus have:

an investment in the growth of the problem. They need homeless young people to support the viability of their projects (Brandon et al. 1980, p. 40).

Of course, this is an oversimplistic interpretation of the situation. Agency workers are usually highly committed to eradicating the problems with which they deal, and when one social problem declines in importance, agencies can simply target their resources elsewhere.

7.3 Politicians' solutions

It is not surprising that solutions are often presented by politicians in the form of a debate. At first sight, the debate is predictable and reflects the opposing political viewpoints of the parties involved. In the UK the political dichotomy is between the Conservative Party, on the Right, and the Labour Party, on the Left, with the Liberal Democrats laying claim to the middle ground. Their solutions to youth homelessness seem to reflect their opposing positions.

The Conservatives tend to adopt an individually based approach to the problem, explaining youth homelessness in terms of the individual behaviour of the young homeless. As such, if homelessness is caused by the individual behaviour of some young people, then it is not the government's role to provide solutions. We saw in Chapter 3 how Margaret Thatcher interpreted youth homelessness:

> **There is a number of young people who choose voluntarily to leave home. I do not think that we can be expected, no matter how many there are, to provide units for them** (*Hansard*, 7 June 1988, vol. 134, p. 713).

Given that many of the young homeless are seen to have voluntarily left home, the obvious solution is for them to return. Michael Spicer expresses a common Conservative view:

> **Many of these people are children, and our first advice to them is, therefore, to go back to their parents** (*Hansard*, 24 January 1990, vol. 165, p. 884).

Blame can also be attached not simply to the homeless individual, but also to the individual's family. As Nicholas Ridley outlined in Parliament:

> **Fundamentally, the causes [of homelessness] are social. They arise from changing values and expectations, and from the loosening of family ties** (*Hansard*, 10 February 1987, vol. 110, p. 184).

This individually based approach to explaining the problem of youth homelessness can also extend to the labour market. There is a feeling that homeless people are work-shy and thus to blame for their homelessness, a view expressed by Anthony Beaumont-Dark:

> **Let us not think that anyone who is homeless is deprived by the Government – often such people do not want to work and do not want to thrive** (*Hansard*, 24 January 1990, vol. 165, p. 884).

Clearly, the adoption of individually based interpretations of homelessness, as opposed to more structurally based interpretations, means that Conservative governments generally perceive the solution to youth homelessness as resting with the individual behaviour of homeless people and their families. As such, the need for government intervention is felt to be a minimal one.

In contrast, on the Left of the political spectrum the Labour Party often advocate quite different solutions, which arise from an opposing explanation of homelessness resting on structural factors rather than individual behaviour. Labour Party spokespeople identify broad structural issues, such as the housing or the labour market, as representing the key to the problem. This was simply expressed by John Cunningham:

> **The severe shortage of adequate, affordable, fit housing is causing the crisis** (*Hansard*, 10 February 1987, vol. 110, p. 178).

Similarly, in the following quote the Conservative government is taken to task for effectively creating the structural conditions that have led to the problem of youth homelessness:

> **While the announcement of a recent package of measures involving opening up a few church halls put a roof over some young people's heads, those measures do nothing to solve the underlying problem that thousands of teenagers are being driven out of their homes by the conditions created by the Government, not least through the stealing of YTS [Youth Training Scheme] allowances and the general cut in benefits** (*Hansard*, 2 July 1990, vol. 175, p. 678).

Evidently, there appears to be a clear dichotomy here, with personal or individual causes and solutions being advocated by the political Right, whereas structural causes and solutions are being advocated by the Left. Similar perspectives can be identified in the USA and elsewhere, where comparable dichotomies exist between the Democrats on the Left of the political stage, and the Republicans on the Right.

In the UK these different perspectives are clearly in line with the wider political ideologies of the two main political parties and with their attitudes towards the welfare state. For example, with the immediate post-war construction of the welfare state in the UK, both political parties of Left and Right adopted a 'post war consensus' towards the welfare state. That is to say, both parties accepted that the welfare state performed a crucial role and approved of continuing government investment in areas such as health, education and housing. However, with the onset of economic 'stagflation' in the 1970s, this 'post war consensus' began to break down. While the Labour Party continued to avow state support, the Conservative Party increasingly adopted the ideas and philosophy of the 'New Right' and attempted to remove all but the most basic welfare state provision, and to emphasise instead a return to individualism and 'family' values (Sullivan 1987).

However, the connection between political philosophy and the solution to youth homelessness is perhaps not as straightforward as this. We have argued elsewhere (see Liddiard and Hutson 1991) that an important factor influencing the approach taken towards a social problem like homelessness is the resource implications of the viewpoint being taken. Undoubtedly, the way that political parties appear polarised in their approach to youth homelessness fits well with their overall approach to welfare. However, there is another crucial difference between the political Left and Right: one party is in power and the other is not. As such, the party in power has some responsibility to house the homeless, which the party in opposition does not have. The significance of this political responsibility can be seen in relation to the measurement of youth homelessness. For example, it should not be particularly surprising that the party in power attempts to minimise the scale of the problem with which they must deal, while the party in opposition provide more generous estimates in order to highlight the effective failure of the government. The Labour Party in opposition, for example, consistently adopt more generous estimates of the scale of youth homelessness than those give by the Conservative government. As Neil Kinnock, then leader of the Labour Party, replied to Margaret Thatcher in 1988:

Does not she realise that in London alone there are 50 000 young, homeless people without secure accommodation, that the hostels are packed, and that there are 1 million fewer places to rent than there were at the beginning of the decade? (*Hansard*, 7 June 1988, vol. 134, p. 713).

Interestingly, however, when the Labour Party were in power, they themselves attempted to minimise the scale of the problem. In 1969 David Ennals, the then Minister of State for Health and Social Security in a Labour government, said:

There has been a great deal of exaggeration of the size of this problem and the numbers involved. I have even seen references to 'three million homeless'. This is really nonsense. In England and Wales there are 3,594 families living in temporary accommodation (cited in Watson and Austerberry 1986, p. 14).

As such, it is clear that the approaches taken by politicians towards the problem of youth homelessness are dependent not simply on their political philosophies, but also on the more pragmatic concerns of whether or not they are in power. The point is further endorsed in the UK by the fact that although the Labour Party frequently adhere to a pro-welfare state stance in attacking the government, when they themselves were last in power, in the late 1970s context of economic 'stagflation', they similarly began to adopt something of a 'New Right' philosophy (Sullivan 1987, pp. 19–21).

Nevertheless, it is clearly unacceptable for a government in power to do nothing about a youth homelessness problem, or at least to be seen to be doing nothing. Subsequently, a common response by the government to opposition complaints about youth homelessness is to detail the voluntary agencies who are working with the problem and to point out that their funding is being increased. This solution – of increasing funding to involved agencies – was illustrated in the government's £15 million response to homelessness in 1990 (see Chapter 4). Throughout the UK, Europe and the USA, youth homelessness is often dealt with through funding agency-run projects in the fields of accommodation, training, counselling and welfare rights.

In most western industrial countries, the response of governments to youth homelessness is in terms of special agency-run projects rather than state policy initiatives that affect the operation of the housing or labour market or the welfare system. A concentration on the former tends to divert attention from the possibility of the latter. In the USA and Europe, for instance, there are few examples of policies or laws designed to protect young people from age-based discrimination in jobs or in housing (Burton et al. 1989a, p. 50). In fact, we have seen that young people are often directly discriminated against by policies. Usually, the main governmental attempts to resolve problems of youth homelessness involve funding agency projects. Yet many agency projects cater to 'special' categories of young people such as young offenders, care leavers, ethnic minority groups or refugees. In such cases, there is a danger that projects will stigmatise and marginalise both young people and the problem of youth homelessness. If wider youth policies on education, jobs, housing and benefits were to be considered then these would evidently have implications for young people who find themselves homeless. Crucially, because these wider youth policies would be concerned with mainstream services, they would not marginalise or stigmatise certain groups. In fact, out of the 12 EEC member states, only the UK and Italy do not have a minister who is in some way responsible for youth policy. In the Netherlands, youth policy is drawn up by a cabinet minister. There is a directorate to draw attention to the implications of general policies for young people and an independent Youth Policy Council for consultation (House of Lords 1991, p. 27).

It is often felt that the solution to youth homelessness lies in changes in legislation – for example, by recognising young people as 'vulnerable' under the Housing Act by virtue of their age, or by reversing the restrictions on benefits that occurred in 1988. However, it is important to remember, as the 1989 Children Act illustrates (see Chapter 5), that legislation in itself cannot provide solutions unless the resource implications are simultaneously dealt with (Karn 1990, p. 95).

7.4 Young people's solutions

It is difficult to make generalisations about how any single category of people interpret the problem of youth homelessness. As we saw in the last chapter, young homeless people are not a homogeneous group. They adopt a wide range of attitudes towards their homelessness, its causes and its solution. Yet it is probably fair to say that many young homeless people – with some notable exceptions – tend to describe the problem and its solution in practical terms rather than in the more campaigning language of agencies. For example, an agency worker described young people's perception of the situation in the following terms:

Their perception is much more practically based – there aren't any proper jobs for them; they haven't got anywhere to live that's suitable.

The reasons for the practical emphasis of many young homeless people are fairly clear and we discussed them earlier. Of course, they may lack the political language of the 'structural' explanations. However, more importantly, young homeless people are clearly in a 'practical' situation. They need accommodation quickly and they need practical help to resolve their homelessness. Policy changes are simply too long-term for their outcomes to be considered. Yet agencies can afford to take a longer-term view and are likely to be involved in homelessness over a longer time span.

We saw in the last chapter that very few young homeless people adopt an explicitly structural approach to explaining their homelessness, although they may refer to structural issues in practical terms. Instead, their interpretation tends to be more individually based. Brandon et al. (1980), for example, found that very few of the young homeless people they interviewed in London emphasised structural issues, such as the housing or labour market, as lying behind their homelessness. Rather, the majority viewed their homelessness as directly arising from their own behaviour or the behaviour of others, and these findings have been broadly endorsed by our own work. Many of the young homeless people we interviewed presented the causes of their homelessness in quite individually based terms, such as family conflict and eviction from the parental home. For many of them, the solution to their homelessness lay not with changing the housing market or the labour market, but with resolving their family conflict and returning home. Ironically, the solutions proposed by some young people often echo those of the Right-wing politician in apportioning personal blame and seeing a return home as a solution.

We have so far assumed that young homeless people see their homelessness as a problem that requires a solution. Yet this is not always the case. For a few young people, their homelessness may not be a problem for them. Subsequently, a solution to their homelessness may be neither appropriate nor desired. There is considerable evidence to suggest that many young homeless people move in and out of homelessness. For some, their homelessness may simply take the form of occasionally having to stay on a friend's floor for a few nights after an argument at home, before resolving their difficulties and returning. Clearly, for some of these youngsters – and indeed some agencies (Liddiard and Hutson 1991, pp. 370–1) – this situation may not be perceived as being particularly problematic or in need of a solution.

In light of the particular emphasis that many young homeless people place on the practical resolution of their homelessness, self-help clearly plays an important role. Young people do not face homelessness simply as passive victims. The wide use they make of their own family, relatives and friends indicate that self-help is often the first reaction to homelessness. Many of their moves through different types of accommodation indicate a desire to improve their situation. After interviewing young homeless newcomers to London, Brandon et al. (1980, p. 192) concluded that, while agencies felt that they were offering an immediate solution to young homeless people with advice and counselling, informal networks and squatting played a much larger part in the solutions actually adopted by young people. However, some of the young people's efforts to resolve their problems can actually compound their difficulties. For example, Robertson (1990, p. 5) found that some young people in Hollywood in the USA sell sex, drugs and thieve when they are homeless. Such short-term and practical solutions to the problem of survival, when work and welfare fail, can obviously create problems in the longer term. Nevertheless, it is evident that many young homeless people prefer self-help to relying on agency intervention. A group for whom this is particularly the case are squatters.

Squatting, on land or in buildings that officially belong to someone else, takes place all over the world and is basic to the survival of millions of poor people (Advisory Service for Squatters 1986, p. 30). While squatting is a major strategy in the Third World (see Chapter One), it is used only by a minority of young homeless people in western industrial countries. Although squatting in the UK and Europe is invariably only a short-term solution, it is distinctive in its self-help element and in the official response it has evoked.

After the two world wars, ex-servicemen and their families squatted on military sites throughout the UK when the 'homes for heroes' failed to materialise. Another wave of squatting began in the late 1960s, and by 1970 many towns in Europe had squatters. In Amsterdam, for example, squatters featured in tourist guides. In the UK, squatting was often tolerated by the authorities because it tended to occur in council properties frequently in need of renovation or redevelopment. Franklin (1984, p. 16) suggests that, at this time, squatting attracted mainly young single people who did not qualify for council housing and it offered groups such as gays, young blacks and women a chance to set up households along different lines of organisation. Although the heyday of squatting in the UK was in the

1970s, it has nevertheless remained as one solution to homelessness. Squatting in England and Wales is still not a crime, as it is in the USA and many European countries. Squatters have certain rights and evictions remain civil actions, although in the UK there are moves to change this (see Hirst 1991; Shaw 1991). However, as the demand for council housing has exceeded supply, councils have increasingly tightened up on their controls and evicted squatters within weeks rather than months. Nevertheless, the Advisory Service for Squatters (1990, p. 1) estimated that in 1987 there were still some 31 000 squatters in London. In contrast to Franklin, they suggest that the characteristics of squatters have changed somewhat. Many are low-paid or self-employed workers, people made homeless through mortgage repossession, students, and even those with children who failed to qualify for housing.

By its very nature, squatting is short-term accommodation. It is generally, but not always, a strategy of young people. It usually requires some degree of organisation and is sometimes undertaken by groups. It may be the main option for those people unwilling to comply with the rules and regulations of hostels or night shelters. It may be, but is not always, associated with an alternative lifestyle. Where this is so, there can be a positive attitude not often found in other forms of homeless accommodation (see Chapter 6). Certainly, squatting is one of the main self-help strategies adopted by young people in order to resolve their homelessness. While squatting is actively discouraged by the authorities, alternatives such as self-build and renovation schemes directly involving young people are few and far between, although there are urban renewal schemes in Germany, with co-operative self-build schemes in the UK and Spain. Interestingly, Burton et al. (1989a, p. 51) suggest that the most successful accommodation initiatives in Europe are those which:

involve young people in defining for themselves the problems they face and which then provide them with support in devising their own solutions.

In conclusion, there is evidently much debate and divergence about what is required to address the problem of youth homelessness. What is not in any doubt, however, is that the current youth homelessness crisis urgently needs to be resolved.

Note

1. The following have been used in compiling Box 7.1 and Section 7.2: Burton et al. (1989b); CHAR (1983) (1987) (1989); Hutson and Liddiard (1991); Karn (1990); NACRO (1981); O'Mahony (1988); O'Mahony and Ferguson (1991); Randall (1988); Rossi (1989); Saunders (1986); Tai Cymru (1991); White (1991); Women's National Commission (1990); Young Homelessness Group (1988) (1991); Young Persons Working Group (1989); Youth Housing Monitoring Group (1991).

8

The Construction of Other Social Issues

8.1 Introduction

This book is ostensibly concerned with the social problem of youth homelessness, and yet in this chapter we consider three quite different social issues – AIDS, child abuse and domestic violence against women. Why is a chapter about these issues included in a book about youth homelessness? In short, we are introducing these three themes to highlight some of the common elements that can be found in all social welfare issues. We have already seen how youth homelessness is variously interpreted and presented by different categories of people, such as the media, agencies, politicians, academics and by young homeless people themselves. We have also considered in relation to youth homelessness the importance of definition, measurement and explanation, as well as setting out the range of suggested solutions. We will now show how three quite different issues can usefully be considered from a similar perspective. In this way, we hope to illustrate that many of the observations that we have made about the construction of youth homelessness as a social problem also apply to other social issues.

These issues – AIDS, child abuse and domestic violence against women – have been chosen because they are contemporary and because, like youth homelessness, they all have a high media profile. The headings we shall use in this chapter are similar to the chapter titles of the book:

- Definitions and measurement
- Explanations
- Public presentations
- Agency viewpoints

- 'Victims' viewpoints
- Solutions

We will begin by briefly outlining the three issues.

8.2 The issues

AIDS

In the USA in 1981 there were announcements of an apparently new disease, termed 'Acquired Immune Deficiency Syndrome' (AIDS). It soon became obvious that the disease was multiplying at an alarming rate and an epidemic was announced (Horton and Aggleton 1989, p. 76). Initially, the disease was reported mostly by gay men. Very soon, however, it was diagnosed in other groups who were seen to be 'at risk' and carriers of the new disease. These groups were injecting drug users, haemophiliacs and Haitians. In 1983 Haitians were removed as a risk group under political pressure (ibid., p. 86). By 1985 it was discovered that AIDS was also widespread in certain African countries where transmission was largely heterosexual (see Chirimuuta and Chirimuuta 1989).

In 1983–4 it was realised that there was an infectious agent that appeared to have close links with AIDS and that was passed through body fluids such as semen or blood. This is known as HIV (Human Immuno-deficiency Virus). The time lag between contracting the HIV virus and the development of symptoms can be many years, and it seems that not everyone who carries the HIV virus will in fact develop the symptoms associated with AIDS (see Volberding 1988). Certainly, the issue of AIDS has been the focus of considerable attention since the mid-1980s for a variety of reasons. In light of the fact that the World Health Organisation expects to see some 30–40 million men, women and children infected with HIV by the year 2000, the high public profile of AIDS seems set to continue.

Child abuse

The physical abuse of children at the hands of their parents or carers has long been recognised, and the National Society for the Prevention of Cruelty to Children was formed in the UK in 1884 (Frost and Stein 1989, pp. 44–9). However, it was not until the 1970s and 1980s that a major media and state interest in child abuse re-emerged, with a series of child abuse cases that hit the British headlines – Maria Colwell, aged 7 in 1973; Jasmine Beckford, aged 4 in 1984; and Kimberley Carlisle, aged 4 in 1986. In each of these cases, young children died at the hands of their fathers or stepfathers and the social services departments involved subsequently attracted a barrage of criticism (Parton 1991, pp. 52–78). However, until the mid-1980s, the sexual abuse of children within the family was not a topic of much public debate in the western industrial world.

In the UK, public attention was drawn to the problem of child sexual abuse in 1986, when a popular BBC programme, *That's Life*, carried out an investigation by asking volunteers to fill in a postal questionnaire about their childhood experiences of abuse. Of the 3,000 questionnaires returned, 90 per cent reported sexual abuse and the largest single category of perpetrators (40 per cent) were fathers (Parton 1991, p. 92). The programme *Childwatch*, which was based on the findings of the research, was watched by 16.5 million people (La Fontaine 1990, p. 3). 'Childline', a national confidential phone-in line, was set up and almost 6,000 cases of sex abuse were reported in just one year (ibid., p. 222).

The high media profile of child abuse in the UK was compounded in 1987 when the 'Cleveland affair' hit the headlines. In five months, 125 children from 57 families in the county of Cleveland were said to have been sexually abused and many were taken into care. The apparent extent of child abuse shocked the public and the professional diagnoses were questioned. The subsequent inquiry highlighted the misunderstandings between the different agencies involved – the police, social workers and doctors (Parton 1991, pp. 79–115). Nevertheless, the whole affair signalled the arrival of child sex abuse as a major social issue in the UK.

Domestic violence against women

Violence in marriage was brought into the public arena by women in the USA and Western Europe in the 1970s. In the UK, a group of women met in Chiswick in 1971, initially to do something about rising prices in the high street. Very soon, however, these women and others began to share their private experiences of violence within the home. These were discussed first in the group and later given a wider hearing via the media. As Erin Pizzey says: 'Every piece of publicity brought more cries for help. Letters were arriving from all over the country' (1974, p. 20).

The first refuge for battered women was set up in Chiswick in 1971, although a split followed between Erin Pizzey and the National Women's Aid Federation (Dobash and Dobash 1980, p. 33). By 1981 there were 200 refuges throughout the UK, the majority of which were affiliated to the National Women's Aid Federation. These refuges provide 'safe house' accommodation, advice and support for both women and their children. In the UK and the USA, the exposure of domestic violence and the setting up of refuges have been directly linked with the wider Women's Movement, whose broad aim was to mobilise women, transform society and free women from male domination (ibid., p. 15). Although domestic violence no longer hits the headlines in the way that it once did, it is now widely accepted as a major social issue.

8.3 Definition and measurement

We saw in Chapter 2 that while definitions and statistics are crucial in constructing and managing the problem of youth homelessness, definitions can vary and statistics can be precariously constructed. This is not surprising as both the definition and measurement of youth homelessness depend partly on the viewpoints and objectives of those constructing them. The same point can be made in relation to AIDS, child abuse and domestic violence against women.

The variation in definitions is best illustrated with child abuse. Definitions of 'abuse' are seldom stated and are clearly open to considerable interpretation. In terms of physical abuse, for instance, definitions are fluid. For example, does one define the physical punishment of a child for a misdemeanour as physical abuse or not? Certainly, if one does, then the prevalence of physical abuse is widespread both in the home and, until recently, in schools. Parton (1985, p. 148) tells us that no actions are 'naturally' child abuse. Rather, actions become established as 'child abuse' as the problem is socially and legally defined and as agencies act on these definitions.

One would have thought that the definition of AIDS would be fairly uncontentious, as it is a medical condition. However, even here there is controversy about how it should be defined – is it signified simply by the presence of the HIV virus, or is it actually dependent on the development of symptoms? Moreover, as Plummer (1988) points out, a multitude of medical, social and political issues are involved in AIDS, which has:

> ... entered the discourses of sex and drugs, of gayness and of prostitution, of race and religion ... of third world and world health, of therapy and trades unionism ... of law and ethics and of power and control. ... Indeed, a myriad of forces have been required to assemble, manufacture, produce and construct 'the AIDS problem' as we know it (p. 21).

We also saw in Chapter 2 that the issues of definition are closely tied to measurement. For example, the way in which an issue is defined will largely determine its scale. Returning to the case of AIDS, if the definition of AIDS is dependent only on the prevalence of the HIV virus, then the number of AIDS sufferers will be considerably larger than if the definition of AIDS is dependent on the prevalence of symptoms. Similarly, how one defines child abuse and domestic violence will obviously determine, to a large extent at least, the subsequent scale of the problem. This is one reason why statistics on social problems can differ so widely.

This variation can be well illustrated by the figures concerned with child abuse. Here, as with youth homelessness, the official statistics are seen by others to be dramatic underestimates. For example, in 1982 the UK official criminal statistics list 230 instances of incest, which Frost and Stein condemn as:

> The most inadequate figures of all ... obviously the proverbial 'tip of the iceberg' (1989, p. 66).

In contrast, a 1985 MORI survey suggested that about 10 per cent of the population had suffered childhood sexual abuse, while a survey of readers of *19* magazine gave a prevalence rate of 17 per cent (cited in Frost and Stein 1989, pp. 66–7). The problems with these figures reflect the problems with youth homelessness figures: definitions vary and are often not stated. Survey methods differ and national rates are often extrapolated from small numbers. In all these issues, there are also particular problems with measuring hidden groups such as victims of child abuse and people infected with HIV. This is also the case with domestic violence.

On the one hand, official figures of domestic violence against women appear high and show that it is the second most common form of all reported violence in two Scottish cities (Pahl 1985, p. 6). This is illustrated in Figure 8.1. However, even these figures are criticised by

FIGURE 8.1 *Offences involving violence dealt with by selected police departments in Edinburgh and Glasgow in 1974**

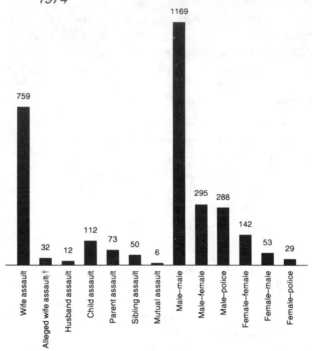

* This includes the reports for all of Edinburgh and one district of Glasgow that were subsequently prepared for and/or dealt with by the courts.

† The term 'alleged' is used by police and courts, but from our reading of the cases there appears to be no significant differences between alleged wife assaults and wife assaults. Hereafter they will be combined.

Source: Dobash and Dobash, 1980, p. 247.

agencies and academic commentators as being too low. Dobash and Dobash (1980, p. 164) suggest that only 2 per cent of assaults on women are ever reported to the police. In this way, domestic violence is a huge hidden problem. The extent to which problems such as these are uncovered necessarily affects the statistics. For example, in child abuse, the size of a problem can grow as it is increasingly recognised and worked with by agencies. As public interest increases and as specialist services are set up, more cases will be reported and the size of the problem will appear to grow. For example, the setting up of a specialist sex abuse referral team led to a flow of referrals from other agencies (Dale 1989, pp. 64–5). Children were referred not just after disclosure of abuse, but also when disturbed behaviour gave rise to suspicions. In this way, a 'hidden' problem is made more visible and more people are counted.

8.4 Explanations

Explanations are important in determining the management of a problem and in apportioning blame. We have noted a dichotomy in the explanations of youth homelessness between those explanations based on the structure of society and those explanations based on notions of individual failure and personal inadequacy. However, we suggested that this 'structural/individual' classification was too simplistic. Instead, we identified a number of approaches that can be adopted in explaining youth homelessness – such as the political model, the individual culpability model, and the pathological model (see Chapter 3).

In a political or structural model, homelessness and other social problems are seen to stem from the structure of society rather than from an individual's actions or behaviour. Yet in a pathology model, the cause of homelessness and other social problems is seen to lie with the individual, although this individual may not be directly responsible – instead, his or her actions may be the result of various problems such as upbringing or poor living conditions. In an individual culpability model, however, the focus is again on the individual, but this time acting as a responsible agent with full control over his or her actions and situation.

We have already seen how these models can apply to the way in which youth homelessness is explained. It is interesting that these three models can also be identified in the explanation of other social problems. For example, it has long been accepted that the incidence of child physical abuse is linked to structural factors such as the social class, poverty and unemployment of the parents. However, looking at the management of child abuse over two decades, it is possible to see how dominant models of explanation can change over time (Parton 1985). Between the late 1960s and the late 1970s, for example, a pathology model of explaining abusing families was dominant in social work in the UK. This was linked to the 'cycle of deprivation' theory, which was current in explaining many social problems. Publicity was given to this idea in a speech by Sir Keith Joseph in 1972 who – in order to explain why poverty persisted in the face of high employment and high welfare spending – related it not to economic factors, but to the poor parenting of children who in turn became poor parents (see Joseph 1972; Kirk et al. 1991, p. 58). The idea of 'dysfunctional families' was commonly used in explaining child abuse at this time. The presence of a single parent or a stepfather was, and is still, seen to indicate risk. If families were intact, then ideas of the psychological misfit of individuals in family roles were used. The response to both models was to treat and rehabilitate the abusers and their families.

After 1972, however, there was a change in the explanation of and response to child abuse in the UK, bringing it more in line with an individual culpability model and laying blame more directly on the abuser (Parton 1985, p. 128). There were calls for social work intervention to be more authoritarian and intrusive. The wider recognition of sex abuse in the mid-1980s strengthened the case for intervention, although state intervention was questioned in the Cleveland affair. In this shift of policy – from treatment to punishment – one can identify the influence of official enquiries following the deaths of Maria Colwell and other children, and the associated media coverage calling for intervention. In addition, feminists were calling for state intervention to compensate for the weakness of children in the face of generalised patriarchal power (see Dominelli 1989).

We have already seen that young homeless people can be blamed for their own situation. This blaming of the 'victim' is particularly prevalent in the case of domestic violence against women and the issue of AIDS. In the former, this can be seen in the commonly asked question 'Why do women stay with a violent partner?' which implies the woman's stupidity or collusion (Hoff 1990, p. 232). It is suggested that women are masochistic or have 'learned helplessness' (Walker 1979). These explanations have been countered by agency workers and academics, who stress the structural reasons behind women's response to domestic violence. For example, they show that the main reason for returning to a violent partner is because of the problem of finding other accommodation (Binney et al. 1981, p. 6). They point out the poverty and isolation often faced by a woman who leaves her partner. They highlight the difficulties that women have with the police and other agencies in both reporting incidences of violence and obtaining services (Edwards 1989). Nevertheless, the inherent blaming of women for staying with a violent partner is still a common response to the problem of domestic violence.

Similarly, in the case of AIDS, although one might expect a straightforward medical model of explanation, the problem is often explained in terms of an individual culpability perspective because of the way in which the disease is associated, at least in the western world, with marginal groups. Homosexuals and drug addicts are often blamed, for their lifestyles are seen to make them responsible for their illness. They are seen as 'carriers', while other categories – haemophiliacs and babies born to HIV-positive parents – are seen as the innocent victims who have 'caught' the disease.

Despite this simplified account of explanations and models, it is important to realise that different categories of people may adhere to very different models and that people may be operating several different perspectives at the same time. We have already shown a mix of viewpoints in the accounts of agency workers (see Chapter 5) and in press coverage (see Chapter 4). The controversies that surround the management of AIDS, child abuse and domestic violence are evidence of alternative explanations being adopted by different groups. Similarly, the mixing of models can be seen in the official indicators that social workers in the UK use to assess whether or not a child is 'at risk' by remaining in their family (cited in Parton 1991, p. 61). These include a mixture of factors drawn from a political model (unemployment, poor housing) and a pathological model (history of abuse, single parent, young mother). Similarly, while feminists may call for legal measures to make a man personally responsible for his violence, they may at the same time feel that structural factors – such as male power in general or the patriarchal family – are to blame.

8.5 Public presentation

The attraction of the media to youth homelessness partly accounts for the way in which the problem has been subsequently presented (see Chapter 4). This is also the case with the issues of AIDS, child abuse and domestic violence. However, not all situations that create personal troubles for people become matters of public knowledge, activity and concern (Gusfield 1981, p. 3). It is not always easy to know why some issues are picked up for public examination and others are not. For example, in terms of mortality statistics, AIDS was not significant in 1985. In the five years between 1982 and 1986, there were 350 AIDS-related deaths in the UK. This compares with some 134 000 deaths from cancer; 190 000 deaths from heart disease; and 5,000 deaths from road accidents in 1985 (Plummer 1988, p. 31). Yet the public concern was about AIDS. Similarly, there is no doubt that child sexual abuse and violence towards women in the family is not new, but it was only in the 1970s and 1980s that they became subjects for public discussion.

These issues have become a focus of public interest for many reasons. One reason is that, like youth homelessness, they all contain elements that make them potentially interesting to the media. For example, in AIDS there is the juxtaposition of death and sex. The death touches the young and the sex is perceived as somehow perverse and promiscuous. Moreover, AIDS is incurable at a time when science is assumed to be all-conquering. Similarly, in terms of domestic violence and child abuse, violence and abuse are the very opposite to what is expected within a family. All these issues are shocking and, as such, they attract a high media profile and public interest.

We discussed in Chapter 4 some of the ways in which the press present social problems such as youth homelessness, and similar patterns can be identified in the context of these other issues. For example, in looking at youth homelessness, we suggested that the press style of presentation exaggerates the non-ordinary, the colourful and the marginal aspects of homelessness. We can see this in the media focus on the links between AIDS and marginal groups, such as gays and drug users (see Watney 1988). Similarly, the Women's Movement is often represented with images of bra burning in the USA and the encampment at Greenham Common in the UK. In this way, complex movements and issues are represented in a few events or symbols. As we saw with youth homelessness, the media are crucial in influencing the way in which a social problem is portrayed and perceived. For example, media reports can lead to a 'moral panic' that can occur when, in the words of Cohen (1972):

A condition, episode or person emerges to become defined as a threat to societal values and interests; its nature is presented in a stylised and stereotypical fashion by the mass media (cited in Watney 1988, p. 55).

Other studies (Cohen and Young 1981; Hall et al. 1978) suggest a connection between 'moral panics' and social control when, in an atmosphere of media-hype, popular consent can be won for measures that require 'more than usual' exercise of state regulation (cited in

Watney 1988, p. 56). In the case of child abuse and AIDS, for instance, public concern through media coverage may have led to greater intervention by social workers into the family and talk of testing, quarantining and segregating in the case of AIDS (Watney 1988, p. 58). Whether or not one fully subscribes to the notion of a 'moral panic', there is no doubt that the media's presentation of social problems is fundamental to how social issues are interpreted.

8.6 Agency viewpoints

In terms of agency involvement, there is a significant difference between youth homelessness and the issues considered in this chapter. In many countries, AIDS, child abuse and domestic violence are the responsibility of statutory agencies. Youth homelessness, however, generally lies outside direct statutory responsibility and is serviced by voluntary sector agencies. The lack of statutory responsibility for youth homelessness in most countries tends to limit the resources available for its solution. This is not to suggest, of course, that statutory responsibility necessarily assures adequate resources. For example, many women living in hostels after experiencing domestic violence fall into a priority group under the UK Housing Act and should be entitled to re-housing. However, surveys have found that, of the women who applied to housing departments for re-housing after living in a women's refuge, many were rejected (see Binney et al. 1981, pp. 77–87; Welsh Women's Aid 1986).

The precise nature of agency involvement varies considerably between different social issues. What is interesting, however, is that common themes can still be identified in the ways that agencies deal with social issues. For example, in Chapter 5 we showed how agency workers in the field of youth homelessness are often faced with a dilemma about how they present the problem to an outside audience. We showed how agency workers might stress, on the one hand, that homelessness is experienced by just a 'vulnerable few' with special problems or, on the other hand, that homelessness is a widespread problem affecting much of the population. Each approach has particular advantages and disadvantages. For example, by defining young homeless people as essentially ordinary, the issue is presented as widespread and worthy of attention. However, if it affects many people, doubt is then thrown on the appropriateness of special funding and intervention. At the same time, an approach that defines these young people as problematic, and thus in need of help, can set them apart from their contemporaries. It may attract funding, but carries with it the inherent danger of marginalising the clients.

The process of marginalisation is particularly clear with the AIDS issue. The illness has generally been closely associated with minority 'at risk' categories, such as homosexual men. Yet there are a number of difficulties with subscribing to a view of AIDS as a problem affecting only marginal groups. Most obviously, it leads to the belief that AIDS is someone else's disease. In this way the lifestyle of the heterosexual majority remains unquestioned (Weeks 1989, pp. 8–13). Similarly, in the case of child abuse and domestic violence against women, the stress on medical and psychological explanations tends to marginalise the abuser – and even the victim – by showing that the abuse is a result of their 'abnormality'. In this way, the 'ordinary' non-abuser and the family structure remain unchallenged. Such marginalisation, as with AIDS, can be contrived by a government or others not wishing to alarm a population or invest resources (Horton and Aggleton 1989, p. 87). Many agencies recognise the problems inherent with presenting AIDS and other social issues as affecting only marginal groups, but also recognise some advantages. Namely, while presenting a social problem as affecting a small minority of the population carries with it the inherent danger of stigmatising these groups, it also has the advantage of attracting funding, because the problem is felt to be small enough to be addressed and even resolved. Certainly, emphasising the close linkage between AIDS and homosexual men has led to an increase in funding for agencies catering for this group, even if it has meant an increase in discrimination towards them.

While some agencies may present a social problem in marginal terms, others may aim to broaden and universalise the issues and to stress the 'ordinariness' of those involved. In the case of AIDS in the UK, while much publicity tended to marginalise the infection to 'at risk' categories, the government education programme tended to stress the risk to ordinary people and the need for safe-sex practices for all. Widening out an issue can be done by showing that it is statistically common and that it affects 'ordinary' rather than 'abnormal' people. Interestingly, this approach avoids marginalisation and can lead to questions about the entire social structure. For example, in the case of child abuse, Kitzinger (1990) shows us that the abuser is not necessarily violent and by implication unusual. She asks us to raise our eyes from the abuser to see the position of all children. In this way it is the powerlessness of all children, rather than the pathology of one adult, that is in question:

> **Abusers rarely have to display any great brutality to get their own way . . . in sensationalising perpetrators' grosser abuses of power we forget the routine use of power over children** (pp. 173–4).

Similarly, by showing that violence by men against women and children is widespread in the family, one is clearly bringing into question the validity of the patriarchal family (see Driver and Droisen 1989). However, there are problems with this approach. If a social problem or issue is widespread and common, the necessary intervention and funding may be unrealisable. Moreover, if a broad approach is adopted it may be ideologically unacceptable to target specific groups.

It is clear that agencies dealing with social problems are often caught in the dilemma of whether to subscribe to a targeted approach – which can bring resources but can marginalise the problem – or subscribe to a more generalising approach – which avoids the problem of stigmatisation, but means that adequate resources may be more difficult to acquire. Because each approach has certain advantages, agencies will variously subscribe to both views – attempting to maximise resources while minimising the degree of stigmatisation (see Chapter 5). What is interesting, however, is the fact that agencies working with very different issues are having to come to grips with this dilemma.

8.7 The viewpoints of 'victims'

In all these issues, the accounts of those directly affected – 'victim' accounts – are extensively used by others. In the media, for example, these accounts are commonly used to bring home the reality of the situation. In the case of AIDS, this can be seen when Silverman (1989) uses a series of short, dull and routine medical exchanges between patients and doctors in a clinic to bring home the reality of the lived experience:

> **Images of contagion and plague have been at the forefront of many press reports and people with HIV infection have been popularly identified as degenerates. . . . In contrast to these views, this study has shed light on a group of frightened, ordinary people** (p. 124).

Personal accounts may be used consciously 'to give people a voice' or to present the reality of private troubles. The suffering of battered wives can be made vivid to the reader through personal accounts (Hoff 1990, p. 62; Pizzey 1974, pp. 26–9). The use of 'victim' accounts by the media – to make vivid a situation and to humanise it – has already been seen in the context of youth homelessness (see Chapter 4).

However, we have suggested that young homeless people can bring distinct interpretations to their homelessness that can contrast with those of agencies and other commentators. Their accounts may be more personal and more optimistic because they are giving accounts of their own lives. It is not surprising that this is the case with other social problems. For example, Kitzinger (1990) is at pains to illustrate that the manner in which victims present themselves is quite different to the way in which agency workers and other commentators may present them. In the context of child sex abuse, for example, Kitzinger (1990) has attempted to show that the young people involved are not helpless and passive, but pursue active strategies. She details the strategies of children for escaping the unwanted attentions of fathers – from staying out of the house, to seeking protection from family dogs or, later on, boyfriends. In doing this, the images of those involved are no longer of the 'limp child with her head in her hand', but of the more ordinary child or adolescent. Similarly, the title of a recent book *Battered Women as Survivors*, with headings such as 'The women as crisis managers' (Hoff 1990, p. 72), indicates that victims of domestic violence should not be seen as simply helpless. It is therefore clear that victims' viewpoints have something useful to add to any examination of a social problem, although it is perhaps surprising that they are not usually considered in their own right.

8.8 Solutions

If people hold different views about society and interpret the same social issue in quite different ways, then it is not surprising that there is often little agreement about how to solve a social problem. For example, a variety of solutions are proposed even in the context of AIDS, which is perhaps surprising given that the issue is explicitly a medical one. One would have thought, for instance, that the solution to AIDS is fairly uncontentious – a medical cure. However, while a medical cure is sought, many groups also see a number of other solutions as being essential, such as removing the stigma from the condition. This may involve changes in definitions of both AIDS and sexuality.

In relation to youth homelessness, we found that broad structural solutions are often deemed to be the most satisfactory by agencies and academic commentators and, to an extent, this is also the case with other social issues. In the context of child abuse, for example, Parton (1985, pp. 198–9) calls for a broad programme of UK policy changes in relation to all children:

> **I have argued that child abuse is far more prevalent and pervasive than official statistics and many professionals admit . . . for a long term strategy, the definition of child abuse should be broad and include all forms of child maltreatment at the individual, institutional and societal level.**

While there is agreement by most campaigners that broad structural solutions are the most desirable, it is acknowledged that such solutions are difficult to achieve because they generally require major shifts in policies. More practical and pragmatic solutions are often the only ones possible. In child sex abuse in the UK, for example, the statutory agency response to a complex hidden problem is to lay out procedures and train workers for dealing with situations that are being newly recognised.

While self-help solutions play an important part in the management of AIDS and domestic violence against women, this is not the case in child abuse and youth homelessness. In the context of youth homelessness, squatting and the self-build movement – both of which offer radical self-help methods – have not generally been approved by the authorities. The use of self-help solutions can have implications for management and bring new methods. An initial self-help response can be radical and in opposition to state services or state inertia. For example, women's refuges are run by the residents who themselves provide the support and therapy. This is more in line with feminist principles than with traditional social work models. The support by women who have themselves experienced the same problems is seen to be essential to consciousness-raising and a new life (Binney et al. 1981, pp. 49–62). Similarly, gay groups in the UK, such as the Terrence Higgins Trust, Body Positive and the Lighthouse, are pioneering methods of patient-centred care in giving support and advice not mediated by the medical profession (Alcorn 1988, pp. 80–1).

Providing state funding to self-help groups can be economical for the state, although state funding can also change the organisation of self-help groups. In the USA, for example, some gay liberation groups from the 1970s onwards were involved in anarchic politics, underground newspapers, and links were made with lesbian groups and the feminist movement. However, state funding for AIDS led to a proliferation of services such as phone lines, clinics, advocacy and public-education projects. As state funding became more available, original self-help groups became involved in 'professional bureaucratic politics with an organisation structure and funding that would rival any corporation' (Plummer 1988, p. 42).

In conclusion, there is a danger, both in this chapter and in the book as a whole, that by focusing on the construction of social problems the personal reality of all these issues will be forgotten. The reaction of the following academic commentator to the issue of child sexual abuse brings this reality starkly back into focus:

I endeavour to maintain an objective attitude to the data, but I am unable to be entirely neutral. My sympathies are engaged. I was angered and appalled when I read about what children, sometimes quite small children, had had to suffer: the physical injuries, the despair and the nightmares represent personal tragedies which should not be tolerated in any society (La Fontaine 1990, p. 18).

9

Conclusions

9.1 Introduction

We began this book with two main objectives. First, to consolidate some of what is currently known about youth homelessness by addressing a number of salient issues. Namely, how is youth homelessness defined and measured? How is it explained? How can it be resolved? By examining the problem of youth homelessness in this way, however, it quickly becomes clear that almost nothing is uncontentious. Youth homelessness, like other social issues, can be interpreted in a number of diverse ways by different groups such as the media, agencies, academics, politicians and by those directly affected – namely, young homeless people themselves. Our second objective was therefore to examine some of the many different interpretations that can be applied to youth homelessness.

Some of this diversity of viewpoint arises from the different interests and experiences of those people involved. For example, one would expect a voluntary agency, which campaigns and provides services for young homeless people, to define and describe their clients differently from a housing department, with dwindling resources and escalating demand. Similarly, it is not surprising that young homeless people should present their homelessness in a distinctive way, because they are talking about their personal lives rather than a theoretical problem. Such differences of opinion are to be expected between such different categories of people. What was more surprising, however, was to find contradictory views coming from the same source. For example, voluntary agency workers can present their clients as just 'ordinary kids' but at the same time point out their 'particular problems', while a press article can simultaneously contain both positive and negative statements about young homeless people.

181

The issue of youth homelessness does not exist in isolation. Discussions about it also involve wider debates about the nature of the family, the economy, welfare and society. In such a situation of diversity and broad topics, it is impossible to set out a single description of youth homelessness. A better approach is to consider the way in which the issue is presented from many different angles and to look for patterns in the way that this is done. Although some of the detail, particularly in terms of legislation, comes from the UK, as do the agencies and young people who gave their views for Chapters 5 and 6, the approach of this book and the issues raised have universal relevance.

The main points of the book are summarised under their chapter headings.

9.2 Youth homelessness in context

While a concern about children and young people on the streets is nothing new, the recognition of youth homelessness as a public problem did not emerge in the western industrialised world until the late 1960s and 1970s. For example, the 1975 television programme *Johnny Go Home* shocked the British public about the risks faced by young people coming to London with nowhere to go and placed the problem of youth homelessness firmly on the public agenda, although policy initiatives were not forthcoming. Behind the widespread rise in homelessness among young people in the 1970s and 1980s were the international problems of youth unemployment, a reduction in benefits for young single people, and a declining supply of suitable and affordable accommodation.

It is important to realise that youth homelessness is only one aspect of a much wider world-wide homelessness problem. We began, therefore, by placing youth homelessness in the context of other categories of people such as runaways, homeless families and older single homeless people, and by making some international comparisons.

The age at which a young person can legally leave home or care (usually 16 or 17), distinguishes runaways from young homeless people. However, runaways and young homeless people face similar risks of sexual exploitation, poverty and offending and the factors that put children at risk of running – a background in care and family abuse and conflict – are also significant in the background of homeless young people. These areas of overlap go some way to explain the lack of distinction made between runaways and young homeless people in the USA and Australia.

Homeless families are in a different situation from young single homeless people because their access to housing and benefits is usually somewhat different. In the UK, for example, the state has a statutory duty to re-house people with dependent children who are unintentionally homeless and have a local connection. However, the applications for re-housing by many families are not accepted and, even if they are accepted, many families must wait for long periods in temporary accommodation such as bed and breakfast.

Attitudes to young homeless people can be influenced by popular stereotypes commonly associated with older single homeless people – 'tramps', 'hobos' or 'vagrants'. The characteristics associated with such people have changed over time from wanderlust and laziness to the medical conditions of alcoholism and mental illness. These connections are made despite evidence that such homelessness is directly related to downturns in national economies. There have been moves to separate youth homelessness in terms of campaigning and services so as to escape these negative stereotypes.

Similar factors lie behind the emergence of young people as a significant category among the homeless in many western industrial countries and similar factors put young people at risk of homelessness. Although the state responsibilities towards homeless people are distinctive to each country, government responses to youth homelessness are often the same – namely, setting up schemes by voluntary agencies for special categories of young people. Whereas homeless people are in a minority position in western industrial countries, in many Third World cities they make up the majority of the population. This fact, together with the economic structures that underlie it, make comparison difficult. However, homeless youngsters in the Third World face many of the same risks as their contemporaries in very different countries, as they move between relatives, institutions and the street.

9.3 Defining and measuring youth homelessness

The study of any social problem must logically begin with its definition. However, there is little agreement about how homelessness should be defined. On an obvious level, the term 'homeless' means not having a 'home'. Yet because there is no agreement about how to define a 'home', so there can be no agreement about how to define the 'homeless'. Because of the way in which it affects the measurement of youth homelessness, the problem of definition is fundamental. How a social problem is defined determines its scale. For example, if one defines homelessness as simply 'rooflessness', so the scale of the problem will be fairly small, certainly smaller than if one adopts a broader definition of homelessness as 'living in inadequate accommodation', which would include young people in a range of housing situations.

Statistics are an integral part of most accounts of social issues, whether they be in the press or in the reports of agencies and academic commentators. The reaction of policy makers to a social problem also depends largely on its size – on the number of people it is thought to affect and whether this is increasing, decreasing or remaining static. However, there are very few agreed statistics on homelessness. First, there are a number of practical difficulties with measuring homelessness, in particular actually locating the homeless. Secondly, measuring homelessness is made extremely difficult by the lack of any agreed definition. Because different groups have different definitions of homelessness, so they also produce different statistics. Because of this, the statistics on a social problem may say more about the organisation collecting them, and how they define the social issue, than they do about the phenomena they are supposed to be measuring. For example, official UK homelessness statistics, because of the way in which homelessness is officially defined, exclude large numbers of homeless people and provide a very misleading picture of the problem. Because homelessness is essentially unquantifiable, it is not surprising that there should be huge discrepancies in homelessness statistics. These discrepancies are not random, but are linked to the definitions used and the aims of the proposer.

The difficulties of measuring youth homelessness can be further illustrated by examining why it is that young women and young black people often appear to be underrepresented in surveys of the young single homeless. The reason is not that young women and young black people avoid finding themselves homeless, but rather that the strategies they adopt when they are homeless are such that their homelessness is often not recorded. For example, many of the statistics on youth homelessness are compiled by agencies working with young homeless people, and yet young women and young black people are often not in contact with these agencies. Subsequently, these groups do not appear to be experiencing a significant homelessness problem, although this is a false impression arising from the manner in which youth homelessness is measured. Equally fundamental and contentious is the question of explanation.

9.4 Explaining youth homelessness

If social issues are to be understood and acted upon, they must be explained. However, explanations of youth homelessness are varied and controversial. Different people explain youth homelessness in quite different ways. A basic distinction can be drawn between 'structural' and 'personal' explanations. Structural explanations explain youth homelessness by reference to societal structures, such as changes in the housing market, changes in the labour market, benefit issues and demographic changes. Because, by definition, homelessness is a housing issue, the housing market is often identified as crucial in explaining the rise of youth homelessness. In particular, recent years have seen a dramatic reduction in the availability of housing that young people can afford, as both public rented and private rented housing have experienced substantial decline. Yet if homelessness is related to the affordability of housing, the economic power of young people must also be an important factor in their homelessness. Both unemployment and low pay are frequently viewed as being integral to homelessness and, since the early 1980s, both factors have come to affect young people in Britain, in the USA and throughout Europe to a significant extent. However, unemployment is not directly the issue – rather, it is a question of the subsequent low income levels that unemployment incurs. As such, the benefit system is also seen to be fundamental to the recent rise in youth homelessness, because young people's benefits have been heavily restricted in a number of ways. These various difficulties have been further compounded in many western industrial countries by a number of demographic changes, such as the expanding numbers of single-person households. Subsequently, while there has been a huge reduction in the *supply* of affordable accommodation, there has also been an increase in the *demand* for such housing.

These four factors – the housing market, the labour market, benefit issues and demographic changes – loosely represent the main 'structural' explanations of youth homelessness, or explanations that specifically relate to the structure of society. However, the problem of youth homelessness is often explained in more personal terms, which relates the cause of homelessness to the individual behaviour of homeless people and those who surround them. A wide variety of such personal factors are often introduced to help explain youth homelessness, such as: leaving home; the experience of care; physical and sexual abuse; mental illness; crime; and alcohol and drug abuse. All of these issues appear to have a close link with the problem of youth homelessness, although there is usually disagreement over why these factors are important and how they should be interpreted.

While a simple division between 'structural' and 'personal' explanations is helpful, such a dichotomy is also too crude. Alternatively, we outlined five broad approaches that can be taken towards the explanation of youth homelessness, each of which has particular strengths and weaknesses.

The first approach is the 'political' model, which broadly coincides with what are usually described as 'structural' explanations and sees homelessness as stemming from the structure of society rather than from an individual's actions or behaviour. The 'individual culpability' model, on the other hand, sees homelessness as having little or nothing to do with society or societal structures. On the contrary, youth homelessness is seen to be a consequence of the individual behaviour of young homeless people themselves, to whom this model correspondingly apportions a degree of blame. The third approach, the 'pathology' model, also sees the cause of homelessness as an ostensibly individual one, but unlike the 'individual culpability' perspective it does not necessarily hold the individual as responsible. Rather, the individual's behaviour is perceived to be a consequence of his or her pathological tendencies. The 'child' model also identifies the key to youth homelessness as being an individually based one and similarly diminishes the responsibility of the individual, who is viewed as possessing childlike qualities and is naive, vulnerable and immature. According to the final approach – the 'spiritual/religious' model – homelessness is related not so much to social or economic privation, but instead to a spiritual poverty in both homeless individuals and society itself.

It is evident that how youth homelessness is defined, measured and explained is open to considerable interpretation. Subsequently, we considered in detail the ways in which three important categories of people – the mass media, homelessness agencies, and young homeless people themselves – interpret and present youth homelessness.

9.5 The public presentation of youth homelessness

There is no doubt that the media is an important source of information about social issues and that the way in which the media presents youth homelessness is widely influential. Some social issues are more newsworthy than others and youth homelessness has certain elements within it that are attractive to the media, such as the stark contrasts, the drugs and the prostitution. These colourful and pathological elements of youth homelessness are then further exaggerated, through a particular journalistic style, to attract the attention of an audience. The sensational, the stereotypical, the emphasis on street homelessness and the human interest story are all part of this press style. However, media presentations are more complex than one would expect. There is often an ambiguity in the manner that young homeless people are presented. They may be portrayed in such a way that both negative and positive interpretations can be made by the reader. TV drama documentaries can add a distinctive approach, as they can present the effect of homelessness over time. These stories are often constructed so as to stress the cumulative risks of homelessness. Interestingly, agency reports and publicity, or even academic comment, also use many of the mass media's techniques, such as concentrating on the sensational, the problematic and the human interest story. This is not surprising because they also need to attract a public audience and media attention.

Although there is agreement that media images are very important, the precise linkage between the media, public opinion and policy making is far from clear. The impact of the media upon the public and public opinion has long been a source of debate – in particular, the question of whether or not the media create or simply reflect the view of their audience. A number of researchers have shown that the public select and interpret media messages according to their existing viewpoints and only those messages that reinforce what individuals believe are selected by the audience. In this way, the same media item can be interpreted in different ways by different people.

It is similarly difficult to elicit the media's impact upon government and policy making. Nevertheless, there is some agreement that wide media coverage can lead to an issue being taken up by policy makers. In choosing to report some items and omit others, the press can set the agenda for action. However, it must also be remembered that policies are made in response to a wide variety of pressures, of which agenda setting by the media is only one.

9.6 Agency viewpoints

Although the state has limited responsibilities towards young homeless people in most countries, the political debate over the issue often revolves around certain pieces of legislation. For example, in the UK it is the 1977 (1985) Housing Act and the 1989 Children Act that set out the statutory duties of housing and social service departments. However, the acute lack of housing and local authority funding severely limits these Acts being implemented in the spirit in which they were written. Subsequently, as in many other countries, the response to single homelessness has come largely from voluntary agencies in terms of providing accommodation and other services. It is these agencies who campaign and play a central role in presenting the issue and their young clients' situations to the press, the politicians and the public.

However, there appear to be interesting contradictions in what agencies say to an outside audience. Despite the obvious hetero-geneity of young people in terms of situation and background, they are often described in one of two opposite ways – either as *ordinary* young people, indistinguishable from their contemporaries, or as *vulnerable* young people with special problems, over and above their immediate homelessness. The adoption of polarised classifications within welfare organisations has been noted before, and it seemed clear to us that these simplified classifications tended to reflect the structure, purpose and resources of the involved agency rather than the characteristics of homeless young people themselves. However, the correlation between agency type and the viewpoint presented is not a consistent or clear one, because the approach taken often differs according to the role and position of the respondent within the organisation. Moreover, agency representatives are using these classifications strategically and there are particular advantages and disadvantages in presenting homeless young people as 'ordinary' or as 'vulnerable'.

Most agencies do more than simply talk about the problem. Many provide direct services for young homeless people and it is this provision of services that justifies their funding. It is often assumed that homelessness agencies are indiscriminate and accept anyone who is homeless and with whom they are in contact. In reality, this is not the case. They must make choices as to who will be included and excluded in line with their particular resources and expertise. Yet the ways in which agency workers categorise their clients and potential clients in terms of who they can and cannot help is complex. We found that clients are often sifted and sorted according to whether or not they are perceived to be deserving or undeserving. In particular, two groups of homeless young people – the 'low risk' and the 'high risk' – are perceived to be undeserving. Most agencies tend to target resources to the middle of their potential client range, avoiding the low risk because of fears of wasting resources and stigmatisation, and avoiding the high risk because of the practical difficulties that they often present to the running of the project.

9.7 Young people's viewpoints

Young people's accounts of their homelessness are frequently used by the media and by agency workers, but seldom considered in their own right. However, it is clear that young homeless people can interpret their homelessness in a quite different manner to agency workers and other commentators. For example, agencies, the media and other commentators tend to stress the dangers of homelessness and often present it as a downward spiral. Certainly, there is some evidence to suggest that the experience of youth homelessness can be a progressively problematic one and many young homeless people agree with this picture, speaking about the problems of finding and keeping accommodation and work. However, some of the young people interviewed in the UK saw their homelessness in less negative terms and spoke about gaining new experiences and new skills. Most young people agreed that the experience of homelessness was unpleasant and risky, yet some also spoke positively about how they themselves had negotiated it. Moreover, given that for some young people homelessness has followed a very difficult home situation, it was not surprising that they may have had positive things to say about their homelessness.

A number of similar disparities can be identified by looking at the way in which young people explained or accounted for their homelessness. While agencies and commentators most often explain youth homelessness in terms of structural factors, young people often explained their homelessness in more individual terms, simultaneously emphasising their role as conscious decision-makers, with a degree of control over their lives. This is in contrast to many homelessness agencies and commentators, who tend to present young people as powerless victims in the face of structural factors.

Despite the difficulties surrounding any definition of homelessness, it is interesting that many commentators assume that young homeless people comply with whatever definition of homelessness is attached to them. Yet this is simply not the case. We found a significant number of young people, described as 'homeless' because of their housing situation, who did not actually accept such a label. The reasons why young people may not see themselves as being homeless are varied. Some did not identify with the negative stereotypes of sleeping rough. Others felt that because they have exercised a degree of choice over their situation, they could not be described as 'homeless'. From this, it is clear that homelessness and the perception of oneself as homeless frequently refers to something more than simply the physical standard of one's accommodation.

9.8 Solutions to youth homelessness

Resolving youth homelessness is the central objective of most people involved in this area. Yet many different solutions are proposed to the problem. On an obvious level, what is seen as the solution to a social problem will depend on what is seen to be its cause. Given that different categories of people explain homelessness in different ways, so solutions will obviously vary.

In all countries, voluntary agencies are one of the most vocal groups in promoting various solutions to the problem of youth homelessness. In campaigning, agencies generally stress the need for broad structural change. If youth homelessness is caused by a shortage of affordable accommodation, a lack of employment and adequate benefits, then policy change in these areas is necessary to eliminate it. However, such broad changes are both difficult to bring about and costly. For this reason, agencies can usually do little except state these solutions in general principles, while they campaign for more specific changes in housing, employment or benefits. Under this heading can be included measures to increase the supply of affordable housing through investing in local-authority housing or, more controversially, encouraging the private sector. There is a call to acknowledge the need for more single-person accommodation in housing programmes and the Foyer model is being borrowed from France. Measures to decrease youth unemployment automatically increase young people's access to accommodation, but these measures are linked to broader economic conditions. The direct connection between homelessness and changes in benefits is clear. For example, the increase in youth homelessness in the UK in the late 1980s followed the removal of Income Support from 16- and 17-year-olds and the reduction in the benefit rate to those under 25. The reversal of these changes, together with the restoration of rent in advance and bonds, would help young people gain and keep accommodation. However, most voluntary agencies are more than simply campaigning bodies. They also offer practical solutions, the most obvious being a bed for the night. This more practical delivery of services is easier to deliver and of more pressing urgency than campaigning.

It is not surprising that politicians often present their solutions to youth homelessness in the form of a debate that reflects the opposing political viewpoints of the parties involved. For example, in the UK the Conservative Party on the Right tends to adopt an individually based approach to the problem, perceiving youth homelessness very much in terms of the individual behaviour of the young homeless. In contrast, on the Left of the political spectrum, the Labour Party interpret youth homelessness and its solution in more structural terms, relating it to the housing market, the labour market and the benefit system. These different perspectives are clearly in line with the wider political ideologies of the two main political parties. However, it would also appear that the approach taken depends not simply on political philosophies, but additionally on the more pragmatic concerns of whether or not politicians are in power and thus whether or not they are directly responsible for funding and managing a solution.

Young homeless people themselves – with some notable exceptions – tend to describe the problem and its solution in practical terms rather than in the more campaigning language of agencies. The reasons for the practical emphasis of many young homeless people are fairly clear. They may lack the political language of the 'structural' and, more importantly, they are clearly in a 'practical' situation. Young homeless people need accommodation quickly and they need practical help to resolve their homelessness. Campaigning for policy changes is usually too long term to be considered by them. Some homeless people feel that the solution to their homelessness lies not with changing society, but with resolving their own family conflict and returning home. Moreover, one tends to assume that young homeless people both recognise their homelessness and see it as a problem that requires a solution. This is not necessarily the case. However, this does not detract from the fact that most young homeless people desperately want to resolve their accommodation difficulties.

9.9 The construction of other social issues

This book concluded with a brief outline of three other social issues – AIDS, child abuse and domestic violence against women. These issues, like youth homelessness, are all of contemporary public concern and have a high media profile. They are included to show that all social issues have common elements, whatever their particular content.

Many of the difficulties with definition and measurement that were outlined in relation to youth homelessness can also be identified in the context of AIDS, child abuse and domestic violence. For example, there is often little agreement about how to define social problems, even AIDS. Yet because the measurement of a social problem is determined in large part by the manner in which it is defined, so the statistics surrounding these social problems vary dramatically. However, as with youth homelessness, the measurement of these issues is also affected by a number of practical difficulties with contacting and measuring groups which are often largely hidden, such as child abuse or domestic violence victims and people infected by HIV.

Earlier in the book we identified a number of broad approaches often taken towards explaining youth homelessness – the political model, the individual culpability model and the pathological model, among others. It is interesting that many of these approaches also apply to the explanation of these other social problems. Similarly, all of these issues have been transformed from private troubles into public problems largely as a consequence of their media treatment. Like youth homelessness, AIDS, child abuse and domestic violence have all attracted considerable media interest and it is apparent that the media often interpret social problems in very similar ways.

In terms of agency involvement, there are some differences between these issues and youth homelessness. AIDS, child abuse and domestic violence are usually the responsibility of statutory agencies, while youth homelessness is generally tackled by the voluntary sector. Nevertheless, there are common themes in the ways in which agencies deal with social issues. For example, there are the same moves either to marginalise or broaden out the problem, given that each approach has particular advantages and disadvantages.

In all four issues, the accounts of those directly involved are often used by others, such as the media. However, these accounts are seldom ever considered in their own right. Nevertheless, it is clear that 'victim' accounts can bring new perspectives to social problems, which can contrast with the views of agencies and other commentators.

If people hold different views about society and interpret the same social issue in quite different ways, then it is not surprising that there is often little agreement about how to resolve a social problem. A lack of agreement and a variety of solutions is common to all four issues. Interestingly, formalised self-help solutions have been important in the context of domestic violence against women and AIDS and, in both, have led to pioneering approaches to the problem.

9.10 The construction of a social issue

It is clear that there are no agreed definitions of youth homelessness, hugely different statistics, contradictory explanations, many solutions, and different national contexts. Moreover, accounts by young people can differ dramatically from agency accounts, and the media presents youth homelessness in its own particular style.

There are, however, connections to be made. There is a logical connection between the way a problem is defined and its size. For example, in the UK the legal definition of homelessness leads to low numbers as most single homeless people are omitted. Explanations and solutions are obviously connected. For example, if a structural explanation is given then the solution will lie in economic or political change. In contrast, an explanation in terms of individual behaviour can lead to personal blame or to the use of counselling as a solution.

In some cases it may be possible to predict the way in which different interest groups will define, measure, explain, present or solve an issue. Agencies and academics tend to stress the structural factors, whereas the press and young people themselves tend to stress the personal factors in youth homelessness, but for different reasons.

Whatever the country, it will often be in the agencies' interests that
the problem be acknowledged as widespread, while politicians in
power will want low numbers. Moreover, these politicians may
explain homelessness in terms of personal behaviour so that blame
can be laid on the individual and not on their policies.

In debating the issue, youth homelessness can be reduced to simple
dichotomies that conceal the complexity of the situation and the
heterogeneity of the clients. For example, explanations tend to be
structural or personal; young homeless people are described as
'ordinary' or 'problematic'; the problem is marginalised or generalised.
This pattern of reduction and selection is often a strategy of debate.
However, there are times when those involved draw on the
ambiguities and complexities of the situation in order to make other
points. Although it might seem possible to predict which position
each interest group will take, one must be cautious in making such
assumptions. Each way of presenting the problem has certain
advantages and disadvantages. One speaker can switch to take
advantage of these and to suit the situation and the audience.

Not all viewpoints have the same strength. The media images of
youth homelessness, with their emphasis on street homelessness with
its sensational and pathological aspects, are perhaps the most
influential. Other categories, such as agencies and academics, often
adopt journalistic techniques as they too wish to reach a public
audience and themselves attract the media. Agencies gain part of
their influence from the contact they have with the media and policy
makers. On the other hand, young people themselves usually have
little opportunity to present their accounts at first hand.

Whatever the viewpoint, much of the debate around any social
issue centres on the national legislation – in the case of youth
homelessness, legislation concerned with housing, benefits and child
care are most relevant. It is in the legislation that definitions,
responsibilities and resource allocations are laid down. The debate
focuses on campaigns and consultations for new legislation, as well as
the interpretation of existing legislation. However, it is clear in the
case of youth homelessness that the way legislation is implemented
rests ultimately on the resources made available whatever the
political context.

By focusing on the ways in which social issues can be interpreted
and the different interest groups involved, there is a very real danger
that we lose sight of the personal tragedy that homelessness
represents for so many young people. Ultimately, it is difficult to

convey with any realism the despair and frustration that so many young homeless people have to face on a daily basis. It is clear, above all else, that the mere existence of a youth homelessness problem in modern society is simply intolerable. That so many young people continue to become homeless is simply unforgivable.

Bibliography

Abrahams, C. and Mungall, R. (1989) *Housing Vulnerable Young Single Homeless People* (London: NCH).

Action on Housing Need (1991) *A Pilot Study of Housing Need in Cardiff* (Cardiff: Action on Housing Need).

Advisory Service for Squatters (1986) *Squatters Handbook*, 8th edn (London: Advisory Service for Squatters).

Advisory Service for Squatters (1990) *Squatting in London Now* (London: Advisory Service for Squatters).

Agnelli, S. (1986) *Street Children: A Growing Urban Tragedy*, Report for the Independent Commission on International Humanitarian Issues (London: Weidenfeld and Nicolson).

Akilu, F. (1991) 'Women's Experience of Homelessness', paper given in Department of Psychology, University of Reading (unpublished).

Alcorn, K. (1988) 'Illness, metaphor and AIDS', in P. Aggleton and H. Homans (eds) *Social Aspects of AIDS* (London: Falmer Press).

Anderson, N. (1923) *The Hobo: The Sociology of the Homeless Man* (Chicago: University of Chicago Press).

Andrews, G. (1987) 'Scarman says Britain in danger of becoming a slum society', *Guardian*, 6 January.

Aptekar, L. (1988) *Street Children of Cali* (London: Duke University Press).

Archard, P. (1979) 'Vagrancy – a literature review', in T. Cook (ed.) *Vagrancy: Some New Perspectives* (London: Academic Press).

Ashton, D. N. (1986) *Unemployment under Capitalism: The Sociology of British and American Labour Markets* (Brighton: Wheatsheaf).

Association of Metropolitan Authorities (1990) *Homelessness: Programme for Action* (London: Association of Metropolitan Authorities).

Atkinson, J. M. (1978) *Discovering Suicide: Studies in the Social Organisation of Sudden Death* (London: Macmillan).

Austerberry, H. et al. (1984) *Homeless in London, 1971–1981* (London: International Centre for Economics and Related Disciplines).

Axinn, J. and Levin, H. (1982) *Social Welfare: A History of the American Response to Need*, 2nd edn (New York: Harper and Row).

Bahr, H. M. (1973) *Skid Row – An Introduction to Disaffiliation* (London: Oxford University Press).

Balchin, P. N. (1989) *Housing Policy: An Introduction*, 2nd edn (London: Routledge).

Barrat, D. (1986) *Media Sociology* (London: Tavistock Publications).

Beacock, N. (1979) 'Campaigning for the homeless and the rootless', in T. Cook (ed.) *Vagrancy: Some New Perspectives* (London: Academic Press).

Belson, W. A. (1978) *Television Violence and the Adolescent Boy* (Farnborough: Saxon House).

Benefits Agency (1991) *Income Support If You Are 16 or 17*, Leaflet IS26 (London: Benefits Agency).

Benefits Agency (1992) *A Guide to Housing Benefit and Community Charge Benefit, Leaflet RR2* (London: Benefits Agency).

Beresford, P. (1979) 'The public presentation of vagrancy', in T. Cook (ed.) *Vagrancy: Some New Perspectives* (London: Academic Press).

Best, J. (1973) *Public Opinion: Micro and Macro* (Homewood, Ill.: Dorsey Press).

Billig, M. et al. (1988) *Ideological Dilemmas: A Social Psychology of Everyday Thinking* (London: Sage).

Binney, V. et al. (1981) *Leaving Violent Men: A Study of Refuges and Housing for Battered Women* (London: Women's Aid Federation).

Bonnerjea, L. and Lawton, J. (1987) *Homelessness in Brent* (London: Policy Studies Institute).

Brake, M. (1980) *The Sociology of Youth Culture and Youth Subcultures: Sex and Drugs and Rock'n'Roll?* (London: Routledge and Kegan Paul).

Bramley, G. (1988) 'The definition and measurement of homelessness', in G. Bramley et al. (eds) *Homelessness and the London Housing Market*, Occasional Paper No. 32, School for Advanced Urban Studies (Bristol: University of Bristol).

Brandon, D. et al. (1980) *The Survivors: A Study of Homeless Young Newcomers to London and the Responses Made to Them* (London: Routledge and Kegan Paul).

Breakwell, G. (1986) *Coping with Threatened Identities* (London: Methuen).

Brynin, M. (1987) 'Young homeless: pressure groups, politics and the press', *Youth and Policy*, no. 20, pp. 24–34.

Burdekin, B. (1989) *Our Homeless Children: The Report of the National Inquiry into Homeless Children by the Human Rights and Equal Opportunity Commission* (Canberra, Aus.: AGPS).

Burrows, L. and Walentowicz, P. (1992) *Homes Cost Less Than Homelessness* (London: Shelter).

Burt, M. and Cohen, B. (1989) *America's Homeless: Numbers, Characteristics and Programs that Serve Them* (Washington DC: Urban Institute Press).

Burton, P. et al. (1989a) *Growing Up and Leaving Home* (Luxembourg: Office for Official Publications of the European Communities).

Burton, P. et al. (1989b) *Accommodation and Social Cohesion in the Urban Environment: The Implications for Young People* (Luxembourg: Office for Official Publications of the European Communities).

Canter, D. et al. (1990) *The Faces of Homelessness in London*, 2nd edn (Guildford: University of Surrey).

Carvel, J. (1990) 'Destitute teenagers face jail penalty', *Guardian*, 3 January.

Caton, C. L. M. (1990) 'Homelessness in historical perspective', in C. L. M. Caton (ed.) *Homeless in America* (New York: Oxford University Press).

Central London Outreach Team (1984) *Sleeping Out in Central London* (London: Greater London Council).

Bibliography

Central London Social Security Advisers Forum (1988) *True Horror Stories: Homeless People and the New Benefit Changes* (London: CLSSAF).

Centrepoint Soho (1986) *Building on Experience: 1986 Annual Report* (London: Centrepoint Soho).

Centrepoint Soho (1988) *Responding to Crisis: 1988 Annual Report* (London: Centrepoint Soho).

Chamberlain, C. and MacKenzie, D. (1992) 'Understanding contemporary homelessness: issues of definition and meaning', *Australian Journal of Social Issues*, vol. 27, no. 4.

CHAR (1983) *Single and Homeless – The Facts* (London: CHAR).

CHAR (1986) *Annual Report 1985–6* (London: CHAR).

CHAR (1987) *Hidden and Homeless: Housing, Single People and the Council* (London: CHAR).

CHAR (1989) *Annual Report 1989* (London: CHAR).

CHAR (1993) *'Plans No Action'* – *Summary of Findings of Preliminary Research into the Children Act and Homeless Young People* (London: CHAR).

Chibnall, S. (1977) *Law-and-Order News: An Analysis of Crime Reporting in the British Press* (London: Tavistock Publications).

Chirimuuta, R. and Chirimuuta, R. (1989) *Aids, Africa and Racism,* 2nd edn (London: Free Association Books).

City of Boston (1990) *Commitment and Compassion: Boston's Comprehensive Policy for the Homeless* (Boston: Emergency Shelter Commission).

Coffield, F. et al. (1986) *Growing Up at the Margins: Young Adults in the North East* (Milton Keynes: Open University Press).

Cohen, S. (1972) *Folk Devils and Moral Panics: The Creation of the Mods and Rockers* (London: McGibbon and Kee).

Cohen, S. and Young, J. (eds) (1981) *The Manufacture of News: Social Problems, Deviance and the Mass Media,* 2nd edn (London: Constable.

Cook, T. and Braithwaite, G. (1979) 'A problem for whom?', in T. Cook (ed.) *Vagrancy: Some New Perspectives* (London: Academic Press).

Cooper, M. (1987) 'The role of religious and non-profit organisations in combating homelessness', in R. D. Bingham et al. (eds) *The Homeless in Contemporary Society* (Newbury Park, Cal.: Sage).

Cowen, H. and Lording, R. (1982) *The Hidden Homeless: A Report of a Survey on Homelessness and Housing Among Single Young Blacks in Gloucester* (Gloucester: Gloucester Community Relations Council).

Crowther, M. A. (1981) *The Workhouse System 1834–1929: The History of an English Social Institution* (London: Batsford).

Cumberbatch, G. et al. (1986) *Television and the Miners' Strike* (London: Broadcasting Research Unit).

Curran, J. et al. (1980) 'The political economy of the human-interest story', in A. Smith (ed.) *Newspapers and Democracy: International Essays on a Changing Medium* (Cambridge, Mass.: Massachusetts Institute of Technology Press).

Curran, J. and Seaton, J. (1991) *Power Without Responsibility: The Press and Broadcasting in Britain,* 4th edn (London: Routledge).

Dale, P. (1989) 'Management implications of child sexual abuse', in P. Sills (ed.) *Child Abuse: Challenges for Policy and Practice* (Wallington: Community Care).

De'Ath, E. (1987) 'Ordinary children – lonely and frightened', *Community Care*, no. 649, pp. i–iii.

De'Ath, E. and Newman, C. (1987) 'Children who run', *Children and Society*, vol. 1, pp. 13–18.

Department of Health and Welfare (1983) *Vagrancy* (Pretoria, South Africa: Department of Health and Welfare).

Department of Housing and Urban Development (1989) *A Report of the 1988 National Survey of Shelters for the Homeless* (Washington, DC: Dept of Housing and Urban Development).

Dobash, R. E. and Dobash, R. (1980) *Violence Against Wives: A Case Against the Patriarchy* (New York: Free Press).

Doherty, R. (1989) 'Displaced and No Home: A Study of Single Homeless Women's Housing Needs and Cardiff Voluntary Sector Temporary Housing Provision', MSc. Econ Thesis (Swansea: University College Swansea).

Dominelli, L. (1989) 'Betrayal of trust: a feminist analysis of power relationships in incest abuse and its relevance for social work practice', *British Journal of Social Work*, vol. 19, no. 4, pp. 291–307.

Donnison, D. (1980) 'A policy for housing', *New Society*, vol. 54, no. 938, pp. 283–4.

Doogan, K. (1988) 'Falling off the treadmill – the causes of youth homelessness', in G. Bramley et al. (eds) *Homelessness and the London Housing Market*, Occasional Paper No. 32, School for Advanced Urban Studies (Bristol: University of Bristol).

Drake, M. (1989) 'Fifteen years of homelessness in the UK', *Housing Studies*, vol. 4, no. 2, pp. 119–127.

Drake, M. et al. (1981) *Single and Homeless* (London: HMSO).

Driver, E. and Droisen, A. (eds) (1989) *Child Sexual Abuse: Feminist Perspectives* (London: Macmillan).

Dutta, R. and Taylor, G. (1989) *Housing Equality: An Action Guide* (London: CHAR).

Edwards, S. (1989) *Policing 'Domestic' Violence: Women, the Law and the State* (London: Sage).

Emms, P. (1990) *Social Housing: A European Dilemma* (Bristol: University of Bristol).

Family Policy Studies Centre (1991) *One Parent Families*, Fact Sheet No. 3 (London: Family Policy Studies Centre).

Ferguson, M. (1983) *Forever Feminine: Women's Magazines and the Cult of Femininity* (London: Heinemann).

Fine, M. (1989) 'Homeless young – our problem?', *The Australian Nurses Journal*, vol. 18, no. 18.

Fopp, R. (1989) 'Press Coverage of the Burdekin Report', *Youth Studies*, vol. 8, no. 4.

Franklin, A. (1984) *Squatting in England 1969–79: A Case Study of Social Conflict in Advanced Industrial Capitalism*, Working Paper No. 37, School for Advanced Urban Studies (Bristol: University of Bristol).

Fraser, P. et al. (1992) *An Evaluation of Area Acommodation Strategies: A*

Study of the Impact of the Home Office Circular 35/1988 Review of Non-Custodial Offender Accommodation (London: Association of Chief Officers of Probation).

Frost, N. and Stein, M. (1989) *The Politics of Child Welfare: Inequality, Power and Change* (Hemel Hampstead: Harvester-Wheatsheaf).

Galtung, J. and Ruge, M. (1981) 'Structuring and selecting news', in S. Cohen and J. Young (eds) *The Manufacture of News: Social Problems, Deviance and the Mass Media*, 2nd edn (London: Constable).

Ginsburg, N. (1989) 'The Housing Act 1988 and its policy context: a critical commentary', *Critical Social Policy*, vol. 9, no. 1, pp. 56–81.

Glastonbury, B. (1971) *Homeless Near a Thousand Homes: A Study of Families without Homes in South Wales and the West of England* (London: Allen and Unwin).

Glauser, B. (1990) 'Street children: deconstructing a construct', in A. James and A. Prout (eds) *Constructing and Reconstructing Childhood: Contemporary Issues in the Sociological Study of Childhood* (Basingstoke: Falmer Press).

Golding, P. and Middleton, S. (1982) *Images of Welfare* (Oxford: Martin Robertson).

Gorder, C. (1988) *Homeless: Without Addresses in America* (Tempe, Arizona: Bluebird Publishing).

Gosling, J. (1990) *Young Homelessness – A National Scandal* (London: Young Homelessness Group).

Greve, J. (1964) *London's Homeless* (London: Bell).

Greve, J. et al. (1971) *Homelessness in London* (London: Scottish Academic Press).

Greve, J. and Currie, E. (1990) *Homelessness in Britain* (York: Joseph Rowntree Memorial Trust).

Gusfield, J. R. (1981) *The Culture of Public Problems: Drinking-Driving and the Symbolic Order* (Chicago: University of Chicago Press).

Hakim, C. (1987) *Research Design: Strategies and Choices in the Design of Social Research* (London: Unwin Hyman).

Hall, S. et al. (1978) *Policing the Crisis: Mugging, the State, and Law and Order* (London: Macmillan).

Hammersley, M. and Atkinson, P. (1983) *Ethnography: Principles in Practice* (London: Tavistock Publications).

Handler, J. and Hasenfeld, Y. (1991) *The Moral Construction of Poverty: Welfare Reform in America* (Newbury Park, Cal.: Sage).

Handler, J. F. and Hollingsworth, E. J. (1971) *The 'Deserving Poor' – A Study of Welfare Administration* (Chicago: Markham).

Handy, C. B. (1976) *Understanding Organisations* (Harmondsworth: Penguin).

Hardoy, J. E. and Satterthwaite, D. (1989) *Squatter Citizen: Life in the Urban Third World* (London: Earthscan).

Harman, L. D. (1989) *When a Hostel Becomes a Home: Experiences of Women* (Toronto: Garamond Press).

Hebdige, D. (1979) *Subculture: The Meaning of Style* (London: Methuen).

Heddy, J. (1990) *Housing for Young People: A Survey of the Situation in*

Selected European Community Countries (Paris: Union des Foyers des Jeunes Travailleurs).

Hendessi, M. (1992) *4 in 10: Report on Young Women Who Become Homeless as a Result of Sexual Abuse* (London: CHAR).

Hevey, D. and Kenward, H. (1989) 'The effects of child sexual abuse', in W. Stainton et al. (eds) *Child Abuse and Neglect: Facing The Challenge* (London: Batsford).

Hill, D. (1989) 'Solstice showdown – on the hippy convoy', *New Statesman and Society*, no. 55, pp. 42–3.

Hirst, J. (1991) 'Public enemies or private neighbours?', *Guardian*, 30 October.

HMSO (1989) *The Children Act 1989* (London: HMSO).

HMSO (1991a) *Homelessness Code of Guidance for Local Authorities 1991*, 3rd edn, Part III of the Housing Act 1985, Department of the Environment, Department of Health, Welsh Office (London: HMSO).

HMSO (1991b) *The Children Act Guidance and Regulations* (London: HMSO).

Hoch, C. (1987) 'A brief history of the homeless problem in the United States', in R. D. Bingham et al. (eds) *The Homeless in Contemporary Society* (Newbury Park, Cal.: Sage).

Hoff, L. A. (1990) *Battered Women as Survivors* (London: Routledge).

Holman, R. (1973) 'Poverty: consensus and alternatives', *British Journal of Social Work*, vol. 3, no. 4, pp. 431–6.

Holmes, C. (1986) 'The worsening crisis of single homelessness', in P. Malpass (ed.) *The Housing Crisis* (London: Croom Helm).

Hombs, M. (1990) *American Homelessness: A Reference Handbook* (Oxford: Contemporary World Issues).

Home Office (1974) *Working Paper of the Working Party on Vagrancy and Street Offences* (London: HMSO).

Home Office (1988) *Home Office Circular 35/1988 Review of Non-Custodial Offender Accommodation* (London: HMSO).

Horton, M. and Aggleton, P. (1989) 'Perverts, inverts and experts: the cultural production of AIDS research paradigm', in P. Aggleton et al. (eds) *AIDS: Social Representations, Social Practices* (London: Falmer Press).

House of Lords, Select Committee on the European Communities (1991) *Young People in the European Communities: A Report* (London: HMSO).

Housing Co-ordinators Group (1992) *Statistical Evidence of Unmet Offender Accommodation Needs* (obtained from G. Wilson, Chair, Housing Co-ordinator's Group).

Howe, L. E. A. (1985) 'The "deserving" and the "undeserving": practice in an urban, local social security office', *Journal of Social Policy*, vol. 14, no. 1, pp. 49–72.

Hutson, S. and Jenkins, R. (1987) 'Family relationships and the unemployment of young people in Swansea', in M. White (ed.) *The Social World of the Young Unemployed* (London: Policy Studies Institute).

Hutson, S. and Jenkins, R. (1989) *Taking the Strain: Families, Unemployment and the Transition to Adulthood* (Milton Keynes: Open University Press).

Hutson, S. and Liddiard, M. (1989a) *Street Children in Wales? A Study of Runaways and Homeless Young People under 18 in Four Welsh Counties* (Cardiff: Children's Society).

Hutson, S. and Liddiard, M. (1989b) *Young People Talking* (Cardiff: Children's Society).

Hutson, S. and Liddiard, M. (1990) 'Homeless young people in hostels – some practical considerations', *Youth and Policy*, vol. 31, pp. 40–2.

Hutson, S. and Liddiard, M. (1991) *Young and Homeless in Wales: Government Policies, Insecure Accommodation and Agency Support*, Occasional Paper No. 26 (Swansea: University College Swansea).

Jenkins, R. (1982) *Hightown Rules: Growing Up in a Belfast Housing Estate* (Leicester: National Youth Bureau).

Johnson, B. et al. (1991) *A Typology of Homelessness* (Edinburgh: Scottish Homes).

Johnson, N. (1981) *Voluntary Social Services* (Oxford: Basil Blackwell and Martin Robertson).

Jones, D. J. V. (1982) *Crime, Protest, Community and Police in Nineteenth Century Britain* (London: Routledge and Kegan Paul).

Jones, G. (1990) *Household Formation Among Young Adults in Scotland* (Edinburgh: Scottish Homes).

Jones, R. (1990) 'Wagon train of Britain's lost tribe', *Sunday Correspondent*, 17 June.

Joseph, K. (1972) *The Cycle of Deprivation*, Paper given at the Pre-School Playgroups Association conference.

Karn, V. (1990) *Homelessness in the USA and Britain* (Wayne State: Wayne State University Press).

Katz, D. and Kahn, R. (1978) *The Social Psychology of Organisations*, 2nd edn (New York: John Wiley and Sons).

Katz, E. and Lazarsfeld, P. F. (1956) *Personal Influence: The Part Played by People in the Flow of Mass Communications* (New York: Free Press).

Katz, M. B. (1986) *In the Shadow of the Poorhouse: A Social History of Welfare in America* (New York: Basic Books).

Katz, M. B. (1989) *The Undeserving Poor – From the War on Poverty to the War on Welfare* (New York: Pantheon Books).

Kenward, H. and Hevey, D. (1989) 'The effects of physical abuse and neglect', in W. Stainton et al. (eds) *Child Abuse and Neglect: Facing the Challenge* (London: Batsford).

Killeen, D. (1988) *Estranged: Homeless 16 and 17 Year Olds and the Social Security Act 1988* (Edinburgh: Shelter Scottish Campaign for the Homeless).

Kirk, D. et al. (1991) *Excluding Youth: Poverty Among Young People Living Away from Home* (Edinburgh: University of Edinburgh).

Kitsuse, J. I. and Cicourel, A. V. (1963) 'A note on the uses of official statistics', *Social Problems*, vol. 11, no. 2, pp. 131–9.

Kitzinger, J. (1990) 'Who are you kidding? Children, power and the struggle against sex abuse', in A. James and A. Prout (eds) *Constructing and Reconstructing Childhood: Contemporary Issues in the Sociological Study of Childhood* (Basingstoke: Falmer Press).

Koch, J. Q. (1987) 'The federal role in aiding the homeless', in

R. D. Bingham et al. (eds) *The Homeless in Contemporary Society* (Newbury Park, Cal.: Sage).

La Fontaine, J. (1990) *Child Sexual Abuse* (Cambridge: Polity Press).

Leach, L. (1979) 'The evaluation of a voluntary organisation attempting to resettle destitute men: action research with the St Mungo Community Trust', in T. Cook (ed.) *Vagrancy: Some New Perspectives* (London: Academic Press).

Leigh, L. (1979) 'Vagrancy and the criminal law', in T. Cook (ed.) *Vagrancy: Some New Perspectives* (London: Academic Press).

Levy, G. (1989) 'The "home truths" that don't add up', *Daily Mail*, 19 September.

Liddiard, M. (1990) 'The Growth in Youth Homelessness: Fact or Fiction?' paper given at the British Sociological Association Annual Conference, Surrey University (unpublished).

Liddiard, M. (1991a) ' "Homeless" or "Homefree"? Youth Homelessness and the Question of Choice,' paper given at a conference, Department of Sociology and Anthropology, University College of Swansea (unpublished).

Liddiard, M. (1991b) 'Young, free and homeless?', *Planet – The Welsh Internationalist*, vol. 86, pp. 83–8.

Liddiard, M. and Hutson S. (1990) 'Youth homelessness in Wales', in C. Wallace and M. Cross (eds) *Youth in Transition: The Sociology of Youth and Youth Policy* (London: Falmer Press).

Liddiard, M. and Hutson, S. (1991) 'Homeless young people and runaways – agency definitions and processes', *Journal of Social Policy*, vol. 20, no. 3, pp. 365–88.

Lipsey, D. (1987) 'Marriage break ups fuel homes crisis', *New Society*, vol. 79, no. 1257, p. 7.

Lipsky, M. (1980) *Street-level Bureaucracy: Dilemmas of the Individual in Public Services* (New York: Russell Sage Foundation).

Lonsdale, S. (1992) 'Patterns of paid work', in C. Glendinning and J. Millar (eds) *Women and Poverty in Britain the 1990s* (Hemel Hempstead: Harvester-Wheatsheaf).

Lunn, T. (1988) 'The Government acts tough', *Community Care*, no. 727, pp. 16–17.

Malpass, P. (1986a) 'From complacency to crisis', in P. Malpass (ed.) *The Housing Crisis* (London: Croom Helm).

Malpass, P. (1986b) 'Housing policy and young people', in P. Malpass (ed.) *The Housing Crisis* (London: Croom Helm).

Marcuse, P. (1990) 'Homelessness and housing policy', in C. L. M. Caton (ed.) *Homeless in America* (New York: Oxford University Press).

McKechnie, S. (1991) *A New Approach: the British Foyer* (London: Shelter).

McMullen, R. J. (1988) 'Boys involved in prostitution', *Youth and Policy*, no. 23, pp. 35–42.

Means, R. (1977) *Social Work and the 'Undeserving' Poor*, Occasional Paper No. 37, Centre for Urban and Regional Studies (Birmingham: University of Birmingham).

Miles, I. and Irvine, J. (1979) 'The critique of official statistics', in J. Irvine et al. (eds) *Demystifying Social Statistics* (London: Pluto Press).

Miller, M. (1990) *Bed and Breakfast: Women and Homelessness Today* (London: Women's Press).

Minford, P. et al. (1987) *The Housing Morass: Regulation, Immobility and Unemployment* (London: Institute of Economic Affairs).

Minns, R. (1972) 'Homeless families and some organisational determinants of deviancy', *Policy and Politics*, vol. 1, no. 1, pp. 1–21.

Morley, D. (1980) *The 'Nationwide' Audience* (London: British Film Institute).

Moses, A. B. (1978) 'The Runaway Youth Act: paradoxes of reform', *Social Service Review*, vol. 52, no. 2, pp. 227–43.

NACRO (1981) *Homeless Young Offenders: An Action Programme* (London: NACRO).

National Assistance Board (1966) *Homeless Single Persons* (London: HMSO).

Negrine, R. (1989) *Politics and the Mass Media in Britain* (London: Routledge).

Neil, C. et al. (1992) *Homeless in Australia* (Canberra: Committee on Homelessness and Housing).

Newman, C. (1989) *Young Runaways: Findings from Britain's First Safe House* (London: Children's Society).

O'Connor, I. (1988) *Our Homeless Children: Their Experiences*, Report to the National Inquiry into Homeless Children (Sydney, Aus.: Human Rights and Equal Opportunity Commission).

O'Mahony, B. (1988) *A Capital Offence: The Plight of the Young Single Homeless in London* (London: Routledge).

O'Mahony, B. and Ferguson, D. (1991) *Young, Black and Homeless in London: The Reality Behind the Myth* (Barkingside: Barnardo's).

Orwell, G. (1933) *Down and Out in Paris and London* (London: Gollancz).

Pahl, J. (ed.) (1985) *Private Violence and Public Policy: The Needs of Battered Women and the Response of the Public Services* (London: Routledge and Kegan Paul).

Parton, N. (1985) *The Politics of Child Abuse* (London: Macmillan).

Parton, N. (1991) *Governing the Family: Child Care, Child Protection and the State* (London: Macmillan).

Picton, C. (1987) 'Australia and the International Year of Shelter for the Homeless', in *Housing Australians: Proceedings of the 1987 Social Issues Conference* (Melbourne: University of Melbourne).

Pizzey, E, (1974) *Scream Quietly or the Neighbours Will Hear* (Harmondsworth: Penguin).

Plummer, K. (1988) 'Organising AIDS', in P. Aggleton and H. Homans (eds) *Social Aspects of AIDS* (London: Falmer Press).

Pollitt, N. et al. (1989) *Hard Times: Young and Homeless* (London: Shelter).

Pottier, J. (1993) 'The role of ethnography in project appraisal', in J. Pottier (ed.) *Practising Development: Social Science Perspectives* (London: Routledge).

Price, V. (1990) *Characteristics and Needs of Street Youth* (Boston, Mass.: Bridge Over Troubled Waters).

Prottas, J. M. (1979) *People Processing: The Street-Level Bureaucrat in Public Service Bureaucracies* (Lexington, Mass.: Lexington Books).

Raffe, D. (1987) 'Youth unemployment in the United Kingdom, 1979–1984', in P. Brown and D. N. Ashton (eds) *Education, Unemployment and Labour Markets* (Lewes: Falmer Press).

Randall, G. (1988) *No Way Home: Homeless Young People in Central London* (London: Centrepoint Soho).

Rees, G. et al. (1989) 'The "new vocationalism": further education and local labour markets', *Journal of Education Policy*, vol. 4, no. 3, pp. 227–44.

Rhodes, E. and Braham, P. (1987) 'Equal opportunity in the context of high levels of unemployment', in R. Jenkins and J. Solomos (eds) *Racism and Equal Opportunity Policies in the 1980s* (Cambridge: Cambridge University Press).

Ritzdorf, M. and Sharpe, S. (1987) 'Portland, Oregon: a comprehensive approach', in R. D. Bingham et al. (eds) *The Homeless in Contemporary Society* (Newbury Park, Cal.: Sage).

Robertson, M. J. (1990) 'Characteristics and Circumstances of Homeless Adolescents in Hollywood', paper presented at the annual meeting of the American Psychological Association, Boston, Mass. (unpublished).

Rose, L. (1988) *'Rogues and Vagabonds': Vagrant Underworld in Britain 1815–1985* (London: Routledge).

Rossi, P. H. (1989) *Down and Out in America: The Origins of Homelessness* (Chicago: University of Chicago Press).

Saunders, B. (1986) *Homeless Young People in Britain: The Contribution of the Voluntary Sector* (London: Bedford Square Press).

Schwarz, J. E. (1988) *America's Hidden Success: A Reassessment of Public Policy from Kennedy to Reagan*, 2nd edn (New York: Norton).

Scott, R. A. (1970) 'The construction of conceptions of stigma by professional experts', in J. D. Douglas (ed.) *Deviance and Respectability – The Social Construction of Moral Meanings* (London: Basic Books).

Sereny, G. (1984) *The Invisible Children: The Shattering Tragedy of the Runaways on our Streets* (London: André Deutsch).

Sexty, C. (1990) *Women Losing Out: Access to Housing in Britain Today* (London: Shelter).

Sharp, C. (1991) *Homelessness, Housing Benefit and the Private Rented Sector*, Housing Research Findings No. 28 (York: Joseph Rowntree Foundation).

Shaw, D. (1991) 'Now squatters will face jail', *London Evening Standard*, 15 October.

Shaw, M. et al. (1990) *Children in Need and Their Families: A Guide to Part III of the Children Act 1989 for Local Authority Councillors* (Leicester: University of Leicester).

Shelter (1989) *One Day I'll Have My Own Place to Stay . . . Young Homeless People Write About Their Lives* (London: Shelter).

Shelter (1992a) *Homelessness in England: The Facts* (London: Shelter).

Shelter (1992b) *The Foyer Project: A Collection of Background Papers* (London: Shelter).

Silverman, D. (1989) 'Making sense of a precipice: constituting identity in an HIV clinic', in P. Aggleton et al. (eds) *AIDS: Social Representations, Social Practices* (London: Falmer Press).

Smith, J. and Gilford, S. (1991) *Homelessness Among the Under-25s*, Housing Research Findings No. 48 (York: Joseph Rowntree Foundation).

Social Security Advisory Committee (1992) *Eighth Report of the Social Security Advisory Committee* (London: HMSO).

Soho Project (1988) *21 Years Working with the Young Homeless* (London: Soho Project).

Spicker, P. (1984) *Stigma and Social Welfare* (London: Croom Helm).

Steele, A. (1989) 'Homelessness: today's youth, tomorrow's tramp?', *Youth and Policy*, no. 28, pp. 9–11.

Storie, J. (1990) *Bed, Breakfast and Social Work*, Social Work Monograph 86 (Norwich: University of East Anglia).

Strathdee, R. (1992) *No Way Back: Homeless Sixteen and Seventeen Year Olds in the 90s* (London: Centrepoint Soho).

Sullivan, M. (1987) *Sociology and Social Welfare* (London: Allen and Unwin).

Sullivan, P. A. and Damrosch, S. P. (1987) 'Homeless women and children', in R. D. Bingham et al. (eds) *The Homeless in Contemporary Society* (Newbury Park, Cal.: Sage).

Tai Cymru (1991) *Report of the Working Party on Single Homelessness* (Cardiff: Tai Cymru).

Thomas, A. and Niner, P. (1989) *Living in Temporary Accommodation: A Survey of Homeless People* (London: HMSO).

Thorns, D. C. (1989) 'The production of homelessness: from individual failure to system inadequacies', *Housing Studies*, vol. 4, no. 4, pp. 253–66.

Thornton, R. (1990) *The New Homeless: The Crisis of Youth Homelessness and the Response of the Local Housing Authorities* (London: SHAC).

Tidmarsh, D. and Wood, S. M. (1972) *Camberwell Reception Centre: Summary of Research Findings and Recommendations* (London: Department of Health and Social Security).

Trenaman, J. and McQuail, D. (1961) *Television and the Political Image: A Study of the Impact of Television on the 1959 General Election* (London: Methuen).

Tuchman, G. (1981) 'The symbolic annihilation of women by the mass media', in S. Cohen and J. Young (eds) *The Manufacture of News: Social Problems, Deviance and the Mass Media*, 2nd edn (London: Constable).

Volberding, P. A. (1988) 'AIDS overview', in I. B. Corless and M. Pittman-Lindeman (eds) *AIDS: Principles, Practices, and Politics* (New York: Hemisphere).

Walker, L. (1979) *The Battered Woman* (New York: Harper Colophon Books).

Washton, K. (1974) 'Running away from home', *Journal of Social Issues*, vol. 30, no. 1, pp. 181–8.

Watney, S. (1988) 'AIDS, "moral panic" theory and homophobia', in P. Aggleton and H. Homans (eds) *Social Aspects of AIDS* (London: Falmer Press).

Watson, E. (1988) 'Vulnerable groups and homelessness', in G. Bramley et al. (eds) *Homelessness and the London Housing Market*, Occasional Paper No. 32, School for Advanced Urban Studies (Bristol: University of Bristol).

Watson, S. (1984) 'Definitions of homelessness: a feminist perspective', *Critical Social Policy*, no. 11, pp. 60–73.

Watson, S. and Austerberry, H. (1986) *Housing and Homelessness: A Feminist Perspective* (London: Routledge and Kegan Paul).

Weeks, J. (1989) 'AIDS: the intellectual agenda', in P. Aggleton et al. (eds) *AIDS: Social Representations, Social Practices* (London: Falmer Press).

Wells, K. (1980) 'I came for the experience', *New Society*, vol. 52, no. 917, pp. 214–16.

Welsh Women's Aid (1986) *The Answer is Maybe . . . And That's Final: A Report about How Local Authorities in Wales Respond to the Housing Needs of Women Leaving Violent Husbands with Comments and Recommendations* (Cardiff: Welsh Women's Aid).

White, M. (1991) *Against Unemployment* (London: Policy Studies Institute).

Wilkinson, T. (1981) *Down and Out* (London: Quartet).

Willis, P. (1984) 'Youth unemployment – 1. A New Social State', *New Society*, vol. 67, no. 1114, pp. 475–7

Wills, T. A. (1978) 'Perceptions of clients by professional helpers', *Psychological Bulletin*, vol. 85, no. 5, pp. 968–1000.

Women's National Commission (1990) *What Chance of a Home? A Study of Homelessness Particularly as it Affects Women* (London: Women's National Commission).

Wright, J. and Lam, J. (1987) 'Homelessness and low income housing supply', *Social Forces*, vol. 17, no. 4, pp. 48–53

Young Homelessness Group (1988) *Unsecured Futures: the Effects of Recent Legislative Change on Young People's Housing Choice* (London: Young Homelessness Group).

Young Homelessness Group (1991) *If Youth Matters Why Are 156,000 Young People Homeless? Are They on Your Agenda?* (London: Young Homelessness Group).

Young Persons Working Group (1989) *Young Single and Homeless* (Leeds: Leeds Polytechnic).

Youth Housing Monitoring Group (1991) *Still in Demand: Second Report on Housing and Support for Young People in Edinburgh* (Edinburgh: Edinburgh Council for the Single Homeless).

YWCA (1989) 'Homelessness: what the YWCA says', *Update – The Magazine of the YWCA*, no.1.

Author Index

Abrahams, C.   37, 101
Action on Housing Need   38
Advisory Service for Squatters
   162, 163
Aggleton, P.   166, 176
Agnelli, S.   20
Akilu, F.   62
Alcorn, K.   180
Anderson, N.   10
Andrews, G.   124
Aptekar, L.   20
Archard, P.   12
Ashton, D.   50
Association of Metropolitan
   Authorities   34, 147
Atkinson, J. M.   33
Atkinson, P.   24, 112
Austerberry, H.   29, 30, 40, 126,
   137, 148, 159
Axinn, J.   150

Bahr, H. M.   12
Balchin, P. N.   50
Barrat, D.   95, 97
Beacock, N.   3, 14, 73, 78, 106
Belson, W. A.   95
Benefits Agency   105
Beresford, P.   41, 74, 75, 87, 89, 91,
   96, 98, 116, 149
Best, J.   96, 97
Billig, M.   113, 116
Binney, V.   172, 175, 179
Bonnerjea, L.   8, 9
Braham, P.   42
Braithwaite, G.   14, 118
Brake, M.   92
Bramley, G.   28, 40
Brandon, D.   29, 63, 65, 67, 68, 69,
   70, 71, 123, 124, 131, 132, 133,
   134, 138, 139, 140, 155, 161, 162

Breakwell, G.   137
Brynin, M.   3, 53, 57
Burdekin, B.   5
Burrows, L.   9, 36, 38, 39, 41, 147
Burt, M.   15, 16
Burton, P.   17, 18, 22, 23, 107, 149,
   152, 159, 163, 164

Canter, D.   127, 139, 140
Carvel, J.   14
Caton, C. L. M.   63
Central London Outreach Team
   129
Central London Social Security
   Advisers Forum   56
Centrepoint Soho   90, 91, 155
Chamberlain, C.   27
CHAR   104, 155, 164
Chibnall, S.   97
Chirimuuta, R. and R.   166
Cicourel, A. V.   32
City of Boston   109
Coffield, F.   3, 135
Cohen, B.   15, 16
Cohen, S.   92, 97, 174
Cook, T.   14, 118
Cooper, M.   109
Cowen, H.   43
Crowther, M. A.   12, 13
Cumberbatch, G.   95
Curran, J.   74, 79, 95
Currie, E.   9, 10, 36, 67, 68

Dale, P.   170
Damrosch, S. P.   21, 109
De'Ath, E.   5, 6, 115
Department of Health and Welfare
   12, 14
Department of Housing and Urban
   Development   15

Dobash, R.   168, 170
Dobash, R. E.   168, 170
Doherty, R.   42
Dominelli, L.   172
Donnison, D.   50
Doogan, K.   52, 69
Drake, M.   109, 127
Driver, E.   177
Droisen, A.   177
Dutta, R.   42

Edwards, S.   172
Emms, P.   49

Family Policy Studies Centre   42
Ferguson, D.   43, 164
Ferguson, M.   95
Fine, M.   17
Fopp, R.   17
Franklin, A.   162
Fraser, P.   104, 155
Frost, N.   166, 169

Galtung, J.   74, 78
Gilford, S.   44
Ginsburg, N.   47
Glastonbury, B.   7
Glauser, B.   20, 28
Golding, P.   95, 97
Gorder, C.   16
Gosling, J.   43, 60
Greve, J.   7, 9, 10, 36, 67, 68
Gusfield, J. R.   173

Hakim, C.   109
Hall, S.   97, 98, 174
Hammersley, M.   24, 112
Handler, J.   8, 118, 153
Handy, C. B.   117
Hardoy, J. E.   19, 20
Harman, L. D.   43
Hasenfeld, Y.   8, 153
Hebdige, D.   92
Heddy, J.   17, 18, 50, 149, 153
Hendressi, M.   6, 61, 62
Hevey, D.   62
Hill, D.   141
Hirst, J.   163
Hoch, C.   73

Hoff, L. A.   172, 178
Hollingsworth, E. J.   118
Holman, R.   118
Holmes, C.   129
Hombs, M.   16
Home Office   14, 104
Horton, M.   166, 176
House of Lords   17, 18, 160
Housing Co-ordinators Group   104
Howe, L. E. A.   115, 118
Hutson, S.   5, 6, 7, 32, 40, 53, 55,
     60, 64, 65, 67, 70, 109, 121, 122,
     124, 125, 135, 137, 152, 154,
     158, 161, 164

Irvine, J.   33

Jenkins, R.   60, 134, 135
Johnson, B.   69, 70
Johnson, N.   107, 155
Jones, D. J. V.   10, 11, 12, 73
Jones, G.   59, 61
Jones, R.   141
Joseph, K.   172

Karn, V.   16, 21, 100, 160, 164
Katz, D.   115
Katz, E.   95
Katz, M. B.   118, 151, 152
Kenward, H.   62
Killeen, D.   55, 59, 61, 114
Kirk, D.   172
Kitsuse, J. I.   32
Kitzinger, J.   176, 177, 178

La Fontaine, J.   167, 180
Lam, J.   47
Lawton, J.   8, 9
Lazarsfeld, P. F.   95
Leach, L.   12, 107
Leigh, L.   10, 14
Levin, H.   150
Levy, G.   86
Liddiard, M.   5, 6, 7, 9, 32, 40, 53,
     55, 60, 64, 65, 67, 70, 75, 109,
     121, 122, 124, 125, 135, 137,
     141, 152, 154, 158, 161, 164
Lipsey, D.   57
Lipsky, M.   110, 111

Lonsdale, S. 41
Lording, R. 43
Lunn, T. 54

MacKenzie, D. 27
Malpass, P. 49, 50, 57
Marcuse, P. 16, 47
McKechnie, S. 150
McMullen, R. J. 62
McQuail, D. 95
Means, R. 118
Middleton, S. 95, 97
Miles, I. 33
Miller, M. 42
Minford, P. 49
Minns, R. 118
Morley, D. 83, 95
Moses, A. B. 116
Mungall, R. 37, 101

NACRO 104, 164
National Assistance Board 10, 63
Negrine, R. 94, 95
Neil, C. 17
Newman, C. 5, 6, 61, 153
Niner, P. 9

O'Connor, I. 4, 5, 6, 7, 17
O'Mahony, B. 6, 38, 43, 56, 58, 59,
    60, 61, 64, 66, 108, 119, 121,
    127, 128, 153, 164
Orwell, G. 10

Pahl, J. 169
Parton, N. 167, 168, 171, 172, 173,
    179
Picton, C. 17
Pizzey, E. 107, 168, 178
Plummer, K. 168, 169, 174, 180
Pollitt, N. 108
Pottier, J. 117
Price, V. 5, 62, 109
Prottas, J. M. 112

Raffe, D. 50
Randall, G. 6, 12, 37, 39, 60, 65,
    66, 71, 108, 111, 112, 125, 130,
    164
Rees, G. 151

Rhodes, E. 42
Ritzdorf, M. 109
Robertson, M. J. 4, 5, 6, 16, 62,
    162
Rose, L. 2, 73, 88
Rossi, P. H. 30, 31, 32, 40, 47, 51,
    56, 59, 63, 65, 66, 144, 148, 152,
    153, 164
Ruge, M. 74, 78

Satterthwaite, D. 19, 20
Saunders, B. 53, 117, 119, 120,
    124, 125, 127, 129, 164
Schwarz, J. E. 152
Scott, R. A. 110, 113
Seaton, J. 95
Sereny, G. 4
Sexty, C. 42, 43
Sharp, C. 55, 148
Sharpe, S. 109
Shaw, D. 163
Shelter 42, 120, 150
Silverman, D. 177
Smith, J. 44
Social Security Advisory Committee
    105, 106
Soho Project 91
Spicker, P. 119
Steele, A. 14, 108, 149
Stein, M. 166, 169
Storie, J. 9
Strathdee, R. 11, 54, 105, 106
Sullivan, M. 158, 159
Sullivan, P. A. 21, 109

Tai Cymru 164
Taylor, G. 42
Thomas, A. 9
Thorns, D. C. 67
Thornton, R. 36, 37, 42, 44, 47, 49,
    53, 54, 57, 59, 63, 64, 67, 128
Tidmarsh, D. 12, 14
Trenaman, J. 95
Tuchman, G. 95

Volberding, P. A. 166

Walentowicz, P. 9, 36, 38, 39, 41,
    147

Walker, L. 172
Washton, K. 119
Watney, S. 174, 175
Watson, E. 60, 64, 65, 66, 104
Watson, S. 29, 30, 40, 137, 148, 159
Weeks, J. 176
Wells, K. 114
Welsh Women's Aid 175
White, M. 152, 164
Wilkinson, T. 10, 87
Willis, P. 59
Wills, T. A. 115

Women's National Commission 164
Wood, S. M. 12, 14
Wright, J. 47

Young, J. 97, 174
Young Homelessness Group 151, 164
Young Persons Working Group 164
Youth Housing Monitoring Group 164
YWCA 149

Subject Index

Note: **bold** type indicates principal references

Abuse   6, 7, 17, 21, 59, 60, **61–3**, 70, 78, 89, 105, 133, 149, 186
Academic commentators   92, 96, 136, 144, 145, 187
Accommodation
  bed and breakfast   9, 28, 55, 140–1, 147, 183
  friends   8, 19, 28, 31, 43–4, 78, 82, 125, 130, 135, 138, 139, 146, 161, 162
  hostels   14, 16, 18, 21, 23, 28, 38–9, 43–4, 55, 64, 65, 67, 93, 106, **107–9**, 116, 119, 120, 126, 127, 139, 140, 149, 163
  squatting   16, 19–20, 28, 38–9, 89, 126, 141, **162–3**
  temporary accommodation   8–9, 28, 29, 78, 82, 94, 146, 183
  see also Sleeping rough
Agencies   5, 21, 29, 30, 32–45, 79, 83, 86–7, **89–92**, 96, 99–122, 123, 124, 125, 126, 131, 132–3, 136, 143–56, 159, 162, 181, 187, 188–9, 190–1
  classifications within agencies   **117–22**, 188–9
  presentations to an outside audience   **110–17**, 188–9
  reports   **89–92**, 187
  solutions   **143–56**, 190–1
  statistics   **32–45**, 184
  statutory sector   29, 33–7, 40–1, **100–6**, 144, 188
  voluntary sector   21, 29, 37–9, 40–1, 92, 93, 104, **106–9**, 131, 144, 159, 181
  see also Careers Service; Housing Departments; Probation Service; Social Services

AIDS   **165–80**, 192–3
  agency viewpoints   **175–7**
  definition and measurement **168–71**
  explanations   **171–3**
  public presentation   **173–5**
  solutions   **178–80**
  viewpoints of 'victims'   **177–8**
Alcohol   12, 15, **66–7**, 69, 108, 109, 119, 121, 183, 186
Australia   5, 6, **16–17**, 74, 78, 98, 104, 183

Bed and breakfast   *see* Accommodation
Begging   2, 83–6
Belgium   18, 149
Benefits   3, 16, 18, 20, 22, 23, **52–6**, 68, 86, 90, **105–6**, 128–9, 144, 145, 146, **151–3**, 182, 185
  see also Housing Benefit; Income Support; Social Fund
Benefits Agency   **105–6**, 129
Black people   *see* Ethnic minorities
Brazil   20

Care   4–5, 6, 7, 18, 21, 55, 59, **60–1**, 63, 70, 102–3, 131, 160, 182, 186
  see also Leaving care
Careers Service   106
Cathy Come Home   7, 73, 87, 89, 97
Child abuse   **165–80, 192–3**
  agency viewpoints   175–7
  definition and measurement **168–71**
  explanations   **171–3**
  public presentation   **173–5**
  solutions   **178–80**
  viewpoints of victims   **177–8**

Children 1–2, 5, 7–8, 9, 10, 16, 17, 18–20, 21, 22, 23, 27, 35–6, 42–3, 61, 93, 100, 102–4, 182
Children Act 1989 11, 37, **102–4**, 144, 160, 188
Community care **63–4**
see also Mental illness
Co-ordination 38, 117, 154–5
Council housing *see* Housing market – state rented
Crime 2, 5, 12, 14, 24, **65–6**, 69, 97, 104, 115, 127, 149, 160, 162, 182, 186

Demography **56–7**, 148, 185
Denmark 148
Department of Social Security *see* Benefits Agency
Domestic violence against women **165–80**, 192–3
  agency viewpoints **175–7**
  definition and measurement **168–71**
  explanations **171–3**
  public presentation **173–5**
  solutions **178–80**
  viewpoints of 'victims' **177–8**
Drugs 12, 15, 16, 18, **66–7**, 69, 74, 78–9, 82, 87, 89, 109, 115, 119, 121, 127, 128, 162, 186, 187

Education 2, 6, 9, 16, 18, 23, 59, 100, 151, 155
Employment *see* Labour market
Ethnic minorities 17, 26–7, **41–5**, 50–1, 121, 160, 162, 184–5
Europe **17–18**, 22, 49, 50, 107, 163, 185
Explanations 6, 8, 11–14, **46–72**, 89, 109, **134–7**, 144, 185–6, 189–90
  child model **70–1**, 134, 186
  individual culpability model 69, 134, 186
  individually based 12–14, **58–67**, 69, 71, 72, 109, 134–5, 136, 156–7, 161, 185–6, 189–90
  pathological model 70, 134, 186
  political model **68–9**, 134, 186

spiritual religious model **71–2**, 134, 186
structurally based 12–14, **46–57**, 59, 68–9, 70, 71, 72, 134–5, 136, 157–61, 185, 189–90

Family conflict 6, 7, 8, 17, 20, 21, 55, 59, 133, 136, 161, 182
Foyers 146, 150
France 18, 49, 51, 149, 150
Friends *see* Accommodation

Germany 18, 49, 149, 163

Health 9, 15, 16, 17, 29, 109, 149
  see also Mental illness
Homeless families 4, **7–10**, 16, 21, 182
  different from homeless youth **7–8**, 183
  explanations 8
  similar to homeless youth **8–10**
  statistics 9
  stereotypes 9–10
Homeless young people
  defining homelessness 29, 123, **137–42**, 190
  'deserving' or 'undeserving' 11, 14, **117–22**, 145, 188–9
  experience of homelessness 123, **124–33**, 189
  explaining homelessness 123, **134–7**, 189–90
  'ordinary' or 'problematic' **110–17**, 181, 188
  solutions 160–3
Homelessness
  defining 3–4, 21, 26, **27–30**, 40–1, 45, **137–42**, 183–4, 190
  explaining **46–72**, 89, **133–7**, 185–6
  'hidden' 22, 29, 31, 38, 41, 43–5, 75–8, 125–6, 131–2
  historical context **1–3**, 182
  'homeless career' **124–7**
  increase in 3, 15, 16, 39, 182
  international context **15–23**, 183
  measuring 26–7, **30–45**, 158–9, 184

Homelessness (*cont.*)
  negative experience   **124–31**, 189
  positive experience   **131–3**, 137,
    163, 189
  solutions   **143–64**
  statistics   2, 8, 15, 16–17, 18, 19,
    21, 26, **30–45**, 86–7, 184
  see also Homeless families;
    Homeless young people; Older
    single homeless; Runaways
Housing Acts   3, 7, 8, 14, 21, 33–7,
    40, 101–2, 160, 188
  1977   3, 7, 14, 21, 33, 101–2, 188
  1985   7, 8, 33–7, 40, 101–2, 103,
    104, 188
Housing Benefit   22, 54–5, 105, 148
  see also Benefits
Housing Departments   229, 40, 99,
    101–2, 103, 114, 181, 188
Housing market   3, 7, 8, 9–10, 16,
    18, 21, 22, 23, 26, 42, 43, **46–50**,
    59–60, 67, 68, 70, 71, 86, 90,
    135–6, 144, **145–9**, 150, 161,
    182, 185
  housing associations   49–50, 104,
    146, 148, 150
  owner occupation   3, 8, 42, 47,
    48–9, 145–7
  private rented   3, 7, 8, 16, 47, 49,
    65, 127, 145, 146, 147
  state rented   3, 8, 9–10, 16, 18,
    42, 43, 47–8, 145–7, 148, 163

Income Support   10, 22, 54–5,
    105–6, 152
  see also Benefits
Information and publicity   146,
    153–4
Interpretivism   23–5
Italy   18, 160

Johnny Go Home   2, 73, 87, 88, 89,
    97, 98, 154, 182

Labour market   3, 18, 19, 20, 23,
    26, 41–2, **50–2**, 59–60, 67, 68,
    70, 89, 135–6, 144, 146, **150–1**,
    152, 156–7, 161, 185
  ethnic minorities   26, 41–2

  women   26, 41–2
  see also unemployment
Leaving care   4–5, 55, 59, **60–1**, 125
  see also Care
Leaving home   4–5, 6, 16, 53, 55,
    58–60, 69, 125, 133, 136, 153,
    156, 186
Legislation   3, 4, 7, 15, 21, 97, 100,
    160, 188
  see also Children Act; Housing
    Acts; State responsibility
Lone parents   10, 105

Media   3, 4, 5, 11, 22, 30, 41, 43,
    53, 62, 66, 71, **73–98**, 112, 123,
    129, 131, 187–8
  effect on policy making   73, **92–4**,
    96–8, 187–8
  effect on public opinion   73,
    92–8, 187–9
  see also Academic commentators;
    Agency reports; Press;
    Television documentaries
Mental illness   12, 16, **63–4**, 108,
    119, 183

Netherlands   49, 153, 160
New Age Travellers   141

Offending   *see* Crime
Older single homeless   4, **10–15**, 21,
    63, 66, 73, 107, 182, 183
  different from homeless youth
    10–14
  explanations   11–14
  historical context   11–14
  similar to homeless youth   **14–15**,
    108
  statistics   12
  see also Resettlement units

Paraguay   20
Physical abuse   *see* Abuse
Policy making   26, 30, 49, 91, **92–4**,
    96–8, 187–8
  see also Media
Politicians   58, 92, 99, **156–60**

Press **74–87**, 91, 93–4, 96–7, 99, 187
  presentation of ambiguity **83–8**,
    93–4, 187
  presentation of contrasts **79**, 91
  presentation of human interest
    stories **79–81**, 93–4, 187
  presentation of negative themes
    78–9, 94
  presentation of stereotypes
    81–3, 91, 94, 187
  presentation of structural issues
    and statistics **86–7**
  presentation of an unfamiliar
    problem **75–8**
  see also Media
Prevention 153–4
Probation Service 29, **104**
Prostitution 2, 20, **62–3**, 78, 79, 87,
    89, 90–1, 187
  see also Sexual exploitation
Public opinion **92–8**, 187–8

Resettlement Units 14, 108–9, 140,
    149
Rough sleepers' initiative 93–4, 159
Runaways 2, **4–7**, 16, 23, 61, 75,
    104, 109, 182
  definition 4–5
  different from homeless youth
    4–5, 182
  explanations 6, 61
  similar to homeless youth **5–7**,
    183
  statistics 6–7

Self-help 19, **162–3**
Sexual abuse *see* abuse
Sexual exploitation 5, 37, 182
  see also Prostitution
Shanty towns 19–20
Single-person households 57, 146,
    148, 185
Sleeping rough 2, 14, 16, 19, 22,
    27, 28, 29–30, 31, 32, 38–9, 40,
    43, 75, 82, 87, 93, 126, 127,
    129–30, 133, 139, 187
Social Fund 56

Social Services 5, 29, 99, 100,
    102–4, 114, 188–9
Solutions **143–64**, 190–2
  agencies **143–56**, 190–1
  homeless young people **160–3**,
    191–2
  politicians **156–60**, 191
South Africa 12, 14
Spain 163
Squatting *see* Accommodation
State responsibility 7–8, 14, 16, 17,
    18, 21–3, 29, 33–7, 100, 106,
    109, 144
  see also Legislation
Stigma 70, 71, 119, 144, 160
Street homelessness *see* Sleeping
    rough

Television documentaries **87–9**,
    187
Third World 18–20, 162, 183
Training schemes 3, 18, 23, 52, 54,
    86, 105, 106, 128, 146, 150–1,
    159

Unemployment 3, 12–13, 14, 17,
    18, 20, 42, **50–2**, 53–6, 59, 86,
    90, 127, 128, 135, 137, 145, 146,
    150, 152, 182, 185
  see also Labour market
USA 2, 3, 5, 6, 7–8, 10, 11–12,
    15–16, 21, 22, 31, 40, 41, 47, 51,
    56, 59, 62, 63, 65, 66, 73, 95,
    104, 107, 109, 144, 151, 152–3,
    163, 183, 185

Vagrancy *see* Older single
    homeless
Vagrancy Acts 11, 14
  1824 14
  1848 11

Women 7–8, 15–16, 21, 26–7, 36,
    41–5, 61, 72, 108, 121, 162,
    184–5
  see also Labour market
Workhouse 2, 11, 100